CRISIS INTERVENTION
and
COUNSELING by TELEPHONE

CRISIS INTERVENTION
and
COUNSELING by TELEPHONE

Edited by

DAVID LESTER, Ph.D.

Stockton State College
Pomona, New Jersey

and

GENE W. BROCKOPP, Ph.D.

Suicide Prevention and Crisis Service
Buffalo, New York

CHARLES C THOMAS · PUBLISHER

Springfield · Illinois · U.S.A.

Published and Distributed Throughout the World by

CHARLES C THOMAS • PUBLISHER

BANNERSTONE HOUSE

301-327 East Lawrence Avenue, Springfield, Illinois, U.S.A.

© *1973, by* CHARLES C THOMAS • PUBLISHER

ISBN 0-398-02641-6

Library of Congress Catalog Card Number: 72-87005

Printed in the United States of America

W-2

CONTRIBUTORS

COREY BERCUN
University of Florida
Center for Crisis Intervention Research
Gainesville, Florida

DIANE BLUM, M.S.W.
Suicide Prevention and Crisis Service
Buffalo, New York

GENE W. BROCKOPP, Ph.D.
Suicide Prevention and Crisis Service
Buffalo, New York

JOHN DOUDS, M.S.W.
Suicide Prevention and Crisis Service
Buffalo, New York

DALE E. FOWLER, M.A.
University of Florida
Center for Crisis Intervention Research
Gainesville, Florida

EVELYN GOLDBERG, Sc.D.
School of Hygiene and Public Health
Johns Hopkins University
Baltimore, Maryland

LEE ANN HOFF, M.S.N.
Suicide Prevention and Crisis Service
Buffalo, New York

BRUCE JENNINGS, M.A.
University of Florida
Center for Crisis Intervention Research
Gainesville, Florida

DAVID A. KNICKERBOCKER, Ph.D.
University of Florida
Center for Crisis Intervention Research
Gainesville, Florida

CHARLES W. LAMB, Ph.D.
The Mary Imogene Bassett Hospital
Cooperstown, New York

DAVID LESTER, Ph.D.
Stockton State College
Pomona, New Jersey

ROGER A. MacKINNON, M.D.
Columbia University College of Physicians and Surgeons
New York, New York

ANN S. McCOLSKEY, Ph.D.
Escambia County Community Mental Health Center
Pensacola, Florida

RICHARD K. McGEE, Ph.D.
University of Florida
Center for Crisis Intervention Research
Gainesville, Florida

ROBERT MICHELS, M.D.
Columbia University College of Physicians and Surgeons
New York, New York

ELLOEEN D. OUGHTERSON, M.A., J.D.
Suicide Prevention and Crisis Service
Buffalo, New York

MARY PACKARD
School of Hygiene and Public Health
Johns Hopkins University
Baltimore, Maryland

CHARLES PALMER, M.A.
Des Moines Child Guidance Center
Des Moines, Iowa

WAYNE C. RICHARD, Ph.D.
Dade Wallace Mental Health Center
Nashville, Tennessee

HERBERT S. ROTH, Ph.D.
Des Moines Child Guidance Center
Des Moines, Iowa

ARTHUR J. SCHUT
Young Men's Christian Association
Des Moines, Iowa

TIM WILLIAMS, M.S.W.
Suicide Prevention and Crisis Service
Buffalo, New York

JOHN W. WILLIAMSON, M.D.
School of Hygiene and Public Health
Johns Hopkins University
Baltimore, Maryland

INTRODUCTION

ALTHOUGH THE GROWTH of telephone counseling services can be traced back to the 1950's, very little interest developed at that time in the telephone as a treatment modality. The early telephone counseling services were located in suicide prevention centers and the thrust of research and writing focused primarily on the suicidal individual. Thus, suicide prevention centers led to an enormous increase in our understanding of the suicidal individual, and this information was widely disseminated. However, the information and experience gained using the telephone as a treatment modality was not codified, published, or disseminated.

Since the 1950's, telephone counseling services have become more and more widespread. As we note in the first section of this book, most communities today have a suicide prevention service, one or more teenage hotlines, a drug hotline or information service, a poison control center, a rumor control center, and more rarely a special service for the elderly. Yet, today, some twenty years after the appearance of telephone counseling services, telephone therapy is still neglected by professionals. As we point out in the second part of this book, therapists seem to have judged telephone counseling to be different from *real* therapy and, hence, did not perceive it as worthy of their attention. A common experience at telephone counseling services is for the professional staff to gradually detach themselves from counseling over the telephone in order to focus on face-to-face therapy, leaving the nonprofessionals to do the telephone counseling.

The editors of this book, working at the Suicide Prevention and Crisis Service in Buffalo, were soon aware of the lack of information and discussion about the problems involved in telephone counseling. Soon after the opening of the Buffalo service, we began a modest journal (*Crisis Intervention*) in which we tried to identify and discuss the possibilities and problems of telephone counseling. We distributed *Crisis Intervention* free of charge to all suicide prevention services and to members of the American Association of Suicidology.

This book is an attempt to further stimulate interest and discussion of the telephone as a mode of treatment and to reach a wider audience than those in the suicide prevention movement. We have used several methods for selecting articles to be included here. First, we have asked experts in various areas of telephone counseling to write chapters specially for this book. Secondly, we have obtained permission to reprint several articles published in professional journals. Thirdly, we have modified and reprinted some of the articles we originally published in *Crisis Intervention*, and finally we have ourselves written chapters specially for this book. As an edited book, therefore, there may be discontinuities in style and uneven coverage of the different aspects of the topic, but we have endeavored to eliminate repetition as much as possible. We have allowed and encouraged disagreement where we felt it was fruitful to do so. In Chapter 12, for example, the two editors have allowed themselves to disagree in public on the treatment of the obscene caller, and in Chapters 18 and 19 we have solicited different perspectives on the selection of telephone counselors. Right and wrong answers are rare in the field on mental health and it is only fair to present different perspectives.

We would like to thank the staff at the Suicide Prevention and Crisis Service in Buffalo, with whom we have worked, for helping to shape our views and modify our opinions; the secretarial staff for assistance in the preparation of the manuscript of the book; and our wives who have continued to encourage our professional preoccupations.

DAVID LESTER
GENE W. BROCKOPP

CONTENTS

PART III

PROBLEM CALLERS

PART IV

THE TELEPHONE COUNSELOR

PART V

EVALUATING TELEPHONE COUNSELORS AND
TELEPHONE SERVICES

CRISIS INTERVENTION
and
COUNSELING by TELEPHONE

PART I

THE VARIETIES OF TELEPHONE SERVICES

INTRODUCTION

In the course of the last decade or so, there has been a tremendous increase in the use of the telephone as a medium for counseling people. The stimulus for this development has two main sources. First, the suicide prevention movement, which began to grow as a result of the opening of the suicide prevention center in Los Angeles in the 1950's, adopted the telephone as the primary mode of treatment due to its immediacy. The individual in crisis, no matter where he is, can usually get to a telephone to call for help. Furthermore, the telephone offers a number of advantages over traditional modes of counseling (see Chap. 5), the major advantage being the relative anonymity it affords the distressed individual. He can seek help without having to identify himself.

The second stimulus came from the development of poison information centers. Again, the telephone is the ideal mode here because of its immediacy. If a person accidentally (or intentionally) ingests some chemical, immediate counseling as to antedotes and treatment can be obtained. Here, the telephone is being used as a way of transmitting information quickly to people.

These two services provided a model for immediate counseling and information-giving twenty-four hours a day by trained staff, and recently the model has been extended into a number of areas. The purpose of this first section is to survey the uses to which telephone counseling has been put.

Before describing the chapters in this section, it would be useful to mention and describe briefly some of the uses to which the telephone has been put as an instrument of counseling. The list below is probably not exhaustive and we would be happy to hear from readers of other ways that the telephone has been incorporated into comprehensive community services.

1. The suicide prevention center. The telephone has always been the major treatment mode of the suicide prevention center. Many centers offer nothing but the availability of counseling by telephone.

2. The crisis intervention center. Many suicide prevention centers soon found that they were being asked to help people in all kinds of crises, not merely suicidal crises. Accordingly, some changed their orientation toward more general crisis intervention and others were set up for the purpose of general crisis intervention.

3. Teen hotlines. Telephone counseling services soon began to orient themselves to particular groups of the population. The most common of these are those directed toward teenagers. These teen hotlines function much as crisis intervention centers except that the kinds of problems that they handle differ. Many teen hotlines do not attempt to provide twenty-four-hour service. Rather they are open for counseling in the late afternoons and evenings.

4. Another population that has been selected for special concern is the elderly. Rescue, Inc. in Boston has run a service for senior citizens in which one call is placed each day to the members. This serves as a protection in case they are ill or there is an emergency. If there is no answer to the call, a volunteer makes a visit to the person's home. Furthermore, the calls are made by senior citizens, so social contacts are initiated and renewed in the process of maintaining the service. The service in Boston is free. In New York City, there is a service which is financed by fees from the participating senior citizens. This commercial service differs from the Boston service in that it restricts the socializing aspects of the service. The service in New York limits calls to about a minute and serves mainly a protective function in case of illness.

5. Some services have been established to help individuals with particular problems. For example, Rescue, Inc. in Boston has started a special telephone counseling service for homosexuals, with a supporting clinic service.

6. Other services have proceeded in a more general direction.

The Suicide Prevention and Crisis Service of Buffalo has opened a problems in living service, which encourages people to call with any kind of problem.

7. The telephone has also come into use as a means to follow up patients discharged from psychiatric facilities. For example, the Mid-Missouri Mental Health Center in Columbia makes follow-up telephone calls to the former patients of the Center's alcoholism treatment program.

8. Another growing special area of counseling is provided by the drug hotlines. These provide information about drugs and their efforts and counseling to those involved with drugs. Not only can they provide general counseling but they can also help the individual who is currently on a "bad trip" with a drug or in a panic state.

9. Moving to the information-giving area, the poison control center is available in many communities to provide immediate counseling on treatment procedures after the ingestion of chemicals of all kinds. These centers were, on the whole, originated by pediatricians to aid in the treatment of childhood poisonings. However, there is now a shift in focus among many of these centers. It has become increasingly obvious that in many cases of "accidental" poisonings, there are self-destructive tendencies at work. Furthermore, the development of suicide prevention centers and drug hotlines has meant that these services must work very closely with the poison control centers to facilitate treatment.

10. Another way in which information can be used to help the community is through the rumor control center. These services were primarily motivated by riots and the need to dampen down the rumors attendant upon such social upheavals. Now, they have extended their information-giving service.

11. Another recent development has come from the cooperation between radio stations and local community groups. In Call for Action, originated by WMCA in New York City, trained counselors endeavored to help listeners with specific kinds of problems; garbage removal, rat and pest control, low-standard housing, voter registration, consumer fraud, traffic safety, pollu-

tion, taxes, and so on. WMCA in New York City concentrated on housing. WWDC in Washington, D.C., concentrated on garbage removal.

12. To these we can add a number of other related telephone services:

Dial-a-prayer
Comforting messenger: In Buffalo, one religious group has reoriented its dial-a-prayer service to include more of a comforting message.
Wake-up services

It can be seen that the range of services is large. In this section we have chosen to describe several kinds of services that we think can serve as models for telephone counseling services. In Chapter 1, the role of the telephone in a suicide prevention center is described, and to illustrate the variety of administrative systems possible, Chapter 2 presents some data from a survey of a number of suicide prevention centers. In Chapter 3, the operation of a teen hotline is described. The telephone does not have to be used in an agency setting, however. The individual counselor can make use of the telephone in facilitating his treatment of patients, and in Chapter 4 the ways in which the counselor can make use of the telephone are discussed.

Chapter 1

AN EMERGENCY TELEPHONE SERVICE:
THE DEVELOPMENT OF A PRESENCE

GENE W. BROCKOPP

SINCE THE LATE 1950's when an emergency telephone service for suicidal individuals was established in Los Angeles, over 200 suicide or crisis telephone emergency services have been founded throughout the country. Most of these services have been initiated by nonprofessional individuals imbued with the need to establish a facility in the community which would provide emergency mental health services where persons could receive assistance at any time of the day or night from individuals, usually volunteers, who were trained to work with people in crisis. Beginning with this concept, each service took on a unique character in its community. What it finally became in the community was a blend of the emergency service concept and the needs of the community in which it was established. What these services will become in the future as their identification as a formal community service becomes established is still unknown, for it is a new concept in mental health—a service designed to respond to a community need, operating outside of the traditional social and mental health agencies and staffed largely by volunteers. Traditional disciplines, boundaries, patterns of services and community needs are not sufficient to explain or define this service. Its phenomenal growth, the individuality of its structure in each community and its developmental pattern defy any global analyses. In this chapter, I will show the development of one center, its historical roots, its present functioning in the community and its goal as a service which will be accomplished through a process of its own extinction.

9

HISTORICAL DEVELOPMENTS AND FUNDING
RELATIONSHIP

The Erie County Suicide Prevention and Crisis Service (SPCS) began in 1966, when at the request of two community agencies, the Mental Health Association and the Psychological Association of Western New York, the Community Welfare Council* appointed a committee to study the need for a suicide prevention service. For over a year the committee collected information on various types of suicide prevention centers throughout the United States and Europe and on the need for such a service in Erie County. In this process, they interviewed all the agencies which were concerned with individuals who might be suicidal. By far the majority of these agencies felt that there was a need for a new service which would focus on this critical area. After considerable study, the committee developed a thoroughly documented plan for a suicide prevention and crisis service. On the basis of this committee report a new independent agency was established.

In November 1968, the SPCS was opened as a separate, autonomous unit operated by a membership corporation with a board of twenty-six directors selected to represent the business, general public and professional community. This corporation contracts with the Erie County Department of Mental Health to provide specialized services in the area of suicide prevention and crisis to the residents of Erie County. Its total operating budget of 245,000 dollars (1971) is obtained through the county mental health department which, in turn, obtains 45 percent of its operating funds from the State of New York and 55 percent from county taxes. The center is now located in a downtown office building in a suite of thirty offices, training and therapy rooms.

The relationship between the county and the SPCS has been an excellent one. The agency has a great deal of freedom within its area of concern, relates to other agencies within the community on an equal basis and has an adequate operating fund through tax monies.

————

* Now the Research and Planning Council.

The Mental Health Department has also profited from this relationship. It works in close operation with an agency that is dedicated to responding to people in emotional or suicidal crisis and one which is characterized by immediacy of assistance for these people. In addition, by having a governing board which is based in the community and which represents most of the business, professional and community facets of the community, the agency represents the needs of the community to the Mental Health Department.

The association between the SPCS and County Mental Health Department has not resulted in a limiting of our service to involvement in a small geographic area. They have urged and supported our move to have an effect throughout the region. We are very active in working with groups and organizations in the eastern United States, consulting with them regarding setting up suicide prevention centers and training people to work in these centers. In addition, the department and the board of the agency has enthusiastically supported the initiation and development of a national journal, *Crisis Intervention*. Published four times a year and devoted to pragmatic, practical and theoretical aspects of the development of centers and the use of the telephone as a therapeutic tool, *Crisis Intervention* is one of three journals published in this area of concern. Presently, this bulletin is being sent out to over 1,400 organizations and individuals who are concerned with crisis intervention and suicide prevention.

PROGRAM GOALS AND PURPOSES

Initially, it was felt that the agency should develop an emergency telephone service through the use of volunteers, have a limited clinical program and initiate research into the problem of suicide. After analyzing the community, its needs, and the present mental health programs in the area and then discussing the potential value of various programs with the Commissioner of Mental Health, it was decided that the agency should have broader purposes and concerns in the area of emergency mental health services. The service was therefore designed to be an innovative unit which would explore new methods of treatment and handling people in emotional crisis through a variety of therapeutic services. In addition, it would provide training and educative programs in crisis intervention in the community and have a comprehensive research and evaluative program within its operation.

Since the SPCS is dealing with suicide and crisis, it operates on a very pragmatic level, viewing mental health problems in a crisis orientation and looking at the community not in terms of the existing services or what has been done in the past, but in terms of what needs to be done both now and in the future to meet the needs of people in crisis. As a result, the agency immediately took on an image of an innovative, catalytic unit which explores new methods of working with patients and new approaches to handling individual problems—an agency which attempts to change the *status quo* and modify the procedures for the care of the emotionally disturbed that presently exist in the community.

The purpose of the agency then is quite different from that of a volunteer group which develops out of an existing community organization. Both as we conceive our role and as the Mental Health Department sees it, we are a unit which is to explore the problems of dealing with people in difficulty, develop new ways of functioning in the community and establish programs to ameliorate the problems people have, with a view toward developing new modes of service and new ways of operation within existing and developing community agencies and organizations. We do not see our role as a continuing one but one which is primarily based on the pragmatics of the situation and one which research will determine as we delineate the problems and move from theory to the modeling of a service entity in the community, then to the educating of existing and developing agencies in handling of these problem situations and finally to a release of this function of the agency into a broader, more comprehensive mental health unit in the community. Our role then is both catalytic and developmental, with the ultimate purpose being the spreading of the concepts of suicide prevention and crisis service throughout all of the organizations related to mental health in the community and with the intent that the Suicide Prevention and Crisis Center as a separate and distinct agency will cease to exist within a short period of time. The dissolution of this center, of course, will be contingent on the development of the methods of handling suicidal patients in existing agencies; but this is the goal of the agency and one which we are committed to achieve.

ORGANIZATIONAL STRUCTURE AND STAFF

The service is organized into three major units: (1) The Crisis Clinic of Erie County; (2) Institute for Training in Crisis Intervention; and (3) the Center for the Study of Personal and Social Disorders. Each of these areas is coordinated by a director, who functions with the Executive Director in administering the agency. Each of the three services will be briefly discussed.

The Erie County Crisis Clinic maintains a twenty-four-hour emergency telephone service available to all individuals in the community. This service is available either through telephone contact or by the individual presenting himself at the clinic. In either case, consultation, therapy or assistance is given to the individual immediately upon request or within a very short period of time. During the day the telephones are manned by trained volunteers and the professional or counseling staff of the center. During the evening and through the night, the telephones are manned by a cadre of trained individuals ranging from housewives to nurses, businessmen to psychologists, who are specifically trained by the center to perform this vital function. The clinic also sees individuals in crisis on a face-to-face basis through a short-term intensive psychotherapy program which uses both group and individual modes.

The Institute for Training in Crisis Intervention is concerned with educating and training both community and professional groups in the techniques of crisis intervention and in assisting them to provide these services through existing agencies. High priority is given to the training of nonprofessional people at the center. Presently, four individuals, selected from the community and having no professional background, are being given specialized professional training to enable them to function as highly trained counselors in the field of crisis intervention. Continuous training programs are being given for new members of our night watch staff and, in addition, training programs of a seminar or workshop type have been given to specific groups in the community, including other agencies, social workers, nurses, the police department, counselors, teachers and psychiatrists.

The third task of the center is to provide systematic research in the area of crisis intervention and suicide prevention. This is accomplished through the Center for the Study of Personal and Social Disorders. The types of calls that are received are continually analyzed as well as the changes in the type of calls over the period of time that the center has been in operation. Investigations are made into completed suicides in Erie County as well as the types of patients and problems that are being seen in the clinic. Research projects are being designed to measure the effectiveness of the center's operation and look into the type of center that should develop in order to meet the specific needs of the community. Programs for the future include research into the disrupting factors in the community and interplay between the social settings and the individual's aggressive behaviors.

To accomplish these varied tasks, the service is staffed by four different types of individuals: (1) Professionally trained individuals who operate out of academic disciplines (including psychology, law, social work, psychiatry, nursing and theology) who, by training and experience, are qualified to work in a center of this nature; (2) trained para-professional people who are selected from the Erie County community and who are trained by the center staff to be mental health counselors; (3) "professional" volunteers who are trained to answer the telephones at night or on weekends and who vary in background from high school graduate to mental health professional; (4) individuals who are in various professional training programs and who work at the center on a full-time or part-time basis for their clerkship, internship or field placement.

The staff of the center consists of eleven professional staff members, five mental health counselors, six secretaries, four counselors in training, one hundred "professional" volunteers, numerous consultants and approximately ten students who are placed here as part of their professional training program.

DEVELOPMENT OF THE TELEPHONE SERVICE

The center began telephone operation on November 12, 1968. To date (November 1971), over 40,000 calls have been received from more than 30,000 individuals in various types of suicidal, personal or emotional crises. Approximately 2,000 calls a month are now handled at the center. In addition, more than 3,000 appointments for face-to-face short-term intensive psychotherapy are made at the center each year.

As a result of our continuous evaluation of our service and the analyses of the calls received at the center, a number of changes in the center and its programs have been made.

In most twenty-four-hour emergency telephone services, the major way of assisting individuals in difficulty is through a telephone, usually publicized under the general rubric of a suicide prevention center, a crisis service, or a combination of the two. Through analyzing the telephone calls of the first six months of telephone service at the Buffalo Center, we noted (as many other centers have noted) that most individuals calling the center are not suicidal or even contemplating suicide. Our figures indicated that 78 percent of the individuals call because of other problems and concerns. Often they will call the center with the disclaimer "I am not going to kill myself but I have this problem and I want to talk to somebody," or "I can't get help anywhere else, maybe you can help me." In looking at the problems people were having through the calls we were receiving, we felt that the designation of the twenty-four-hour telephone emergency service under the term "Suicide and Crisis Service," could be a stumbling block for individuals and may prevent them from calling the center with other problems they have (which may have a suicidal aspect although they were not defined as such by the people calling) because of the ethical and religious connotations which the community attached to suicidal behavior.

We decided to explore other ways to label our telephone service to facilitate the movement of individuals with problems to the center and then through the center to a helping network of people. Our initial movement was to develop a broader designation that would allow individuals with a wider range of problems to feel that they could call the center. Out of the many choices that were available, we selected the term "Problems of Living" since it defined problems in a nonpsychiatric manner, gave them sense of normality, and did not circumscribe problems according to age, sex, or type of difficulty.

The second differentiation was in terms of specific problem areas or age groups. Again analyzing the phone calls received at the center, we felt there was a need to contact or to develop a telephone service which would focus on the teens and twenties population. It was felt that the teens population would be more likely to call a telephone service if it was designated specifically as a teen line. Also, we felt that many of the telephone therapists on the Suicide Prevention Line, even though they would be facilitative in assisting people with more severe problems, would have a more difficult time handling the problems of the teenagers who call on the suicide line since the adults tend to define these problems in a nonserious way. By beginning a separate line we felt we could train volunteers to focus on the problems of youth more effectively.

One of the problems with which we became concerned after developing the three telephone numbers, was that we were moving rapidly toward a proliferation of telephone numbers, each one designed to reach a specific problem population. We were on the way to flooding the community with a mass of emergency telephone numbers, implicitly forcing them to make discriminations among the numbers to call for assistance.. When we were asked by the Mental Health Department to consider developing a number designed to reach individuals with drug problems, we became acutely aware of this problem, for in less than eighteen months we would have given the community four numbers designated as problem or emergency numbers—four different telephone numbers to be called by individuals with various types of difficulties.

In attempting to work out a solution for this problem, we came back to the Problems of Living number, which because of its ambiguity and breadth, could be used to encompass the drug problem with which we were concerned or any other problem that might develop in the community in the future.

With this in mind, we took the following direction in the differentiation of our phone numbers:

The Problems of Living line is designated by the number 854-5655 and is a series of numbers from 5655 through 5660. By splitting this series of numbers into units of three numbers each; e.g. 5655, 5656, 5657, 5658, 5659, and 5660, we could advertise the second series; 854-5658 as the drug line and answer it as the drug line. In the future, by merely changing the last digit from 8 to 5, we could effectively more the number back into the Problems of Living units, and again leave the last series of three numbers available for a new kind of problem whenever one has been defined in the community. This would allow publicity to be developed for a specific number designated by a problem area, and it would keep the proliferation of telephone numbers to a minimum, since, as the problem area became less "hot" in the community, it could be subsumed under the Problems of Living line and could be advertised as such in the community.

We feel for any telephone therapy service to be effective, the service must be defined in such a way as to facilitate the movement of individuals to the telephone service. Therefore, the way the phone is listed must be defined in a way which is seen as facilitative by the individuals who are in difficulty or in a way which encompasses their problem and allows them to feel that they can receive the assistance that they need from this service. To accomplish this, it appears to us that the differentiation of the telephone line from a suicide prevention or crisis service into both broader areas and specific problems (as they become defined) is essential if the service is to be responsive to the needs of the community.

The concept of telephone therapy is still a new one in the professional community. How it will develop and differentiate and what will be the best ways in which it can be defined is still to be determined. It is apparent from our work in Buffalo that each community must find its own way to define its telephone emergency service, and that their service must be defined in terms of the problems the community has, so that the service can facilitate the movement of an individual in difficulty to the appropriate resources.*

TELEPHONE SERVICE DATA

The following tables show the types of calls that we respond to on the four telephone services. It can be seen from the table that there is some differentiation (age, sex, severity of problem) in who uses each line and in the way the lines are used.

TABLE 1-I

ANALYSIS OF TELEPHONE CALLS TO THE SUICIDE
AND CRISIS SERVICE

	Total	Suicide*	Teen†	Pl‡	Drug§	Male	Female
Name							
Anon	40%	32%	50%	42%	55%	43%	38%
first name	35%	38%	36%	25%	17.5%	28%	38%
last initial	4%	6%	3%	—	2.5%	3%	5%
full name	21%	24%	11%	33%	25%	25%	19%
Age							
0-9	—	—	—	—	—	—	—
10-19	46%	21%	95%	4%	42.5%	30%	53%
20-29	18%	27%	2.5%	25%	30%	16%	18%
30-39	11%	15%	—	29%	10%	25%	6%
40-49	6%	11%	—	4%	—	2%	8%
50-59	4%	5%	—	8%	—	3%	4%
60-69	.5%	1%	—	—	—	—	1%
70-79	.5%	1%	—	—	—	2%	—
80-99	—	—%	—	—	—	—	—
unknown	14%	19%	2.5%	29%	17.5%	22%	11%
Mean age in Years	23	28	16	31	17	26	22
Sex							
male	28%	29%	17%	58%	42.5%	100%	—
female	72%	70%	83%	42%	57.5%	—	100%

---

* Suicide calls. 128 first calls taken randomly over a two-week period 5-1-71 to 5-15-71.

† Teen calls. 81 first calls taken randomly over a 2-week period 5-1-71 to 5-15-71.

‡ Problems of living calls. 24 calls—all new cases in May 1971.

§ Drug hotline calls. 75 first calls in May 1971.

---

* In addition to the emergency telephone service, the center provides a Care-ring service and full range of clinical out-patient services to the Erie County community through face-to-face counseling in both individual or group mode. Other related services include outreach program in the community under the concept of "Night People" and educational, training and research programs of a wide variety. As this book is focusing on telephone counseling, it would be inappropriate to go into these many services in detail. The reader should be aware, however, that the center is much more than a telephone answering service.

	Total	Suicide*	Teen†	Pl‡	Drugs§	Male	Female
Calling For:							
self	86%	82%	92%	83%	75%	93%	93%
other	8%	16%	4%	—	11%	—	—
self & other	6%	7%	4%	17%	16%	7%	7%
Marital Status							
single	57%	38%	96%	21%	42.5%	45%	63%
married	21%	25%	4%	63%	10%	28%	19%
separated	5%	8%	—	4%	—	8%	3%
divorced	5%	9%	—	4%	2.5%	3%	6%
widowed	1%	3%	—	—	—	2%	1%
common law	1%	2%	—	—	2.5%	—	1%
unk.	9%	15%	—	8%	42.5%	13%	7%
Crisis							
acute	16%	20%	14%	4%	—	17%	16%
chronic	21%	25%	12%	33%	—	20%	22%
neither	32%	29%	43%	17%	—	25%	35%
not checked	30%	26%	32%	46%	—	38%	27%
Suicidal History							
unknown	50%	44%	58%	50%	—	43%	52%
none	10%	12%	9%	8%	—	13%	9%
ideation	3%	5%	—	4%	—	5%	3%
threats	1%	3%	—	—	—	2%	1%
attempts	7%	12%	2%	—	—	3%	9%
not checked	28%	24%	31%	37%	—	33%	26%
Current Suicide							
none	64%	61%	68%	63%	—	57%	66%
ideations	4%	7%	3%	—	—	5%	4%
threats	2%	4%	1%	—	—	3%	2%
attempt	2%	4%	—	—	—	2%	2%
not checked	28%	24%	31%	37%	—	33%	26%
Traced	1.5%	3%	—	—	—	3%	1%
Police Called:	1.5%	2%	1%	—	—	2%	1%
Hour							
unknown	2%	1%	1%	0%	0%	0%	1%
midnight to 3 AM	10%	13%	6%	12%	0%	8%	9%
3 AM to 6 AM	4%	5.5%	0%	4%	2%	4%	4%
6 AM to 9 AM	2%	3.5%	1%	0%	0%	0%	3%
9 AM to noon	10%	6.5%	14%	21%	11%	17%	10%
noon to 3 PM	13%	12.5%	17%	12%	16%	17%	12%
3 PM to 6 PM	15%	14%	20%	4%	25%	10%	17%
6 PM to 9 PM	22%	19%	19%	16%	26%	20%	19%
9 PM to midnight	24%	26%	21%	30%	20%	25%	24%
Mean Length of							
Call in Minutes	16.8	20.5	9.8	21.3	12.9	19.4	15.3

Problem	Total Primary	Total Mentioned as a Problem	Suicide Primary	Suicide Mentioned	Teen Primary	Teen Mentioned	Pl Primary	Pl Mentioned	Drug (see Table 1-II)	Male Primary	Male Mentioned	Female Primary	Female Mentioned
alcohol	3%	5%	5%	9%	0%	1%	0%	0%		2%	3%	2%	5%
anxiety	0%	15%	9%	18%	9%	12%	8%	13%		7%	13%	10%	18%
depression	8%	18%	9%	24%	2%	5%	21%	29%		8%	17%	9%	20%
drugs	5%	9%	7%	13%	4%	5%	4%	4%		8%	10%	2%	6%
employment	1%	5%	1%	3%	0%	0%	0%	4%		0%	2%	1%	3%
family	18%	28%	15%	27%	23%	30%	21%	29%		17%	23%	21%	31%
financial	0%	1%	0%	1%	0%	0%	0%	4%		0%	0%	0%	2%
homicide	0%	1%	0%	1%	0%	0%	0%	0%		0%	2%	0%	1%
info	9%	12%	10%	13%	9%	12%	8%	8%		8%	13%	10%	12%
legal	1%	3%	0%	2%	0%	0%	8%	13%		2%	13%	1%	3%
lonely	7%	11%	9%	16%	4%	4%	13%	13%		8%	13%	8%	12%
ment. dis.	2%	5%	4%	6%	0%	2%	0%	13%		7%	10%	8%	2%
pregnancy	2%	3%	0%	0%	6%	7%	0%	0%		0%	2%	3%	3%
school	2%	3%	1%	2%	2%	5%	0%	0%		3%	3%	1%	3%
sexual	7%	9%	6%	9%	6%	9%	13%	17%		15%	18%	5%	7%
suicide	9%	18%	17%	31%	0%	2%	0%	4%		8%	17%	7%	15%
boyfriend	11%	13%	3%	3%	26%	32%	4%	4%		5%	7%	14%	17%
other	3%	5%	1%	2%	6%	9%	0%	4%		2%	5%	3%	5%

Line	Male	Female
suicide	55%	51%
PL	23%	7%
teen	22%	42%

Disposition	Total	Suicide	Teen	Pl	Drug	Male	Female
unknown	.5%	2%	—	4%	—	2%	—
hung up	12%	16%	8%	38%	9%	16%	10%
ventilate	39%	34%	48%	17%	33%	37%	42%
SPCS appt.	8%	10%	3%	4%	2%	10%	8%
pt. call back	8%	9%	6%	—	11%	7%	9%
clergy	.5%	1%	—	—	—	—	1%
M.D.	3%	3%	3%	8%	5%	—	3%
psychiatrist	2%	1%	1%	4%	—	3%	1%
friend/relative	9%	2%	22%	4%	7%	5%	11%
Meyer/Buf. State	2%	2%	1%	—	2%	—	2%
police	2%	2%	—	8%	—	2%	2%

family serv.	1%	1%	—	—	—	2%	1%
NYS Emplm.	.5%	1%	—	4%	—	—	1%
Bflo. Housing	.5%	—	—	—	—	—	1%
family court	.5%	1%	—	—	—	2%	—
lawyer	.5%	1%	—	—	—	2%	—
Bell Teleph.	.5%	1%	—	—	—	—	1%
Children's Aid	.5%	—	1%	—	—	—	1%
E.C. Health Dept.	.5%	1%	1%	—	—	—	1%
E.C. Mental Health	.5%	—	—	4%	—	2%	—
SPCS	3%	4%	1%	4%	—	3%	1%
Salvation Army	.5%	1%	—	—	—	—	—
library	.5%	—	1%	—	—	2%	—
A.I.D.	.5%	2%	—	—	7%	—	1%
Parents/w.o. Part.	.5%	1%	—	—	—	2%	—
Plan. Parenthood	3%	2%	4%	—	—	3%	2%
Comm. Drug Abuse ctr.	.5%	1%	—	—	—	—	—
newspaper	.5%	1%	—	—	—	—	1%
TV programs	.5%	—	—	—	2%	—	—
guidance counsel	—	—	—	—	2%	—	—
narcotics guidance	—	—	—	—	7%	—	—
methadone clinic	—	—	—	—	13%	—	—

Appointments

	7% of all calls	10% of all calls	2% of all calls	8% of all calls			
show	65%	62%	50%	67%	0%	80%	64%
fail	24%	23%	50%	33%	0%	20%	18%
cancel	11%	15%	0%	0%	0%	0%	18%

TABLE 1-II

ANALYSIS OF CALLS ON THE DRUG HOT LINE*

Problem	Primary	Secondary
Contemplating use	5%	5%
Overdose	2%	2%
Relief from immediate effects	20%	22%
Relief from habit	20%	22%
Information	42%	60%
Lonely	2%	6%
Lost methadone dose	6%	9%
Other	2%	5%

Method of Taking	
Oral	42%
Injection	17%
Smoke	5%
Sniff	2%
Other	2%
Unknown	31%

Drug Involved

Pot	7%
Psychedelic	20%
Narcotic	24%
Barbituate	7%
Amphetamine	16%
Alcohol	2%
Minor Tranq.	—
Major Tranq.	—
Unknown	24%

Information About

Availability of drugs	—
Legal aspects	—
Physical effects	22%
Speakers wanted	2%
Printed material	9%
How to deal with user	5%
Where to get help	11%
Drug identification	5%
Other	2%

————

* Based on 75 first calls in May 1971.

SUMMARY

I conceive of a suicide prevention center as a unit involved with crisis intervention, suicide prevention or mental health problems in the community which may lead to crisis or suicide. It attempts to do this through the development of a presence in the community, through exploring and delineating problem areas, and defining what is necessary to ameliorate the condition. Its task also includes modeling the new process or method and then moving these out into the broader, more comprehensive units of mental health services.

To accomplish these goals we have established an organization which is flexible, open to change, has a good resource in terms of money and a close association with both the community and the Mental Health Department. Staff who were not tied to traditional methods of service were selected—staff who would be able to examine very carefully and critically what they were doing with a view toward changing and remolding the structure of the telephone and clinic services to meet the community needs. As a result, the agency and the emergency service of the center have changed quite rapidly and thoroughly throughout the past thirty-six months of its existence and has become, itself, a model of change.

I feel that of all the organizations in the world, a dynamic and pragmatic concept such as a suicide prevention center should not be allowed to die simply because of tired blood or through the strangulation of bureaucratization. I feel that when an organization such as this has performed its function in a community, that is, when it has established a presence in the community, served as a catalytic unit in the development of broader community mental health centers, and has provided for the community, it should be allowed to go out of existence. In this way, the presence and the process of fresh, new, dynamic and innovative approach to mental health problems can remain alive or be reborn under the aegis of a new organization which will be committed to goals similar to those which this suicide prevention center has been committed; to isolate, define, understand, and meet the needs of a lonely, detached, dispairing and hopeless segment of humanity and thereby be instrumental in their search for a more meaningful and richer existence.

Chapter 2

A SURVEY OF TELEPHONE ANSWERING SYSTEMS IN SUICIDE PREVENTION AND CRISIS INTERVENTION AGENCIES

RICHARD K. MCGEE, WAYNE C. RICHARD, AND COREY BERCUN

THE CHIME-LIKE TELEPHONE bell starts to ring: 'Ping, pong.' Simultaneously one of the lines on the white telephone console begins flashing. A woman picks up the receiver and in a soft voice answers: 'Suicide Prevention and Crisis Service. Can I help you?"

Thus begins nearly every newspaper feature story ever written about a local suicide and crisis service. Throughout the country such services have been advertised to the public through the newspaper feature writers who tend to emphasize the drama of the ringing telephone and the availability of someone on the spot to answer it. The telephone service has come to be taken for granted by many program planners and managers, and few people seem to realize the complexity of the issues surrounding the kind of service required by a twenty-four-hour telephone answering program. It would surprise many citizens who have never called to learn that in many centers which advertise twenty-four-hour availability to the public, it can be a difficult, time-consuming, frustrating, and annoying process to get a

This study was conducted through facilities supported by Grant No. MH 16861 from the Center for Studies of Suicide Prevention, National Institute of Mental Health, to the University of Florida.

The authors are grateful to Mr. David Willens for his assistance in completing this study.

A shortened version of this chapter appeared in *Life-Threatening Behavior*, 1972, Vol. 2, No. 1.

"helper" on the telephone. In some instances, it is actually impossible to complete a call.

The purpose of this chapter is to identify and discuss some issues related to setting up a telephone answering service and to report some results of an actual survey taken to determine the effectiveness of the systems being operated in nineteen different programs in the southeastern United States. In this study "effectiveness" is defined as the time taken to complete the connection to the crisis worker. It should be recognized that this is a very important, but by no means the only aspect of the total effectiveness of a crisis center.

COST OF TELEPHONE SERVICE

Naturally, a primary consideration in establishing any new program is the relative cost of each major component. However, it is often overlooked that maximum coverage on the telephone by crisis personnel does not result in additional telephone charges. Rather, it requires an office where someone can be on duty around-the-clock. The office need not be large. The only added space necessary is room for a daybed to be used by the night watch in case it is possible for them to sleep during the early morning hours of the shift. Rent money and adequate physical space are the most importance cost issues in telephone services covered around-the-clock in the center's office.

It is interesting to observe that some centers consider around-the-clock coverage to be unfeasible. They use the next best thing —part-time coverage by a commercial answering service. The costs of answering services vary considerably, but rarely does any suicide prevention program pay the full rate usually charged commercial or professional clients. Nearly always the answering service will trim their charge as a public service to a nonprofit organization. Sometimes, answering services have been known to provide the service completely gratis because of good public relations developed by physicians who serve on the crisis center board of directors. Naturally, anything so valuable, offered free, becomes a highly valued and often unexamined component of the program. Few crisis service directors have taken time to determine how much they are "paying" for these free or reduced-rate services. Observations of telephone systems to be reported later indicate that using a commercial telephone service, during even a part of the twenty-four-hour period, may be a penny-wise and pound-foolish economy.

MANPOWER ISSUES

A second set of issues related to the operation of the telephone service concerns who is available to serve on an around-the-clock basis. Whereas most suicide and crisis services throughout the country have made appropriate use of the nonprofessional volunteer, there are some complications to their being available for the night watch. There are centers existing in places where the office is not considered a safe place to be at night. Usually, this means that the housewives who volunteer for the daytime and early evening shifts would not be comfortable spending the night in the center. Such a conclusion should not be allowed to generalize to all volunteer workers, however. Many of the male volunteers would find no problem with this at all. Further, if they can get a few hours sleep, they generally find it no more of an inconvenience to their work the next day than if they are interrupted two or three times during the night while on duty at home.

There is always the question of whether or not professional workers should be the ones to take the telephone calls during the evening hours. It has been very interesting to observe that this issue can be rationalized either way, as necessary to suit the biases of the program directors. In one program, professionals did not want to be disturbed in their regular daily clinical practice in a community mental health center, so they "allowed" the volunteers to cover for them during the office hours. At night, however, they reasoned that the calls would be more serious and would require the expert handling of the professional. In another center, the clinic staff accepted it as their responsibility to cover the service during the day when they would be in the office, but they brought in volunteers to handle calls at night when the professional staff didn't want to be bothered by calls at home. Arguments related to the differential desirability of mental health professionals over nonprofessional volunteers as telephone crisis workers have been included elsewhere in this book. However, it should be remembered that there is no substantive evidence that any professional practitioner of any discipline is superior in his handling of suicide or crisis calls to the properly trained volunteer. Furthermore, the utilization of professional personnel as telephone workers on the grounds that they are members of a clinic staff, and therefore the only ones available, is a practice which denies a community the full range of helping resources which are potentially available within its midst.

Finally, a frequently under-utilized source of valuable manpower for suicide and crisis services is the local university or college. College students find that taking duty in a crisis center is a meaningful role in their social action oriented lives. In between calls they frequently are able to spend much of the time doing the studying or term paper writing that they would be doing at home. If a center has some additional funds, college students will take night watch duty for a few dollars a night for a little extra spending money, but they work equally well for no pay at all.

RECORD KEEPING

A major problem which has been faced by most crisis services is how to collect and store case information about clients when the calls are not taken in the center office. It is frequently necessary for a worker on the evening shift to open a new case, and then someone in the office must handle certain follow-up aspects of the case the next day. The worker who opened the case must then take his information forms and notes to the office early in the morning, or he must mail them in. Or, he may carry them around for a few days until it is more convenient to drop them off at the office. In the meantime, the management of the case is severely impaired because all of the client data are not in the office. The problem is even worse if the case was opened previously by another worker, and the file which the worker needs is in the office while he is at home. From the standpoint of adequate clinical service, it is absolutely necessary to provide continuity of information about the case. This can be done if each crisis worker has his own private caseload of clients which he manages in the professional therapy model. This system has great liabilities for crisis intervention programs, whether the personnel are professional or volunteer. The only adequate method of insuring maximum clinical management of crisis cases is to have all records and all case work performed in a central place twenty-four hours a day. Attention to this issue should automatically dictate the type of telephone system to be employed.

PUBLIC RESPONSIBILITY

There is a further issue which will need more and more attention in the future growth of existing crisis programs as well as in the development of new ones. This is a moral and/or ethical issue. It relates to promising the community an image of a service through public advertising and then delivering something less than the public expects. An advertisement which says in effect that a person can call day or night and find someone to talk to about his problems does not lead to the expectation that he may have to go through several different procedures before finally getting to the helper. The caller has the right to expect that the person who answers the telephone will be the one who will help him. Similarly, if the advertising prompts suicidal people to reach out in their ambivalence to grasp at a slim ray of hope before taking a self-destructive act, then such a caller should not have to experience a series of delays in the helping process. To provide a system with less than the maximum in efficiency and rapidity for getting caller and crisis worker together is tantamount to a violation of the contract which should exist between a suicide prevention service and the community. Of course, it is highly doubtful that any crisis service deliberately misleads its public, but it is very risky for a director to delegate to anyone else not under his direct control (i.e. an external answering service) the responsibility for assuring that his commitment to the public is being met. This is an ethical issue which crisis centers must begin to face.

A SURVEY OF NINETEEN EMERGENCY
TELEPHONE SYSTEMS

The preceding paragraphs have attempted to discuss some of the issues which should be taken into consideration in the planning and operation of a suicide and crisis telephone service. Admittedly, the position taken is one which advocates an idealized type of service. It is important to determine how many centers actually operate this way, and in those which do not, what problems, if any, occur in their systems. For this reason, a study was made of a sample of suicide and crisis intervention services known to be operating in the Southeast.

Programs Included in the Sample

The list of centers included in this study is not intended to be a complete list of all services in the region. However, they include all programs which the authors knew were in operation during December 1970. The nineteen centers included in the study are located in Nashville, Knoxville, Memphis and Chattanooga, Tennessee; Atlanta, Georgia; Birmingham and Montgomery, Alabama; Greenville, South Carolina; Greensboro, Sanford and Halifax County (Roanoke Rapids), North Carolina; Pensacola, Jacksonville, Gainesville, Orlando, Eustis, St. Petersburg, Brevard County (Rockledge), and Miami, Florida.

Among this group, ten were programs developed by or within community mental health centers. In some, the suicide and crisis service served as part of the required emergency service component. The remaining nine programs were separate and independent agencies.

Methods and Procedures

The primary purpose of the survey was to determine two things: (1) what procedures or steps are involved in getting through the answering system from initial ring of the phone to actual contact with a crisis worker on duty; and (2) how much time is required to get a response from a helper. Two time intervals were recorded. The first interval was the length of time elapsing from the point where the caller first detected the ringing of the number he called to the point where that number was answered by someone. This interval was designated as "Time to Answer." The second time period also began at the same point as the first, but continued until the caller was able to determine that he had actually contacted a person who identified himself as the "crisis worker on duty." This period of time was designated as "Time to Reach Worker."

It is believed that timing the intervals with the first ringing of the number called yields results exactly comparable with those which would have resulted had all the calls been placed locally. However, a different problem resulted when the answering system required the caller to give his number and wait for the worker on duty to return the call. Here, of course, an increased time interval was required because the experimenters gave instructions that the worker should return the call "collect." Thus, the call had to be handled by a long distance operator and could not be dialed directly. It was presumed that this additional time was fairly standard for all communities using such a system and did not unfairly prejudice data from any center. It is also reasoned that nearly every crisis center advertises its service on radio and television stations whose reception area extends beyond the limits of the toll-free telephone service in their community. Hence, it is very likely that real calls are received from persons on a long distance basis. In such cases, the data gathered in this study would accurately reflect the service such callers received.

The experimenters determined in advance that certain ethical problems must be satisfied in the design of this study. First, it was felt that research activities do not justify the placing of "fake" emergency calls, nor should the impression be given that an emergency existed when such was not the case. Such procedures are considered a violation of the confidence of crisis workers who deserve to be treated as if they are on duty for serious business, not for what they are very likely to perceive as "fun and games" procedures of experimenters. Therefore, every effort was made to urge the system to function as rapidly and as normally as possible, without falsely causing the worker to mobilize emotional energy and anxiety which should properly be reserved for a genuine emergency he might have to face later. Further, it was considered incumbent upon the investigators to avoid any deception of any kind, and all questions asked by the workers were answered completely and honestly.

It was recognized that complete honesty might dictate that program directors should be notified prior to the study and given a chance to refuse to be included in the investigation. However, such a procedure would also have provided the opportunity for them to alert the workers and encourage them to "look good" during the time of the study. Then, long distance calls from a given city would have automatically signaled that the call was a research call, and less faith could be placed in the generalizability of the data obtained. It was thus decided that no prior announcements would be made, but that all program directors would receive a complete and anonymous report of the findings when they were completed.

The final methodological question concerned when to place the calls. Again, it was decided that the procedure should permit the least possible contamination due to notice circulating within the worker group that someone was doing a study of the telephone system. Therefore, all calls were placed within the same twenty-four-hour period. The intervals chosen were designed to permit observation of the various systems (1) during weekday office hours, (2) during early evening hours, (3) during middle-of-the-night hours, and (4) during the weekend. To allow for these observations the calls were placed on consecutive days as follows:

Period I—Between 3 PM and 5 PM, Friday
Period II—Between 7 PM and 9 PM, Friday
Period III—Between 1 AM and 3 AM, Saturday
Period IV—Between 10 AM and 12 noon, Saturday

The experimenter's procedure on each call was as follows:

When the first call was answered, he asked, "Are you a crisis worker on duty to talk to people with a problem?" If the answering person was not the crisis worker, the caller stated, "I would like very much to talk with a worker as soon as possible." If questioned directly, he stated, "This is not an emergency, but it *is* important that I speak with a person on duty. Could you get one for me, please?"

When a person was reached who identified himself as the worker on duty, the experimenter said, "First, I want you to know that this is not an emergency call. However, I am conducting a study of several suicide prevention and crisis intervention programs to find out how their telephone systems operate at this time of the day." He would then proceed to ask a few questions about the system to satisfy himself that he correctly understood the steps through which the contact had been accomplished. The experimenter tried to remain alert to the feelings of the worker and attempted to respond to them, especially expressing appreciation and regret for having to disturb the worker during the midnight hours of Period III.

Results of the Survey

As a result of the study, eight different telephone systems were identified during the seventy-six calls. They are identified as follows:

A. The call is answered directly by the crisis worker on duty.
B. The call is answered by an operator or receptionist in the office, who then switches the call to the crisis worker on duty.
C. The call is answered by a commercial answering service which then patches the call through the switchboard to the worker on duty at home.
D. The call is answered by a commercial answering service which takes the caller's name and number and notifies the worker, who returns the call.
E. The call is answered by personnel in another agency who

take the caller's name and number and notify the worker, who returns the call.

F. The phone is answered by personnel in another agency who give the caller the name and number of the worker on duty and instruct him to redial the call.

G. A mechanical recording device informs the caller of another number which he can dial to reach a crisis worker on duty.

H. There is no answer at all after several attempts (including a request for assistance by the long distance operator).

Table 2-I shows the frequency with which each of these systems was encountered during the four calling periods. It is evident from these data that most centers use more than one of the several systems. In fact, only five of the nineteen centers used the same procedure during all of the four periods. Five centers employed as many as three different systems during the four periods, while the remaining programs had two different systems in operation.

TABLE 2-I

UTILIZATION OF VARIOUS TELEPHONE SYSTEMS
DURING A 24-HOUR PERIOD

Type of Answering System	Period I	Period II	Period III	Period IV
A. Direct to worker	10	6	6	5
B. Switchboard to worker	4	1	0	0
C. Com. A.S./Patch to Worker	0	4	5	4
D. Com. A.S./Worker return	3	6	5	5
E. Other agcy/Worker return	1	2	0	0
F. Other agcy/ref to Worker	0	0	1	2
G. Recording ref to Worker	1	0	1	2
H. No answer	0	0	1	1

Table 2-II is a complete accounting of the time intervals recorded for obtaining the first answer and for reaching a crisis worker in each of the nineteen centers during the four calling periods. Data recorded in this table are in minutes and seconds; thus a time of three minutes, fifteen seconds would appear as

TABLE 2-II

RELATIVE EFFICIENCY OF THE NINETEEN TELEPHONE SERVICES

Center	3 to 5 PM Friday			7 to 9 PM Friday			1 to 3 AM Saturday			10 to 12 N Saturday		
	Type of System	Time to Answer	Time to Worker	Type of System	Time to Answer	Time to Worker	Type of System	Time to Answer	Time to Worker	Type of System	Time to Answer	Time to Worker
1	A	00:11	00:11	A	00:02	00:02	A	00:04	00:04	A	00:03	00:03
2	A	00:06	00:06	D	00:05	06:00	D	00:13	15:32	D	00:05	14:20
3	B	00:11	03:10	D	00:07	16:20	D	00:18	08:16	D	00:03	39:12
4	D	00:14	17:30	D	00:13	12:15	D	00:16	13:41	F	00:05	n.c. a
5	A	00:03	00:03	A	00:08	00:08	A	00:05	00:05	A	00:06	00:06
6	A	00:08	00:08	C	00:30	01:10	C	00:10	01:00	C	00:17	02:42
7	D	00:11	15:00	C	00:14	01:30	C	00:15	01:10	C	00:06	00:57
8	G	00:10	06:10b	A	00:05	00:05	G	00:03	01:05	G/B c	00:05	02:10
9	E	00:06	08:00	E	00:13	49:00	F	00:14	03:18	F	00:11	n.c. d
										E	00:28	07:45
10	B	00:15	01:30	D	00:12	09:15	C	00:10	02:00	C	00:12	02:35
11	B	00:06	01:00	C	00:08	01:09	C	00:08	00:53	C	00:07	01:12
12	D	00:06	05:35	D	00:07	07:16	D	00:17	n.c. e	D	00:06	11:16
13	A	00:04	00:04	B	00:11	01:20	A	00:18	00:18	A	00:06	00:06
14	B	00:06	01:25	C	00:02	01:49	C	00:15	02:25	D	00:05	06:52
15	A	00:09	00:09	D	00:14	04:20	D	00:12	05:20	D	00:08	11:35
16	A	00:04	00:04	A	00:05	00:05	A	00:06	00:06	A	00:07	00:07
17	A	00:18	00:18	A	00:09	00:09	A	00:11	00:11	A	00:05	00:05
18	A	00:04	00:04	E	00:04	05:35	A	00:04	00:04	H	—	—
19	A	00:04	00:04	A	00:04	00:04	H	—	—	G	00:03	02:50

a . . . e See discussion in text for explanation of unusual events on these calls.

03:15. Since it was evident that the different types of answering systems required markedly different times to reach the crisis worker, Table 2-III was developed to permit an easier comparison of the different systems. It is evident in Table 2-III

TABLE 2-III

COMPARISON OF VARIOUS TELEHONE SYSTEMS ACCORDING TO
MEAN TIME TO REACH A CRISIS WORKER

Telephone System	Number Calls Attempted	Mean Time (min:sec)	Range of Times	Number Calls Not Completed
A	27	00:06	00:02-00:18	0
B	5	01:41	01:00-03:10	0
C	13	01:35	00:53-02:42	0
D	19	12:32	04:20-39:12	1
E	4	17:35	05:35-49:00	0
F	3	03:18	-	2
G	4	03:04	01:05-06:10	0
H	2	-	-	2

that the most immediate response to a call is permitted under System A, where the call comes directly to the worker on duty. In such cases neither nonhelping people nor time delays are inserted into the process of getting help. However, only minimal delays were found with systems which utilized switchboard transferring of calls. Systems B and C yielded relatively short delays. Somewhat longer delays and considerably greater inconvenience were encountered in Systems F and G, which required the caller to place a second call in order to contact the worker on duty. However, all of these systems are vastly superior to Systems D and E which require taking the caller's name and returning a call to him. It is also noteworthy that System F resulted in two of the three calls not being completed.

Table 2-II indicates that five of the calls resulted in special circumstances which merit more elaborate description. On the Period IV call to center number 4, the answering service which had taken the previous calls informed the caller that there was no service on the crisis line during the weekends, but that he might get some help if he called another number. That number proved to be that of a secretary at a hospital across the street from the Mental Health Clinic. She accepted the caller's name and number and agreed to have a call returned. However, after a one-hour lapse in time, a call was placed back to the hospital a second time. This time the caller was informed that the doctors at the hospital had decided not to return the call because they did not recognize the caller as one of their patients. People who call this particular service during weekends are usually calling their own doctors, and unless this is the case, no service is readily available for them. One would have to conclude that the Mental Health Clinic which operates this unusual system does not feel a need to provide complete emergency telephone service to its community.

The Period I call to center number 8 resulted in an unusually long delay not otherwise found in the System G procedures. This was due to the fact that when the caller redialed the new number provided by the recording, he found the line busy on the next four attempts. These attempts were scheduled at approximately one-minute intervals. When the line was clear, it took an additional brief period to get the worker on the line. This event points out another difficulty of having workers take their calls at home. Frequently, other members of the family need to use the telephone and the line is not always kept free for crisis cases.

The Period IV call to the same center resulted in a combination of systems. First the recording redirected the caller to the Community Mental Health Center. There a clerk had to redirect the call once more to the nurse on duty in the Alcoholic Rehabilitation Unit, who was assigned to serve as the crisis worker for that shift. The time to reach a worker was not long, but the many steps which were required served to insert nonhelpful and irrelevant events into the process of calling for help.

The Period IV call to center number 9 resulted in a failure of the system to function. The initial call was answered by an officer on duty in the local police station. The officer only gave the caller the name of the worker on duty and advised him to obtain the telephone number from the local directory. When the caller explained that the call was originating long distance, the policeman promptly hung up the phone. A second call was then placed to the same agency, and this time a different officer answered and executed System E, which resulted in a call eventually being returned.

Finally, the Period III call to center number 12 represents the problems which can occur with the System D type of operation. The answering service operator took the caller's name and number and agreed to have a call returned. However, after one hour no call had been received, and the caller placed a second call to the same service. He was told the answering service had a large back-up of calls to relay and only two emergency lines available, hence his call could not be relayed immediately. A second commitment was made that a call would be returned. Fifty minutes later when no call had been received, the investigator made a third call to the service. He was informed it had still not been possible to relay the call because of the heavy traffic through the answering service, and he then asked that the call be cancelled. It is entirely possible, of course, that the answering service failed to respond in this case due to their annoyance at receiving out-of-town calls at this hour. Or they may attempt to function as a screening unit to keep the crisis workers from being disturbed unless, in their opinion, it is really justified. Or, it may be that the answering service was really as busy as the operator repeatedly indicated. In any event, this system is hardly providing an acceptable service for the crisis agency whose clients apparently cannot depend upon getting through.

DISCUSSION OF THE STUDY RESULTS

The data presented in the preceding section clearly indicate that it is not safe to relinquish the responsibility for the telephone answering system to someone outside of the crisis agency. One can never be certain that the system will function the way it is supposed to. There were only two complaints about this survey. One came from a center director who felt it would have been more ethical to inquire of the directors how the telephone system operated. The fact that this director operated the center number 12 where the incomplete call occurred during Period III completely demonstrates the rationale of the study design. She would never have described this event, not because she wanted to distort the facts, but because she could not have known what happened on that event. The experimenters are themselves associated with one of the centers included in the survey, and thus they might describe how that service *should* operate. Nevertheless, their own center was also called, without the prior knowledge of the crisis workers on duty, in order to determine what *really happens* when people call for help.

The delays encountered under Systems D and E could be due to several possible factors. There could have been a delay in the answering service relaying the call because their switchboard was busy. They could have encountered difficulty locating a worker, or the worker could have delayed in returning the call.

The data suggest that the commercial answering service is not always an inefficient system. The remarkable difference between the efficiency of System C, which utilizes a patch through the board, and System D, which requires a return call, must not be overlooked. However, it must be pointed out that no center can officially contract for the System C type of service. Patching by use of cross-connectors is not permitted legally under Federal Communications Commission regulations. Nevertheless, many answering services perform this function when the operators consider it to be an emergency situation. They are willingly placing themselves, and the service manager, in jeopardy by doing so. A few answering services, through their good will and appreciation for the crisis service and their lack of regard for what they consider to be an unreasonable and inappropriate regulation, automatically define any call to their crisis service client as an emergency matter. Such an answering service can be a real asset to the crisis center.

On the other hand, the mechanical patch does have other liabilities. It requires the operator to break in on the line periodically in order to determine if the conversation is still in progress, since no disconnect signal is possible under this arrangement. If the operator should not disconnect after a call is completed, the crisis worker's home telephone line is non-functional, and he would be unable to initiate a call to rescue services, police, or other helping resources if such were needed.

There is one hopeful note in these data. Five of the centers contacted (numbers 1, 13, 15, 16, 17) began operations during 1970. Of the twenty calls placed to these new centers, sixteen were answered directly by the crisis worker on duty. Perhaps it may be concluded that because these newest programs have instituted this type of system, we may expect more and more agencies to move in this direction in the future.

Admittedly, the results of this survey have been interpreted in a critical manner, and some agency directors may naturally feel defensive, if not outright angry. The authors recognize that these data are limited; it would be much better if there were ten calls to each center during each time period. A great deal of faith is being placed in a very few calls which, by taking maximum advantage of chance events, may give a disproportionately bad picture of a center operation. There is no malice intended in these findings nor in their interpretation, but there is a desire to provoke and stimulate crisis service telephone systems to strive towards the best possible service to the public. What matters here is not that a particular finding occurs only once in every 1,000 calls; what matters is that the event *can* occur at all, because it *did* in fact occur. Of course, no system can ever be foolproof. Telephone equipment is such that the operation of light and bell signals is dependent upon local electrical power. Hence, a worker who is alert and on duty would not even know when the phone is ringing during a power blackout, unless auxiliary power is available. There are some low-probability contingencies which are beyond control of any center. However, the fact that a center operates effectively most of the time is not adequate justification for permitting defective service to occur *through use of a system which is not maximally effective at its best*.

These data clearly show that the only certain method of delivering around-the-clock emergency telephone crisis intervention services is to provide a trained crisis worker on duty full-time at the point where the calls are received. This is by far the most efficient procedure and the one which yields the greatest personal satisfaction to the staff of the crisis center. It is the only system which maximizes control over the program in the hands of the people who are responsible to the community for delivering what they promise in their publicity.

It is the authors' conclusion, based upon the results of this survey, that the type of telephone answering system employed often reflects the interest and motivation of a crisis center for performing a quality job in the community. The telephone system also reveals the level of development of the service itself. The growth and development of individual community suicide and crisis services may be charted by the history of their autonomy and control over the answering of the initial call.

SUMMARY

The telephone service established by directors of suicide prevention and crisis intervention services is generally given little careful consideration. Many agencies take their telephone systems for granted, assuming that almost any system will function adequately if an operator is available and a crisis worker is on call. There are a number of important issues at stake which should be carefully considered before a program is established which uses any system other than full-time coverage by the trained crisis worker at a permanent location. In order to investigate just what really happens under the various systems which are in use, a series of seventy-six calls were placed to nineteen different emergency crisis services in the southeastern United States. Times were recorded to show how long it took to get an answer to the first call, and how much time was required, through what various systems, to get an actual crisis worker on the line. There were marked differences in the latter variable across the seven different systems identified. The results clearly indicate that crisis services are in danger of unknowingly providing inferior and dangerously low-quality service unless they maintain maximum control over their own telephone answering system twenty-four hours a day.

Chapter 3

COMMUNITY YOUTH LINE: A HOTLINE PROGRAM FOR TROUBLED ADOLESCENTS

H. S. ROTH, CHARLES PALMER, AND ARTHUR J. SCHUT

T HE NEED FOR A crisis service had been recognized by professionals in the Des Moines community for several years, but it was not until late summer of 1969 that a specific impetus began to evolve. It was at that time that a member of the Des Moines Child Guidance Center staff encountered a telephone crisis-line service operating very effectively in the San Diego area. This concept was transplanted to Des Moines and a small group of professionals began reviewing the appropriateness of a similar program for that metropolitan area.

The Des Moines community, although located "safely" in the middle of the conservative middle west corn belt, was neither isolated nor immune from effects of the ever-growing youth culture. Much fear and controversy was attached to the problems of youth in the Des Moines community, with the drug scene taking a central focus in most conversations regarding youth. It was out of this sense of community concern and anxiety that the Des Moines Child Guidance Center and the Y.M.C.A. decided to mutually direct their efforts toward the establishment of a call-in counseling service for young people. This service was called Community Youth Line. Many service titles were suggested and considered—Crisis Line, Drug Line, Suicide Line—but it was felt that a service defining itself on a broad base as a

An earlier version of this paper was presented at the 22nd Annual Meeting of the American Association of Psychiatric Services for Children in Philadelphia, November 1970.

41

program concerned with the entire spectrum of youth problems would be preferable. It was not the intent of the developers of the program to restrict themselves to any particular or specific segment of the youth population, either by nature of particular types of problems, age, sex, location in the city, or philosophical orientation.

Both the Y.M.C.A. and the Child Guidance Center had been impressed with the reluctance of young people to use the established helping services already available within the community. The reasons for this reluctance seem to center around the youth's fear of exposure, general distrust of professionals, and agency policies regarding parental involvement and other regulatory procedures that distanced the young persons from the "helping establishment." It was hoped that Youth Line could avoid these problems by assuring anonymity through the use of the telephone. By making use of trained lay volunteers whose expertise was in concerned listening and not in advice giving nor in "psychotherapizing," it was assumed that some of the resistances to formal professional help might be overcome. No restrictions were placed on eligibility for service; all the young person needed was a telephone, the Youth Line number, and motivation enough to dial it.

The working relationship between the Child Guidance Center and the Y.M.C.A. seemed to be an ideal marriage of agency input, not only because mutual input between differing agencies is often rare but also because these agencies brought particular resources to bear on a counseling program of this type. The Child Guidance Center's unique contribution seemed to evolve from its clinical and training expertise. The center directly provided the counselor training component of the program, volunteering two of its staff members to be responsible for the nature and quality of the preparation that the lay counselors would receive prior to and during their involvement in the program. An emergency back-up system was also devised whereby a volunteer on the phone could be in contact with a professional within minutes of the time of encountering a self-defined emergency on the Youth Line phone. This system utilized an emergency paging device that was always in the possession of an on-call professional. The psychological training consultants and the program director operated as emergency back-up staff, with other Child Guidance Center staff members being available during instances of critical need.

The Y.M.C.A. seemed particularly well suited for moving into a program of this nature due to their program emphasis on productively engaging youth in the community. This agency had been doing street and outreach work on a regular basis for several years and was more acquainted with and accepted by the members of the Des Moines' youth culture than any other agency in the area. The Y.M.C.A.'s role in the joint undertaking would be to provide the administration of the program. Thus, the services of at first a half-time and subsequently a full-time Youth Line director were volunteered and provided from the Y.M.C.A. staff. Of note, the San Diego program, after which Des Moines' Community Youth Line is modeled, is a Y.M.C.A. sponsored and operated program; the service which we are here describing is, on the other hand, supported by the several agencies but in actuality a separately incorporated nonprofit organization.

As Youth Line had significance for the entire community, neither the Child Guidance Center nor the Y.M.C.A. were solely responsible for the creation or continued operation of the program. As the development of the concept and specific planning for the start of the program began to unfold, other interested parties and youth-involved services began to make their input and impact on the program. St. Paul's Episcopal Church volunteered the use of its facilities for the location of the program's telephones and interview rooms. Representatives of the Drake University faculty and campus ministry, Planned Parenthood, and various other social agencies participated in early planning discussions and contributed in varying degrees with expertise and enthusiasm.

The church location was ideally suited to the initial needs of the program, as St. Paul's is centrally located in downtown Des Moines. The church has a street level entrance directly adjacent to the Youth Line rooms, allowing ease of entry on the part of counselors and users of Youth Line without disturbing the general programs of the church and without causing the youth the unnecessary discomfort of walking past numerous strangers. Although the program emphasizes the telephone as its counseling medium, it does not discourage face-to-face sessions within the counseling office. Thus, no attempt was made to keep the location of the service confidential. A small amount of walk-in service was anticipated, but neither promoted nor discouraged. The central location of the office plus the general acceptability of St. Paul's amongst the youth of the community (a coffee house had been operated there for several summers) made it an ideal location.

A positive and mutually trusting relationship between Youth Line and local law enforcement officials seemed to be a prerequisite for effective operation. Thus, conferences were held with the county attorney, police chief, and vice squad members. These were arranged through the juvenile court's chief probation officer, who operates in an advisory capacity to the Youth Line program. In the conferences with law enforcement officials, matters of policy and procedures were mutually discussed and established. Matters of particular concern to law enforcement officials seemed to center on the program's approach to felons and drug users. In talking these matters through, all parties seemed to establish a mutual understanding relative to the procedure of the other party, and it was established that each would operate in his own way without interference from the other. Continued liaison with law enforcement was seen as essential, as many rumors and myths spring up around a program of this type in regard to its sometimes clandestine-appearing or quasi-legal actions. Open communication clarifies these matters immediately.

It was also considered necessary to inform key persons in the helping professions about the exact nature of the program, particularly around the role of the volunteer counselor. The planners of the program anticipated greater resistance to the idea of using volunteers in a service of this type than was actually encountered. In point of fact, few medical or mental health professionals stated discomfort with the plan to deal with the concerns and situations that would be presented to them by telephone. A number did, on the other hand, raise questions regarding the referral policy of this new program; it was explained that while Youth Line did not see itself as primarily a referring agency, it would not hesitate to aid a youth in seeking out help from another service in the community when that service would seem to be particularly appropriate to the concern of the moment. Such referral would be strictly at the option of the youth.

As the Youth Line program envisioned itself as at times a liaison between establishments—the adult service-giving establishment and the youth establishment—efforts were made to fully educate both groupings in the community. Thus, many meetings and conference and talks were held with a wide range of groups, explaining the purposes and nature of the program. Members of youth groups as well as adults working in different capacities spread the word regarding the developing program. In an attempt to acquaint our volunteers with services in the community that deal with youth and might be used on a referral basis, as well as acquainting those services with the volunteers, a part of the early training involved visits by those volunteers to the agencies. The volunteers were responsible for establishing a procedures book which would delineate the policies and procedures of the other agencies as well as how a Youth Line counselor might best help a caller use a service of the other agency. This procedures book is kept up to date in the Youth Line office and is immediately available for reference by a Youth Line counselor.

As the educational efforts of Youth Line spread, both the newspaper and radio-T.V. media began to pick up interest in the program. Articles, spot announcements and interview programs have been very valuable in educating the public about the program. Particularly useful were articles appearing in high school papers throughout the city. Student interest was quite high, with many students preparing class term papers on the program and then presenting them to their fellow students. Thus, the word-of-mouth communication throughout the youth group was very successful in making the availability of the program clear. Youth Line cards were printed explaining the program's scope of services as well as assuring confidentiality and the free and voluntary nature of the program. The cards also listed the location of the office, the times the program would be in operation, and the telephone number to be used. These cards were not distributed until the first day of formal operation, although subsequent to that time more than 100,000 have been distributed to such community locations as hamburger stands, restaurants, school counselor's offices, and other places patronized by youth. The cards themselves were donated by local businesses, with a recent multicolored and very attractive revision contributed by a youth-oriented advertising agency.

As the planning for the opening of Youth Line began to take shape, efforts were directed toward the recruitment of a high quality volunteer staff. The need for volunteers was communicated from a number of sources, ranging from radio requests to church service announcements to presentations in university classrooms. Des Moines is fortunate in having a centralized Volunteer Bureau which aided greatly in publicizing the need for volunteers and securing volunteers for the program. As the need for volunteers was made public from many different sources, the types of individuals responding to the need varied greatly in all variables. This was, of course, what was hoped by the program planners as they saw the volunteer group as being best established on a broad heterogeneous basis representing all factions of the community. Initial screening and orientation sessions were established, with the finding that only in rather extreme situations could the definitive judgment be made about who should or should not be a Youth Line counselor. Thus, with a few exceptions, the screening sessions proved to be a self-screening procedure. The primary qualifying restrictions placed on counselors had to do with age and commitment to the program: although initially age eighteen was considered the minimum, this was later raised to twenty years as some feeling was developed regarding the maturity and objectivity of the eighteen- and nineteen-year-olds showing interest in volunteering for the program. The volunteer's time commitment included not only the three hours per week of scheduling on the telephone, but also regular attendance in the twice-a-month orientation and personal development training sessions of three hours each, as well as occasional special substantive training sessions. Volunteers were asked to apply only if willing to commit themselves to at least three months' participation in the program.

The initial response to the need for counselors was gratifying, with the program being over-subscribed with volunteers by Thanksgiving time, thus allowing several months of training to have been provided prior to opening the program on February 15, 1970.

On the day the telephone lines opened, Youth Line had forty-four primary counselors plus about a dozen people who were considered secondary counselors, that is, not yet trained to the point of counseling readiness. The volunteer counselors and everybody concerned with the fledgling program were enthusiastic and excited, and anticipations and anxieties were high as we wondered whether we would have any calls or not during the initial phases of the operation. As noted above, there had been several newspaper articles, but we had been quite hesitant to distribute any of our Youth Line cards to the public prior to the actual opening date, for fear that youth might be contacting us and not finding "anybody home" on the telephone. Accordingly, we had waited until that first day of operation to even place Youth Line cards in the hands of the counselors for general distribution or to publicize the calling number. We were, therefore, surprised by thirty-three telephone calls during that first day of operation, a Sunday afternoon and evening in February.

The calls of that first day covered the entire range of problem categories which we have subsequently found ourselves dealing with, although perhaps a little more heavily at the very beginning on drug-related issues. At the time, Des Moines had no drug abuse program or drug contact houses and Youth Line (not through its own design, but because we were "the only game in town") was identified as a drug crisis stopping point. Therefore, many of our initially presented problems and requests for information were related to drugs, but we also had child-parent, student-teacher, boy-girl, and other interpersonal and intrapsychic difficulties from the very beginning of the program. We also had quite a few callers, of course, who were simply checking us out to see if we were for real.

A few days later, during that first week, both the Des Moines Register and one of the high school newspapers had inquiring reporters asking around town about what people thought of this new counseling service; without exception, both young people and adults said things on the order of: "We think it's great. Of course, I don't think I'll ever use such a thing, and I don't know the kind of people who might have the sorts of problems that would need to contact Youth Line, but it sounds like a real good idea." Not only did it sound like a good idea, but apparently there were quite a few of "that kind of people," because Youth Line has been used to an extent which far exceeded the wildest expectations of any of us involved in its development and operation. Table 3-I reports our statistics relative to the kinds of calls and clientele that we have received during the entire first year of operation.

A few comments are appropriate about the place of research in the Youth Line operation. They are not intended as apology, but as explanation of an interesting aspect of an exciting program. Youth Line operates entirely on donated funds; although the budget was raised four times during that first year to its final figure of 30,000 dollars, in actual fact we *raised* less than 20 percent of that amount of money. And research is *not* a primary function; "our thing" is the delivery of a counseling service staffed by volunteers, the training of those volunteers, and simple day-to-day maintenance of the program. Accordingly, we have developed a wealth of data on the Youth Line program, but these data are not presently available for presentation here. Hopefully, some day some graduate student will want to do a master's thesis or a doctoral dissertation on our program, and we are trying to keep our records in such a way that the informa-

TABLE 3-I

STATISTICAL ANALYSIS OF CONTACTS DURING THE FIRST YEAR OF
OPERATION—FEBRUARY 15, 1970 THROUGH FEBRUARY 14, 1971

Item	N	%
1. Total Volume of Contacts		
a. Counseling contacts for which client information sheets were written	10,968	54.5
b. Noncounseling business contacts, e.g. requests for off-duty counselors, for speakers, for information about the program, volunteer application. Figures reflect only those calls received on counseling line, not those made via business office number	2,567	12.8
c. Hang-ups, prank silence, wrong numbers	6,589	32.7
Total	20,124	100.0%
2. Age Categories and Sex of Clientele (Based on (a) and (b) above)		
Girls to age 18	8,550	63.2
Boys to age 18	2,948	21.8
Mothers with parent/teenager problems	249	1.8
Fathers, as above	73	0.5
Other adult, above age 18 with personal problems, nonparent	1,715	12.7
Total	13,535	100.0%
3. Counseling Contacts (Based on 1(a) above)		
Face-to-face, including scheduled visits and "walk-ins"	673	6.2
Telephone	10,295	93.8
Total	10,968	100.0%

tion can be retrieved; at this point, all we can present is preliminary data of the most basic sorts.

Remember also that our clientele are not required to give any personal information. We encourage their telling us their names, addresses, phone numbers, ages, schools, all the basic information and whatever they might be willing to provide, but in actual fact we do not require these as a condition of service. Therefore, our statistics have some limitations; what we present in this paper has to do with the total volume of contacts during that first twelve months of operation, that is to say, every telephone call including those which, when answered, were responded to with dead silence and heavy breathing and a hanging up or the simple click or hum which may or may not have been a wrong number. You'll note on our statistical summary that we had a total, including those hangups, of 20,124 contacts during that first twelve-month period. Roughly ⅓ were these hangups, and we have no way of knowing whether they were pranks or false alarms or a need being met by the simple expedient of knowing that there was an available listening ear. But even aside from these, Youth Line has averaged more than 900 counseling contacts per month during this reporting period, contacts for which client information sheets were written.

The statistical presentation of Youth Line activity is derived primarily from data recorded on forms referred to as client information sheets. We have gone through several changes on these, but one of the tools which serves both an administrative-training and clinical service function has been this information sheet which each counselor writes up relative to every therapeutic contact. In this way, checks and balances are provided in terms of administrative and professional staff having knowledge of what the volunteer counselors are doing, who they are doing whatever they are doing with, and the nature of the counseling service being provided. Regularly and routinely, the counselors are given feedback in the form of written reports back to them, relative to the statements that they made about what went on in the counseling session. It is readily apparent that the client information sheet is only secondarily used for research purposes, although our research findings are almost entirely based on the information on these and a few other minor records (a "head count" sheet and a "request for other counselors" log) kept on each shift.

Another category of research presented in Table 3-I has to do with the age and sex of our clientele. Many, of course, do not divulge their age, just as many do not give their names. We are working on some preliminary age curves, and it looks as though sixteen seems to be the modal age for male and female clientele. We were quite impressed with the discovery that there are approximately two female contacts for every male calling, although it now appears that this is a common occurrence in other and similar hotline programs. This ratio seems to hold for adolescents, parents, and other adults with self-referent problems.

Table 3-II refers to information derived from 10,968 client information sheets. We also had over 2,500 noncounseling business contacts during our first twelve months, the majority of which were, in fact, young people calling and wanting to talk with a particular counselor who was not on duty at that time. These calls were handled differently with different counselors at different times; most often, if the counselor is willing, the one on duty will call that counselor at home. Last names and home phone numbers are never given out to the clientele, and the counselor at home makes the decision about whether he prefers to return the call at a time other than his scheduled on-the-phone shift. Some very good on-going counseling relationships have been developed in this way, and this also allows for additional Youth Line telephone output. (Youth Line calls may run anywhere from a few minutes to five hours, and the telephone company, after monitoring our lines for services, reports that we average over 100 busy-signals per day.)

TABLE 3-II

CATEGORIZATION OF PROBLEMS PRESENTED BY CLIENTELE OF COMMUNITY YOUTH LINE IN TELEPHONE AND FACE-TO-FACE CONTACTS WITH COUNSELORS FEBRUARY 15, 1970 THROUGH FEBRUARY 14, 1971

Problem	*N*	*%*
1. Relationships not elsewhere classified, including such problems as peer pressures, wanting to help someone, arguments, feelings hurt by someone, shyness, feeling unloved, wanting to be better liked.	1,017	9.3
2. Home life, including general and specific problems with parents and siblings, worry over family distress, running away or kicked out of home.	1,433	13.1
3. Dating and marriage, except sex-related problems, but encompassing general questions and fears, boyfriend/girlfriend or spouse difficulties, wanting more dates.	2,186	19.9
4. Sex and pregnancy, ranging from requests for contraception and abortion information to concerns above venereal disease, pressure from boyfriend to have sexual relations, homosexuality, techniques, general fears.	1,014	9.2
5. School grades, teachers, kicked out, thinking of dropping out, problems with assignments.	161	1.5
6. Legal and draft problems, such as requests for general legal info, problems with probation or arrests for drug or other issues, concerns about military status.	170	1.5
7. Drugs, except for legal problems, but including medical information and emergencies, "tripping" and wanting to talk or needing help with a "bummer," fears and concerns regarding own or other's drug use, alcohol problems.	876	8.0
8. Resources and Referrals relative to areas not covered above, such as requests for nondrug or V.D. medical help, needing a job or money or a crash pad, wanting to know how to contact or about other community resources.	799	7.3

9. General Personal Counseling not specifically or primarily
   related to any of the above categories, encompassing everything from "just wanting to talk" to boredom, guilt,
   depression, suicide, fears of insanity, sensitivity about
   physical appearance.   3,312   30.2
                                         Total   10,968   100.0%
   _____

   Note: These categories developed by A. D. Feinstein, San Diego, California.

Rather than go into any detail on problems presented by
Youth Line clientele, attention is directed to Table 3-II. While
these summary categories may not be as interesting (except for
their impressive volume) as case histories and narrative accounts
of counseling, it is our experience that confidentiality can be
protected in no other way. With the numbers and variety of
counseling contacts in our program, attempts to appropriately
disguise any particular case result in it resembling yet another
real case! And so, the findings are grouped rather than disguised,
despite the possible loss of information or reader interest.

One noteworthy finding, however, is that drug-related problems—for all the publicity and concern of our contemporary
culture—are far from our most important contact area; dating
and marriage, home life, and particularly the category of general
personal counseling over a whole range of categories far out-
weighs drug-related issues as, for that matter, do concerns about
sex and pregnancy. Those topics which seem to hit the popular
press, i.e. drugs, draft, and school-related student discontent
have not, during the first year of Youth Line, been the primary
contact focus areas.

In addition to the concerns about program development and
the presentation of client-counseling statistics, there are several
other vital facets of the Youth Line program. The balance of
this paper will focus on the training which is provided for Youth
Line counselors and on these wonderful people who are the
recipients of the training and are the backbone and body of the
Youth Line program. Youth Line counselors are a heterogeneous
lot, as you will note in Table 3-III. Not only do they run the
gamut of the young to elderly with all the various occupations
and amounts of education; in appearance, Youth Line counselors
range from hip to mod to rather square, politically from rigid

right to radical left, with racial and religious representation fairly proportionate to that of the greater Des Moines community.

TABLE 3-III
YOUTH LINE COUNSELORS

Characteristics	N
Applicants, through February 14, 1971	201
Withdrew and rejected. Persons who applied but terminated their Youth Line connection prior to completion of the initial training orientation phase and prior to ever being assigned as secondary or primary counselors.	81

Active Youth Line Counselors. (All secondary and primary counselors ever scheduled during the first year.)

	N
Currently active as of 2-14-71	61
Inactive as of 2-14-71*	59
Total	120

Sex

	N
Male	61
Female	59

Age Distribution

	N
Under 20 years	3
20 to 24 years	46
25 to 29 years	22
30 to 34 years	11
35 to 39 years	10
40 to 44 years	12
45 to 49 years	7
50 to 59 years	6
60+ years	3
Range: 18 to 68 years	
Median: 26 years	
Mean: 31 years	

Marital Status

	N
Single	53
Married	59
Separated, Divorced, Widowed	8

Education

	N
High school only	12
Some college (includes current students)	41
Bachelors degree	30
Some grad work (includes current students)	22
Masters degree (includes current students)	13
MA+ (includes Ph.D.)	2

Occupations

The occupational status of the counselors does not lend itself to easy categorization, but includes administrative assistants and administrators, an architect, Avon lady, author, banker, bookkeeper, counselors and caseworkers from various social agencies, a cab driver, construction worker, CPA, editorial assistant, factory foreman, film maker, Girl Scout executive, many housewives and homemakers, a hospital orderly, lab technician, ministers, mailroom clerk, public health nurse, pharmacists, parole officer, university

professor, painting contractor, personnel supervisor, realtor, secretaries and stenographers and receptionists, social workers, students
(college, graduate, nursing, medical, and technical), sales clerks
and store managers, a systems analyst, a number of teachers at
various levels, some unemployed people, VISTA volunteers, YMCA
workers and executives, a Job Corps training specialist, and many
others . . . really a heterogeneous lot!

---

* Note: Counselors defined as inactive, not currently scheduled, include
those who have permanently terminated their relationship with the program
because of moving, other interests, personal reasons, and those on extended leaves
of absence, e.g. maternity leave, sabbaticals, military service, time schedule
conflicts, who have announced intentions of returning to the program in the future.

Perhaps the training and activity of the counselors can most
ideally be described in the sequence from initial application to
full and active participation. The prospective Youth Line counselor, upon making inquiry, is directed to the Volunteer Bureau
noted previously or to the Y.M.C.A., where he can get an application form. This, upon completion, is sent to the director who,
when sufficient applications have been received, schedules an
initial group interview. Presently, such initial group sessions are
being conducted every five to six weeks, with anywhere from
ten to eighteen or twenty new people being scheduled each time.
This session is for the primary purposes of giving prospective
counselors a richer familiarity with the Youth Line operation
while at the same time affording the director a preliminary opportunity to engage and interact with and subjectively evaluate the
candidate's potential as a Youth Line counselor. Several experienced active counselors are also present and participating during
these sessions.

Subsequent to that first meeting, those persons electing to
continue with the program (and few are rejected at this stage
except for very blatant reasons) are scheduled for two to four
weekly, three-hour formal orientation sessions and one intensive
day-long workshop. Each candidate is issued a handbook con-
taining information on the rules, regulations, and procedures of
Youth Line together with over 150 pages of additional training
materials, mainly reprints of journal articles applicable to lay
counselors. The primary focus is on "in-the-now" orientations,
with Rogerian and experiential counseling, reality therapy, and

Gestalt therapy and theory being most heavily represented in the assorted papers.

Simultaneously, the groups are becoming familiar through lecture, study, and practice with the issues and problems to which Youth Line is addressed. They may hear lectures on abortion or drugs, study the latest information on suicides or how to deal with the telephone-calling masturbator, visit one or more of the social service agencies around town, spend some time actually observing at the Youth Line office, and throughout the period, be engaged in role-playing sessions on the various problem presentations. An invaluable and frequently used training aid is a phone company tele-trainer which allows the group to practice, to listen in on, and later to discuss the handling of hotline calls. Role play is probably the chief precounseling assignment training device and, in fact, continues as long as a person remains a Youth Line counselor.

Ultimately, the indoctrination sessions are completed and the new Youth Line person is assigned to one of the ongoing orientation and personal development (O. and P.D.) groups, at the same time being put on the counseling assignment schedule. Although it is possible at this stage to be assigned primary counseling duties and responsibility, most typically the person is designated a secondary counselor, on the schedule but not yet being allowed to do the work. He must make his shift, but may not initially handle any phone calls; rather, at this point, he is observing and listening and talking with and learning from the primary counselors with whom he is assigned, possibly sitting in on a face-to-face contact, reading client information and feedback sheets on the other counselors, and sometimes being the "gopher"—the one who goes for cokes, coffee, or whatever.

Attendance at the three hour, every other week, O. and P.D. session is required of every Youth Line counselor for as long as he continues in the program. Although there are some differences between the various groups because of the individual styles of the particular trainer/leaders, in most instances the sessions begin with attention to any administrative problems or dissemination of any administrative information that may have come up during the intervening weeks. This is often followed by discussions, role playing, or other means of attending to problems and problem categories encountered by the counselors—essentially a client-oriented and counseling technique-oriented time in the training session. And then the remaining time, anywhere from one to two hours of the meeting, is devoted to the personal development part of the counselor, with training in self-awareness, most frequently through the application of encounter and human relations training laboratory techniques. The psychological consultant and group leaders themselves vary in orientation from psychoanalytic to Gestalt, and the training sessions therefore reflect on eclecticism not often seen in established training programs.

As time passes and the newly designated secondary counselor becomes known and more knowledgeable about the program, he is gradually phased into a more active role. The primary counselor with whom he is assigned may, for example, take a call and then ask the novice to speak with the client, giving him such information as the age, sex, and general presenting problem. Later, after several opportunities to deal with and discuss the calls, he may be asked to simply take the next call, and throughout this there is constant formal and informal feedback, discussions with other counselors, and the opportunity for self- as well as administrative evaluation. Ultimately, if all goes well, the person is assigned primary counseling responsibility (the entire process to this point having taken an average of 8 to 12 weeks).

Youth Line primary counselors are assigned to the schedule in three-hour shifts, continue with the O. and P.D. sessions, and are often included in such other activities as speaking before community groups, helping with the new training groups, and fund-raising. More experienced counselors may be asked to take the responsibilities of counselor-coordinators on shared cases (some of our clients have been known to call as many as 14 different workers on a regular basis); others may be invited to share in the writing of feedback sheets or to participate in other clinical/supervisory activities. Case conferences are scheduled weekly and professional consultation is readily available to each counselor—that consultation ranging from personal to mental health professional to legal, medical, theological, or whatever else is requested by the counselor.

And that pretty well introduces the Community Youth Line phenomenon. We might mention one final aspect of our program in this context, and that is the fact that we regularly schedule parties so that Youth Line people from different backgrounds and the various training groups can get to meet and know each other. It was noted earlier in this paper that this was the first volunteer-staffed program in the annals of Des Moines' volunteerism which was oversubscribed before we ever started; after attending a Youth Line party, one lady from the Volunteer Bureau remarked that, "other organizations have volunteer guilds or volunteer groups, but you people have a cult!" And that does very much touch on the spirit of this group of volunteers who are not merely doing a job, but doing some personal growing and moving along as they participate in their very worthwhile Youth Line activity.

This paper has addressed itself to Youth Line's six month gestation and first year of life. Youth Line may still be in its infancy, and there is no question that we will look forward to our own personal growth and development as a program, but it is a healthy and husky infant. A little one-page information sheet which we distribute throughout the community pretty well tells the story: we are free, we are voluntary, we are confidential, we are available, and we are very, very busy.

Chapter 4

THE ROLE OF THE TELEPHONE IN THE PSYCHIATRIC INTERVIEW

ROGER A. MacKINNON AND ROBERT MICHELS

THE TELEPHONE PLAYS an important role in contemporary psychiatric practice. At first glance the topic seems too simple or straight-forward to warrant careful consideration. However, it involves an area of clinical work with patients and therefore should be subject to study. Since the topic is not usually discussed in the training of psychiatrists, it is an area where the personal style of each interviewer will emerge without self-scrutiny, and countertransference problems can easily be recognized.

Most patients make their initial contact with a psychiatrist via the telephone and often have subsequent occasion to call. Telephone calls during the interview also present a problem: some psychiatrists accept telephone calls while interviewing a patient; others never accept telephone calls in this situation; a third group occasionally accepts telephone interruptions, with varying criteria for the decision. In addition, the telephone can be used for psychiatric interviews, both in emergencies and on a long-term basis. This paper will consider four issues: (1) the relationship between the doctor and the patient who is telephoning, (2) the effects of telephone interruptions on the interview, (3) the patient who telephones with an acute psychiatric emergency but refuses to come to the doctor's office, and (4) conducting regular therapy sessions by telephone.

Reprinted from *Psychiatry*, 33:82-93, 1970, by permission of the authors and the William Alanson White Psychiatric Foundation, Inc.

THE PATIENT TELEPHONES THE DOCTOR

The Initial Telephone Call

Each doctor has his own way of handling an initial call from a prospective patient. Most psychiatrists expect some information concerning the patient before making the first appointment. Often this has been provided by the referring physician, but not infrequently a person whom the psychiatrist does not know telephones requesting an appointment. If this person does not spontaneously volunteer some information, the doctor will usually determine if the caller is himself the patient, and how he obtained the physician's name.

In gathering this basic information the doctor often develops clinical "hunches" about the patient, and in some instances he may ask a few questions. Patients sometimes reveal their problems in a typical manner at this point. The paranoid patient may ask more than once if this is really Dr. Jones, or whisper, or even make overt references to delusional material. The obsessive patient often attempts to control the doctor while making his first appointment, by suggesting a list of times when he would be available, or by asking the doctor's fee. The phobic patient asks for information about matters pertaining to travel and safety. The very dependent patient may cling excessively on the telephone while asking for directions, and so forth.

Calls Following the First Interview

Different issues are involved when the patient telephones the doctor following the first visit. Something discussed during the interview may have upset the patient, and if this is not explored, the patient might be frightened away from treatment. On other occasions the patient telephones because he feels that he "got away with something" during the session. He might say, "Oh Doctor, I forgot to tell you," or, "I made a mistake in telling you thus and such," or, I would like to add the following to what I reported." Such comments indicate that the patient was dissatisfied and may have felt that the doctor did not understand him or did not accept the patient's view of himself. The physician might comment to that effect and then suggest that the issue could be explored further during the next appointment. Another patient may use the telephone to "confess" some embarrassing or humiliating information which he was unable to disclose face-to-face during the interview.

Phobic patients frequently telephone after the first hour complaining of their symptoms and expressing a desire for reassurance. The physician could remark to the patient, "Something during the hour must have upset you; this is not unusual, and your anxiety will pass." It is essential to offer this type of reassurance to the phobic patient in the initial phase of treatment in order to help establish a working therapeutic relationship.

Covert hostile reactions to the therapist are evident in the patient who calls after the first session to say, for example, "This is Miss Smith, the patient that you saw on Thursday morning at 10:00." The implication is clear that so little emotional contact was made that the doctor might not remember the patient. The interviewer may choose not to respond to this aspect of the comment until the next interview. However, on occasion, he may ask, "Do you feel you made so little impression on me that I do not remember you?" A less challenging comment would be, "Yes, of course, I remember you."

At the end of the first interview a patient may ask the physician for his home telephone number. The patient might be asked if he is anticipating an emergency, as that is usually the reason for such a request. The doctor could explore what type of emergency he expects and how he has coped with such situations in the past. It is essential that the psychiatrist tell such patients that his answering service is able to contact him in the event of an emergency. Depending on the physician, the answering service either will offer his home telephone number when the patient calls or will telephone the doctor, who will then return the patient's call.

The authors subscribe to the minority view which favors allowing the patient to obtain the number directly. This implies to the patient that the psychiatrist is not afraid of the patient's dependent needs, nor will he feel unduly troubled or bothered if the patient has an emergency. The authors' experience has been that patients rarely abuse the doctor's privacy at home. The ability to contact the physician quickly may relieve the patient's anxiety and actually decrease the frequency of his calls.

Severely depressed or suicidal patients are often so fearful of being a burden that they need definite permission to ask for the physician's help. The psychiatrist may provide this permission by giving his home telephone number directly to the patient rather than indicating that it can be obtained from the answering service. However, if the physician gives his home telephone number because of his insecurity and anxiety, he may actually precipitate a crisis.

Some patients interrupt the doctor with telephone calls in order to demonstrate the hostile and inconsiderate nature of their personalities. Rather than become angry or abrupt with such patients, it is better to show them consideration, even though they are incapable of reciprocating. This helps the patient to adopt the physician as a new ego ideal. One can say in a polite and friendly tone, "I'm busy just now. Could I call you back in a little while?"

On occasion the physician must decide whether or not to telephone a patient who has missed an appointment without notifying the doctor. During the initial interviews it is a good idea for the physician to telephone the patient under such circumstances. Such behavior on the patient's part indicates a problem in the transference which requires immediate therapeutic intervention.

When a patient has telephoned, it is usually helpful to refer to the call in the next session. The patient is then afforded the opportunity for discussion of his reactions to the telephone conversation and exploration of its deeper meaning to him. The therapist will gear his analysis of the unconscious meanings of the call to the patient's capacity to develop insight. With more seriously ill patients, this uncovering may be deferred until late in treatment.

TELEPHONE INTERRUPTIONS DURING THE INTERVIEW

Telephone interruptions can be considered in terms of their effect on the on-going interview rather than upon the relationship between the doctor and the patient who is calling. Many doctors feel that this problem can be circumvented by never accepting telephone calls when they are with a patient. This has both advantages and disadvantages. The interviews are never interrupted; the patient and physician are never distracted by an irrelevant conversation. However, not accepting calls during an interview caters to the infantile omnipotence of the patient, encouraging his fantasy that he is the only person of concern to the doctor. Some doctors who follow such a system permit the patient to hear their telephone ring before it is answered by a secretary or an answering service. Furthermore, they may continue with the interview, ignoring the telephone as though it had not intruded. The patient is less likely to comment on the distracting influence of the telephone if the doctor attempts to ignore it, but he may nevertheless be disturbed.

Other psychiatrists have an arrangement whereby they may turn off the bell, allowing a light to flash instead. The usual practice is for the light to be placed where it will be visible to the doctor, but not to the patient. It is then possible for the doctor to accept or not accept telephone calls, depending on the patient, the situation, and his own mood. If the physician is not accepting calls during an interview, it is preferable that the patient be unaware that the telephone is ringing. In practice, the authors do not permit more than one telephone call during any given session.

In the treatment of more seriously disturbed patients, the physician's telephone conversation can help the patient to improve his reality testing and his recognition of emotions. For example, a psychotic patient may grossly misinterpret the nature of the call. The telephone interruption is useful if the doctor reconstructs the conversation and attempts to determine how the patient came to his conclusions. The physician can point out gross distortions and then disclose the true nature of the call.

The doctor thereby helps the patient to cope with reality by improving his ability to communicate and to interpret the communications of others. As the patient demonstrates improvement, his speculations become more perceptive and accurate. Situations in which the patient continues to misinterpret are indications for further therapeutic work. The principles are similar to those used in working with the patient's reactions to other people in a therapeutic group.

During the first few sessions of treatment the patient most often shows no reaction to a telephone interruption. In more advanced stages of therapy, reactions to a telephone call become obvious. These responses are manifestations of the transference and accordingly are subject to analytic study and interpretation. Hearing the doctor talk with another person on the telephone gives the patient an opportunity to experience a side of the physician's personality different from that which is elicited to the patient's personality. This may lead to a discovery that the doctor is capable of expressing tenderness, warmth, anger, and so forth, and in the later stages of treatment may help the patient achieve a more realistic image of his therapist. For example, one patient had abandoned his career as a teacher because of his feeling that it was a passive, feminine, and hence, demeaning profession. He overhead his doctor's brief telephone conversation one day and deduced that his therapist was also a teacher and that in this capacity he was able to function effectively as a man. This helped the patient to work through his neurotic conflicts.

The effects of a telephone interruption on any given interview depend upon the problems of the patient, the personality of the psychiatrist, and the specific events at the time of the interruption. The doctor who has a thorough knowledge of all the factors can predict his patient's reactions to a given telephone interruption. When he feels an interruption would have an unfavorable effect upon the therapy, he can turn off the telephone.

Consideration will now be given to specific reactions which patients and therapists have to telephone interruptions.

The Patient's Reactions to the Interruption

Relief

Patients may experience relief after telephone interruptions for several reasons. They may discover that other people have problems similar to their own. The doctor's willingness to accept urgent phone calls from others gives permission for this patient to call the doctor in time of need. A third basis for relief is the reaction which the patient describes "saved by the bell." This typically occurs when the patient has started to discuss or is just about to discuss some very difficult material.

In the first instance, the interviewer might explore the feelings underlying the patient's surprise at learning that others have problems similar to his own. Similar exploration would be indicated when the patient is relieved to learn that it is permissible to call the doctor in time of need. However, the patient who feels "saved by the bell" requires a different approach. He is using the telephone call as a method of resistance. Sometimes the doctor can merely direct the patient back to the comments he was making when the telephone rang. On other occasions, it is more useful to explore the patient's feelings of relief at the interruption as a way of making the patient more aware of his resistance. If the patient continues to react in this manner to telephone calls, the psychiatrist can simply turn off the telephone, particularly when the patient is discussing difficult material. The phobic patient will typically react with this type of resistance.

Distraction

The typical "distracted" response is characterized by the question, "Where was I when the phone rang?" or, "What was I saying, Doctor?" Such a reaction also indicates resistance, although this patient is less likely to accept an interruption. Compulsive talking, which superficially resembles free association, may be used as a defense against the emergence of disturbing thoughts. An unexpected interruption may bring such material to the patient's attention. After the call the patient attempts to reconstitute his defenses by resuming his previous discussion. Rather than exploring the resistance aspect, it is more useful to ask the patient what he was doing while the telephone conversation was in progress. Often illuminating material will be obtained in response to such an inquiry.

Frequently it is appropriate for the physician to say nothing, thereby giving the patient the opportunity to pursue his own free associations. During the period of initial history-taking, the doctor might completely ignore an interruption and merely help the patient to continue with what he had been saying. The therapist must exercise care in following the latter course since the "simple distraction" is frequently a defense against concealed responses of anger or curiosity about the telephone conversation. Once this is recognized by the doctor, he may work with the deeper feeling.

Anger

Angry responses to the telephone interruption include direct angry statements and indirect sarcastic remarks, such as, "Can't you afford a secretary, Doctor?" or, "You owe me three minutes." It is important that the interviewer not respond with anger or defensive behavior. Explanatory remarks deflect the treatment from the important issue. The doctor either listens while the patient ventilates his rage and then continues with the interview or interprets the patient's feelings that he is being cheated or deprived of the interviewer's complete attention. Such comments are supportive of the patient's anger and will help him feel that the doctor really does understand him. If the call lasts more than a minute, the interviewer might ask the patient if he could stay a few minutes at the end of the session. Obsessive or paranoid patients are most prone to feel overtly angry in response to interruptions.

Denial

The characteristic example of denial is the patient who ignores the call, seeming to remain in the state of suspended animation until the interviewer concludes his conversation. The patient will then finish his sentence as though there had been no interruption. This response is designed to conceal either the patient's anger or intense interest in every detail of the telephone conversation and fantasies concerning the call. Some patients will use fantasy formation to avoid overhearing the conversation. Such denial is a defense against expression of forbidden impulses. The denying patient also manifests a striking lack of distraction, and it is useful for the interviewer to comment, "You seem not to have been distracted by the telephone call." If the patient denies having distracting thoughts, the interviewer could comment, "It's interesting that you were able to keep your mind on the very word you had started to say." This type of response may occur in the hysterical patient who was interrupted in the middle of a rehearsed drama, or with the obsessive patient who was busily following his mental notes. If the interviewer successfully uncovers the patient's resentment, the focus of the interview is shifted to this issue.

Guilt or Feelings of Inadequacy

Responses of guilt or feelings of inadequacy immediately reveal that the patient has carefully listened to the conversation. His typical remarks will be, "You have such important responsibilities, " or, "Why do you bother with me when there are other people who need you so much more than I do?" The patient may even offer to step outside while the physician is in the middle of the telephone call. These responses basically stem from anger which the patient turns inward against himself. The patient's self-esteem is very low and he does not feel entitled to ask for much in life. Underneath he resents the necessity that he share the doctor with other people, who he believes have problems which are considered more important than his own. Because of his profound sense of inadequacy he feels that he has no right to complain. Therapists are often tempted to interpret the patient's underlying resentment and usually encounter failure. Instead, it is more helpful to comment to the patient that even in his illness he seems to feel that he is a failure, that his symptoms are less interesting or his case is less challenging than that of someone else.

The patient who reacts in this manner also suffers from hidden feelings of intense competitiveness. His response to the telephone interruption provides a ready opening for discussion of such feelings. Initially the patient may only accept the idea that competitiveness is a mental attitude through which he is constantly making unfavorable comparisons between himself and others. Later he may acknowledge that competitiveness is associated with a feeling of resentment that one is always in the losing position. The patient may be more willing to accept this if the doctor does not immediately attempt to focus the feeling of resentment upon himself. Hostile feelings are easier to accept when directed toward someone not immediately present. The interviewer's position as a figure of authority and a potential source of supportive care also inhibits expression of hostile feelings by such patients.

The response of guilt or inadequacy is characteristic of the depressed patient or the patient with a masochistic character.

Envy or Competition

The openly envious or competitive response is a variation of the overtly angry reaction. After listening to the telephone conversation, the patient may ask, "Why can't you be that way with me?" The interviewer's warmth or friendliness to the caller has aroused feelings of competition and jealousy in the patient. The patient feels that the doctor does not care enough about him. Such feelings may be more subtly expressed with the comment, "That must not have been a patient!" When the patient is asked why or how he made such a determination, he replies that the interviewer sounded "so friendly." As in treating openly angry reactions, the interviewer should not attempt to defend himself or convince the patient that he is not being deprived. Instead, he might encourage the patient to further express his feelings of deprivation.

Paranoid Responses

A typical paranoid response would be, "Were you talking about me?" or, "Was the call for me?" The interviewer will learn more if he does not hasten to correct the patient's misinterpretation. First, he might explore the patient's fantasy and then determine the process through which the patient came to his decision. This avoids provoking the patient into an angry defense of his views. Exploring the content of the fantasy will elucidate important transference feelings, while pinpointing the distortions in the thought process may be useful in helping the patient improve his reality testing. The paranoid patient does not know whom to trust. He compensates for his inability either by indiscriminate trust or by trusting no one. The physician might inquire, "Who did you think I was talking to?" and, "What did you think we were discussing?" The fantasy revealed by the patient provides useful information concerning the psycho-dynamics of the patient's emotional disorder. After the inter-viewer has fully explored the patient's ideas, it is useful to show him where he misinterpreted the conversation.

On occasion a call may be about the patient. In this situation it is wise for the interviewer to indicate to the patient the identity of the caller as soon as the interviewer has determined who is calling. This can be done by addressing the caller by name and then proceeding with the conversation. This gesture helps the patient to recognize that the physician is not willing to hold "secret" discussions.

Curiosity

Curiosity, like denial, is a type of response in which the patient has no awareness of any conscious emotional reaction. He has become involved in the conversation, but he is only aware of an interest in what is going on between the doctor and the caller. Typical remarks would include, "Was that your wife who called?" or, "Is everything all right at home, Doctor?" or, "I hope that wasn't bad news." The curiosity is usually a defense against a deeper emotional reaction, such as residual childhood curiosity concerning parental bedroom activities. Remarks displaying curiosity offer the interviewer an opportunity to comment: "Let's take a look at your curiosity in this area." Rather than answer such questions it is better to establish with the patient that he does have curiosity concerning such material. Another approach would be to explore the meaning of the patient's curiosity and to trace it back into his childhood.

Sympathy

The sympathetic response is elicited when it becomes apparent that the caller is in distress. The patient in the office may comment, "I hope that person will be all right," or he might volunteer to relinquish his appointment to enable the doctor to see the other person. Such reactions are frequently defenses against experiencing angry, envious, or guilty feelings. Interpreting the underlying emotion is difficult; the therapist can do very little at that time except continue the interview. Perhaps he may thank the patient for his good intentions. Responses of sympathy are more common in depressed or masochistic patients.

Fright

At times when it is appropriate for the physician to express anger to the caller the patient in the office may react with fear. An illustration of this occurred when an insurance agent interrupted a psychiatrist for the third time and seemed unwilling to accept the doctor's statement that he was not free to speak. Instead he insisted on completing his rehearsed speech. When the doctor became angry and abruptly terminated the call, the patient appeared shocked and said, "You certainly weren't very nice to that person!" The patient feared that he also might evoke an angry response from the doctor. Patients who inhibit their own aggression often fear that as a result of therapy they might lose control of their impounded rage and cause injury to others. Any indication that the doctor can get angry will increase this fear.

A variation of such a reaction might be characterized by the patient's disappointment in the doctor. This could happen when some unattractive aspect of the physician's personality is demonstrated before the patient for the first time. The physician might cope with such reactions in different ways, for example, interpreting the patient's disappointment that the physician is not perfect, or helping the patient to recall previous experiences of disappointment in persons he admired.

Pleasure

The patient is sometimes pleased with the way in which the doctor conducts himself on the telephone. He may, for example, experience vicarious pleasure hearing the doctor express his anger in a way which the patient is unable to emulate. In this situation, the doctor could direct the interview toward the patient's characteristic ways of expressing anger which prevent him from a more open type of emotional expression.

Another situation in which the patient might be pleased occurs when the doctor has obviously received good news. This reaction would require further discussion only if it was apparent that the patient was insincere in his expression.

The Interviewer's Reactions to the Interruption

It is important that the interviewer be aware of his own emotional reactions to telephone interruptions. He may experience relief from boredom or relief if the patient has been expressing hostility. He might be distracted and then experience guilt feelings for having lost the continuity of the interview. He could react by feeling happy or sad in response to good or bad news. He may become angry for several reasons: as a result of the interchange with the caller, or merely because of the particular time at which the interruption occurred. He can recognize countertransference in some reactions, as, for example, when he has used a telephone call in order to enhance his status in the eyes of the patient in his office.

Customarily, when answering the telephone, the interviewer indicates that he is not free to converse. However, if a brief conversation is unavoidable, the physician can find useful therapeutic opportunities if he closely observes the patient's behavior during the call.

On rare occasions the interviewer may ask the patient to leave the consultation room when he receives a telephone call. An example would be a call involving a serious emergency in the personal life of the physician. Under such circumstances the doctor would place an undue burden upon the patient by the unnecessary disclosure of his personal problem.

Someone seeking to reach the patient may call the doctor's office. If the patient is in the office at the time, the doctor can simply hand the telephone to the patient. Should the patient not be there, he may take the message and convey it to the patient. If the matter was not sufficiently urgent to warrant the interruption, the doctor could analyze the patient's motivation for allowing such unreasonable behavior from friends or relatives.

On some occasions the patient may ask to use the doctor's telephone. If the request is made at the end of the session and would cause the doctor to be late for his next appointment, it could be suggested that the patient call elsewhere. If the request is made at the beginning of the session, the doctor might permit the call but then direct the patient's attention to his reasons for not locating a telephone before his appointment. The use of the doctor's telephone, however, can be therapeutically valuable. In one example a patient asked to use the telephone and proceeded to phone her stock broker, placing several "buy and sell" orders in an arrogant manner. Before the interviewer could comment on this unusual behavior, she volunteered, "Doctor, you have just observed a portion of my personality of which I am very ashamed—I hope you will be able to help me."

Telephone Calls from Patients Relatives

Relatives of the patient may occasionally telephone the interviewer and ask either for an appointment or for information concerning the patient. Information concerning the patient should not be divulged, but the relative could be told, "I would like to tell John that you called and expressed an interest in his problem." At times the relative may ask the doctor to promise not to reveal the call. If the doctor agrees to such requests, he is placed in an untenable position and therapy is inevitably damaged.

The therapist may accurately suspect the caller wishes to interfere in the therapy. The authors consider it an error to refuse to speak to him if he is close to the patient. Frequently the caller exercises important influence over the patient's life or the patient is dependent upon him. Alienating such persons can only injure the patient. If the patient gives his consent, an interview with the relative could be arranged with or without the patient present.

TELEPHONE EMERGENCIES

A patient may telephone the doctor in a state of serious depression or acute anxiety which constitutes an emergency. It is apparent that the psychiatrist is at a disadvantage in treating a patient over the telephone. His examination is limited to auditory material and he is unable to utilize other sensory impressions of the patient. Rather than work under such handicapped circumstances, some physicians insist that the patient come for a personal examination or they refuse to aid the patient.

Such rigidity seriously limits a physician's usefulness. Surely the patient is also aware that a personal interview is preferable to a telephone call. In an emergency, however, even a brief positive contact with the physician may be of life-saving benefit to the patient. It is essential, therefore, that one respond to such a patient with the same degree of respect and dignity shown in a personal interview. Many doctors react to the telephone inter-interview with annoyance and resentment which are quickly communicated to the patient. Frequently, the telephone call is the patient's test to determine if the doctor is an accepting or rejecting individual. It is a prejudice of many therapists that all requests for telephone interviews are manifestations of resistance. This is not always valid.

The physician might begin by obtaining the patient's name, address, and telephone number, if the patient has not already identified himself. The patient may be reluctant to provide some of this information. In this situation, the patient can be asked why he feels it is necessary to conceal his identity.

It has been our experience that the "telephone" patient has often had prior contact with a psychiatrist. It is therefore useful to make inquiry about such contacts early in the interview. This is particularly true of the patient who refuses to disclose his identity.

After obtaining a brief description of the presenting problem, it is useful to ask the patient if he has considered arranging for a personal interview. If it becomes apparent that the patient is psychotic, the doctor can ask if the patient fears that a personal visit might lead to hospitalization. If so, the therapist might then investigate specific symptoms which the patient feels might require hospital treatment. After such a discussion it is frequently possible to assure the patient that these symptoms do not require hospitalization. Such a patient can be told that treatment, in order to be successful, requires the cooperation of the patient, and that treatment forced upon the patient probably will not help. The doctor may further assure the patient that he indeed seems to have some motivation to receive help since he has called a physician.

Patients resort to telephone interviews for various reasons. The problem of physical distance prevents some patients from coming in person. Other frequent motivations for telephone interviews are the fear of inordinate expense associated with psychiatric help or the fear of humiliation as the result of discussing embarrassing material face-to-face. Some patients experience such intense desire to commit suicide that they fear that they may not live long enough to be interviewed in person and, therefore, are using the telephone contact as a measure of true desperation.

On rare occasions, at the conclusion of a forty-five-minute interview on the telephone the doctor realizes that a patient who still refuses to come for a personal appointment is seriously in need of help. It may then be useful to make an appointment for a second telephone interview. After several such telephone interviews, the patient usually will be willing to come for an appointment in person.

If someone other than the patient is calling it is necessary to determine the relationship between the patient and the person on the telephone. In a recent example of this, one of the authors was telephoned by a very distraught colleague. Fifteen minutes of clinical presentation had transpired before it became apparent that the patient was the colleague's wife and not a case from his practice. This was not a simple misunderstanding. It arose out of the colleague's strong need to detach himself from his own personal relationship describing his wife merely as another patient about whom he was concerned.

It is important that the interviewer ask the age of the person to whom he is speaking early in a telephone contact. Meeting the patient in person provides visual clues about his age, making it unnecessary to inquire explicitly. Errors of many years can easily be made if estimates of the patient's age are based on the sound of his voice. Other basic identifying data that the physician routinely obtains when speaking to the patient in person are also frequently overlooked during the telephone interview.

An obvious but often neglected technique for reducing the handicaps inherent in a telephone situation is to ask the patient to describe himself physically. While no one answers such a question objectively, certain patients tend to distort more than others. This tendency is based on how they feel about themselves. It is possible for the physician to reduce such distortion by asking the patient if the answer he has given is more a reflection of how he appears to others or how he actually feels about himself.

A doctor may decide to summon the police in response to a telephone call from a severely suicidal or homicidal patient who is on the brink of losing control of his impulses and cannot come to the hospital. This should be done openly, with the patient informed of the action. If the patient objects, the physician can increase the patient's responsibility for this decision, pointing out that he made such action possible through the disclosure of his name and address.

For example, a patient may telephone the doctor and announce that he has just ingested a full bottle of sleeping pills. Obviously the doctor asks the patient his name, address, and telephone number at once and then asks the name of the medication and the approximate number of pills. If he has taken a dangerous dose, the physician can advise him that the police will be sent immediately and that the patient should open his door to facilitate their entry. The physician might inform the patient that he will call back as soon as he has summoned the police. He can also inquire about the name and phone number of the closest neighbor in the event that the police are not immediately available.

If the patient refuses to disclose his name and address, the doctor might comment, "You must have some uncertainty concerning your wish to die or you would not have called me. There are only a few minutes remaining in which you can change your mind. You have taken a fatal dose and it may already be too late to save your life, but we can still try." Realizing that the outcome is already uncertain, the patient may allow "fate" to intervene and may provide the identifying data.

An analogous situation could occur with the patient who is on the verge of homicide.

A special problem of the telephone interview is silences, which occur as they do in conventional therapy. It is often difficult for the telephone interviewer to allow these silences to develop during the conversation. This is a reflection of the interviewer's discomfort, dissatisfaction, or impatience. Only through experience can a therapist relax and be professionally at ease while conducting a telephone interview.

In the later portion of the telephone interview, the physician may inquire if there is anyone else with whom he can converse; by obtaining another person's view of the patient's problems, the therapist may gain information that would help him to assess the clinical situation.

CONDUCTING REGULAR THERAPY SESSIONS BY TELEPHONE

On rare occasions a psychiatrist may elect to treat his patient by telephone. For instance, a patient might be forced to move to some part of the country where psychotherapy is unavailable. Under these circumstances regular treatment sessions might be continued by telephone.

Three brief vignettes illustrate some major points. In the first case, a middle-aged depressed woman who has had several years of therapy went to Nevada for six weeks to obtain a divorce. Her marriage contributed to her depression, but she was unable to face the prospect of the divorce without the emotional support of her therapy. Her treatment was successfully conducted twice a week for six weeks on the telephone.

The second case was a thirty-year-old depressed woman with anxiety and hypochondriacal trends. After one year of treatment she became pregnant and seemed likely to miscarry. Her obstetrician insisted that she remain in bed for three months. Her home situation was intolerable and she lived too far away to receive psychotherapy at home. The psychiatrist treated her twice weekly by telephone during this period.

The third case involves a more unusual situation in some respects. The patient was a thirty-year-old phobic housewife who moved to the suburbs after several years of treatment. One day a severe snowstorm forced a cancellation. The patient waited until her appointed hour to telephone, as she had hoped to find some means of transportation. The physician sensed that she was eager to terminate the call and commented to that effect. The patient revealed disturbing thoughts about the doctor which she had successfully suppressed while in the office. As the patient would have isolated her feelings if the matter had been left until the next appointment, it was discussed at that time. Subsequenly the patient deliberately sought a "telephone" session when more difficult material emerged. That time the physician refused as it was clear that the patient's request was a form of resistance.

Admittedly these are all special situations, but nonetheless they are scarcely unique. The arrangement to continue a patient's treatment by telephone implies that the patient's dependence upon the doctor is realistic. In situations where this would be undesirable, telephone sessions are not indicated.

As the reader has surmised, the telephone consultation presents many challenging and difficult problems. The physician who has developed skill and flexibility in this situation will be able to work more effectively with a wider variety of patients.

PART II

CRISIS INTERVENTION AND COUNSELING BY TELEPHONE

INTRODUCTION

IN THIS SECTION we have endeavored to point to the unique qualities of telephone counseling, the advantages and disadvantages, and the errors that are easy to make as a telephone counselor. There are many ways, of course, in which the skills acquired as a face-to-face therapist are applicable to therapy and counseling with the telephone. This section does not concern itself with these general skills. The reader can turn to one of the standard texts on therapy for this information.

Telephone therapy by itself is often able to resolve the crises of some individuals. However, more often, it is but one facet of a comprehensive treatment program. We have seen in Chapter 4 how the psychiatrist can utilize the telephone in providing adequate treatment for his patients. In Chapter 13 we will mention how mildly disturbed individuals can be maintained in the community with the support of a telephone counseling service, whereas without this support they might have to be institutionalized.

Recognizing the need for telephone counseling to be incorporated into a network of resources and treatment modes, two chapters in this section discuss the kinds of auxiliary services needed to complement a telephone counseling service.

Chapter 5

THE UNIQUE CONTRIBUTION OF TELEPHONE THERAPY

Tim Williams and John Douds

Most systems of psychotherapy assume that face-to-face interaction is necessary for effective therapy. This assumption is taken for granted as a *sine qua non* for "genuine" therapy. In agency statistics a face-to-face interview is called therapy, but a telephone conversation is often given the status of a "contact," as if it does not deserve recognition as equivalent to a genuine therapy session. Although a telephone contact is accepted as better than nothing, it is judged as a depersonalization of true therapy.

The purpose of this chapter is to explore the unique contributions of telephone therapy. Our intent is not to attack the supremacy of face-to-face therapy, but rather to heighten an awareness of the unique value of telephone therapy as a treatment dimension useful for particular client life-styles and problems. We believe that telephone therapy provides a new dimension of therapeutic service and deserves recognition as a special way to link certain people with a helping service. The helping service provided by most agencies reaches individuals who are moderately distressed, but excludes others whose problems make it difficult for them to seek help. A telephone counseling service provides greater penetration into the community, for an individual is as close to a helping contact as he is to the nearest telephone.

The telephone has unrealized potential as a therapeutic instrument which can reach many people who might otherwise not receive counseling. It is surprising that a profession whose essential tool is interpersonal communication has for so long ignored the possibilities offered by the telephone. The business world seized upon the invention long ago, using it as an aid in business transaction. (Conference telephone calls, for example, are very common today.) In politics, too, the telephone plays a crucial role. The famous Kremlin-White House hotline exploits to the full the major benefits of the telephone, linking people at all times of crisis, regardless of their geographical distances from each other. This is what McLuhan means when he calls the telephone a "hot" medium.

We shall explore the potential of telephone therapy from two perspectives: first, the unique qualities of telephone therapy, and secondly, the value of telephone therapy for people with certain life-styles and problems.

THE UNIQUE QUALITIES OF TELEPHONE THERAPY

Telephone therapy differs from conventional face-to-face therapy in the following ways: (1) the client has more control, (2) the client can remain anonymous, (3) geographic and personal barriers can be bridged, and (4) the therapist can remain anonymous.

Client Control

A person in distress may be so overwhelmed psychologically that he does not have sufficient psychological energy to visit a helping agency. The act of visiting an agency demands certain resources and strengths. To apply for help at a strange agency requires contacting the unknown, which is a fearful step for most of us. The client has to meet another human being, which can be difficult especially when a person feels an inner helplessness in relation to his problem. Upon entering the agency structure, the person is faced with the fact that the dominance relationship is set so that the agency and the counselor are in command. This compounds the patient's feeling that, to some degree, he is at the mercy of the counselor. The client is often required to give out personal information, information which few of us like to give to someone whom we do not know.

Paradoxically, at the beginning of the therapeutic contact the patient is asked to give more of himself than is the therapist. Furthermore, the client has no choice of who his helper will be. There are very few of us who would accept these conditions happily.

Our point is this: coming for help may in some instances be positively humiliating. It becomes understandable why many people who need help will not seek it unless driven by desperation. Under these circumstances, the telephone offers a unique advantage as an instrument of help.

In the first place, the client has some power or control when he contacts the helping person on the phone. Should the helping person be too threatening to the patient, the latter is in a position to hang up. The knowledge to the patient that he could always cut off the therapist if things become too threatening to him gives him a feeling of freedom that he won't necessarily become a victim to an unknown source. In the office situation, however, we doubt that the patient feels any of this power. If things do not work out well, the patient ends up imprisoned in a strange office with a threatening source whom he must submit to or attack.

Client Anonymity

Experience has affirmed the value of anonymity in the helping process. The advantage of being able to hide one's identity may facilitate greater self-revelation and openness on the part of a patient. Opening oneself up to another person is an act of vulnerability and can, in fact, increase one's feelings of inadequacy and helplessness. Anonymity is useful here, for the patient can feel secure, in that he has some control over the potential negative consequences of his self-revelation when his name is not known by the counselor. The value of anonymity in facilitating self-revelation is illustrated by the fact that strangers are often able to reveal themselves to each other on a temporary basis. In a context of anonymity, self-revelation does not threaten normal role functioning. Anonymity reduces the fear of being ridiculed or abused while in a vulnerable position and can reduce the loss in social status involved in presenting oneself as someone in need of help. The reduced threat, therefore, opens the door for help to some clients.

Bridging Geographic and Personal Barriers

Many psychologically distressed people are restricted in their geographic mobility. It may be threatening to leave a place in which they feel secure and rooted. They have established their psychological space within a familiar area. All novel stimuli, whether positive or negative, may initially be experienced as threatening. In order to maintain a very unstable equilibrium, such people have exchanged the possibility of growth and adventure for a form of rigid, closed-in safety. They have locked themselves in to feel safe and secure, but have paid the price of locking out new creative experiences.

For this type of individual, the telephone may be the one opportunity to begin a new process. From his island, the client can begin to talk with other human beings in a safe way. In the words of one man: "I have lived so much inside myself for the past three years, that I believe that I have forgotten even how to approach and talk with other human beings." The telephone represents to this person a safe means by which to begin social interaction. He can do this at a safe distance and on his own terms. There are people who call a telephone counseling service five or six times a day. This could be viewed as too great a dependency. Yet we might note that each of us needs a certain amount of social interaction each day to keep going. Four or five calls each day by an isolated person may be quantitatively no different from the social contact any of us needs. From this perspective, the isolated person is simply focusing the normal need for social interactions onto one agency because it is available to him in his immediate environment. Given this support, the patient may be able to develop confidence that he can eventually begin to seek social interactions in other ways.

Recently Rescue, Inc. in Boston instituted a Life-Line service for the elderly. Once a day the staff of Life-Line call each elderly person on their service. The telephone service is free. Elderly people who wish to become a part of the telephone network simply have to contact Rescue, Inc. and request the service. Life-Line serves two purposes. The daily telephone calls serves as protection for the elderly when they are ill or when there is an emergency. If the phone is not answered, a Life-Line volunteer will visit the home of the person for a routine check. Secondly, Life-Line brings the elderly together. All daily telephone calls are made by the elderly to each other. The daily telephone calls start new friendships and often renew old ones.

This type of service may seem minimal compared to intense psychotherapy. However, according to the Census Bureau in New York City there are an estimated 750,000 people living alone in the city. Recently, again in New York City, some psychiatrists have developed a diagnostic category: loneliness. A Life-Line service, therefore, provides a vital service for a community.

Therapist Anonymity: The Power of Positive Transference

Thus far, we have discussed those aspects of telephone therapy which make initial contact easier for the patient. Now, we shall look briefly at another aspect of telephone therapy which can play a significant role, both at the moment of initial contact and at later stages of telephone therapy.

We have already indicated the advantages of the patient remaining anonymous. The other side of that coin is that the therapist may remain anonymous. When a patient contacts a helping agency, he doubtless has some idea of what will happen to him and some notion of what the therapist will be like. (This notion may, of course, not be realistic.) If the client does not know what to expect, he may imagine, consciously or unconsciously, how he would like the therapist to be. Reality may be better than the patient's expectations. He might have expected an impersonal technician, but instead been greeted by a warm and sympathetic human being. In face-to-face therapy, the chances are, however, that reality will not match his fantasy. And the psychologically distressed individual cannot, in his present state, withstand the shattering of his illusions. His illusions give him a sense of security.

Of course, the telephone therapist will not be whatever the patient wishes him to be. However, he will be far more like the patient's ideal than the face-to-face therapist, since the patient is presented with only a part of the reality. On the telephone, we receive none of the visual clues about a person that we receive in a face-to-face contact. We have no idea what the person we are talking with looks like, nor can we see facial expressions, and, finally, we get none of the body language clues to his thoughts, feelings, and personality that we generally receive in a face-to-face contact.

The important point is that the telephone contact, much more than the face-to-face interview, permits the patient to make of the therapist what he will. This has the crucial implication that he can make of the therapist what he *needs*.

For example, one of us had a long series of telephone contacts with a teenage girl trying to break a habit of frequent soft-drug use. She seemed to be making progress and attributed this to the "firm line" that the therapist was taking with her. She thought of the therapist as a well-built, tall, muscular individual. Actually, the therapist did not fit this description at all, and he had done very little in the way of taking a firm line on the drug question. He had, in fact, concentrated more on other areas. It seems, however, the girl had projected onto the therapist the strong, forceful, masculine qualities she was seeking in someone who could control her behavior. The medium of the telephone contact provided her with the opportunity to do this.

Of course, there are disadvantages in allowing an individual to dwell too long in a world of fantasy. However, if the therapist is aware of what is happening, he can begin to present the patient the reality of the situation when he feels that the patient has sufficient strength to accept reality.

In summary, the anonymity of the therapist facilitates the development of transference, which can be used, within limits, to facilitate positive growth on the part of the patient.

THE USE OF TELEPHONE THERAPY AS A TREATMENT MODALITY WITH CERTAIN CLIENTS

There are particular kinds of patients for whom telephone therapy provides a particularly useful treatment modality. We have identified four patient or situational categories which appear to respond best to telephone therapy. They are (1) the adolescent, (2) the isolate, (3) the desperate, and (4) the one-shot caller.

The Adolescent

The adolescent needs to spend a good time in self-involvement, attempting to master new impulses and experiences. A great deal of energy is tied up in tentatively testing out new roles in an effort to discover his unique identity in a complicated world. It is part of his life process to be perpetually ambivalent about everything and everyone. He has a pervasive indecisiveness and ambivalence about reality, and thus he finds it very difficult to reveal, even to describe, the facets of his inner life. At this point in his development, self-revelation becomes very difficult. He is spending a great deal of time trying to create a social image, and does not want to reveal "weaknesses" that threaten his image. A feeling of independence and self-sufficiency is a vital part of the self-image. Those experiences which even suggest dependency, vulnerability, weakness, and lack of self-confidence are all viewed as threats to his self-esteem. The world of appearances is very crucial to the adolescent.

In view of this, therefore, it can be seen that asking for and receiving help can be tremendously threatening to the adolescent. A telephone counseling service provides the possibility of helping the adolescent in a way that is less threatening to his self-image, since the patient can remain anonymous and has a great deal of control.

The Isolate

Telephone therapy is revelant to the needs of the severely distressed person who is simply unable to enter a new situation. A great danger for this person is his ultimate isolation from the world. A telephone contact with a counselor is perhaps the only step he is capable of taking in order to obtain help. It is a social input in an otherwise barren existence.

Although the availability in the community of a telephone counseling service may facilitate the isolate's search for help, the great problem with this kind of individual is that he is unlikely to respond to this passive service. Communities need an active outreach service that can identify and make contacts with isolates. The isolate, all too often, has lost the motivation even to call a telephone counseling service. However, a telephone counseling service provides a potential contact with a helping agency for the individual who is falling into greater and greater isolation. If the contact is made, it can, hopefully, prevent his complete isolation.

The Desperate

There are many people who need immediate help as a result of a sudden psychological shock which tips their mental balance to a point where they are overwhelmed by feelings of disorientation. A parallel and more dramatic type of situation is actual physical wounding on a field of battle, where the individual is unable to do anything but cry for help. The effects of psychological shock may be similar. For the person who is faced with such a crisis the presence of a telephone counseling agency becomes a life-line to reality contact. The very sound of a caring, thoughtful voice can provide emotional support, analogous to the giving of a blood transfusion to the physically wounded.

The One-shot Crisis Contact

Finally, we believe that there are many relatively normal people whose sense of pride and integrity is threatened by coming to an agency. Such a person may identify coming for help as being sick. His fear of a loss of self-esteem acts as a barrier to seeking help openly. Furthermore, he may perceive his need as quite temporary, in the sense that he momentarily needs the presence of someone else so that he can think through his situation better. He does not want to become involved in a longer-term theraputic relationship. A telephone counseling service is, perhaps, the only means by which such individuals can receive help.

CONCLUSION: BUILDING INTERPERSONAL BRIDGES

We have attempted to describe the unique value of telephone therapy in relation to the special needs of patients in crisis situations. Its special usefulness lies in the fact that the therapist can use it to build interpersonal bridges to human beings who, because of their psychological state or external circumstances, simply cannot visit an agency for help.

The telephone serves as a means for a patient to seek help without having to run the gauntlet of bureaucratic procedures (appointments, waiting lists, information disclosure, and so forth) which are necessary for the orderly running of an agency, but which often serve to screen out many of those people most desperately in need of help.

The agency and the patient build psychological barriers which hinder their reaching each other. The telephone can facilitate the bypassing of these barriers. It can enable contact on terms which threaten neither the patient nor the agency. Many people who have been unable to seek help through conventional modalities have been able to receive psychological support and counseling from a telephone counseling service.

Professionals must not continue to underrate the telephone as a therapeutic modality. The telephone counseling service can provide a crucial service for the psychologically distressed individuals in the community. Telephone therapy should not be viewed as a substitute for face-to-face therapy, but rather as a preferred mode of treatment for particular individuals who are in certain kinds of crisis situations.

Chapter 6

CRISIS INTERVENTION: THEORY, PROCESS AND PRACTICE

Gene W. Brockopp

It may appear to be tautological to say that the technique of crisis intervention is the most appropriate method for dealing with people in crisis. Yet, of all the theories of behavior, methods of psychotherapy, and techniques of intervening into people's problems derived from them, the theory and technique of crisis intervention is the method of choice when working with a person on the telephone who is in crisis.

As both the concept and the technique are recent additions to the armamentarium of the mental health worker, crisis intervention is often misused in emergency telephone services. In this chapter, I will focus on crisis intervention as a process, showing why it is a useful theory and how it can be applied to the telephone emergency service. I will also develop some of the technical aspects of its use in the crisis intervention center. The application of this process to specific types of cases or problems will be shown in subsequent chapters.

THEORY OF CRISIS INTERVENTION

The theory of crisis intervention has been developed by Lindemann (1944) and Caplan (1954), although important contributions have been made by Wolberg (1965), Bellock and Small (1965), and extensions of the therapy are to be found in the writings of Hauseman and Rioch (1967), Jacobsen (1965) and Hansell, *et al.* (1970). The conceptual framework of crisis theory, as expressed by Caplan is based upon the hypothesis that an individual is normally in a state of psychological equili-

89

brium, that is, he is able to balance the inner tensions and the outer stresses in a way which is appropriate to him and thus maintain himself without too great an expenditure of energy. This state is maintained through the use of behavioral patterns with which the individual is familiar and which allow him to interact with the environment, solve his problems and maintain the homeostatic balance or a point of equilibrium on an abstract concept called the "continuum of mental health." One end of this theoretical continuum represents mental illness and the other mental health. Where any person would be on this continuum would depend on his life-style, the way he handles crises, the type of living he does, his normal response to stress, and so on. When facing a problem in his everyday life, a person may become upset, but is usually able to return to his point of balance on this continuum. These temporary upsets are generally solved by means of previously learned problem-solving behavior or various means of coping. When the person is confronted by a problem situation in which the previously used methods of restructuring his life or environment are either not available to him or not successful in his solving the problem, the person is confronted by a critical situation, that is, one in which he is uncertain about the end or resolution of the problem. Since he is unable, through the use of his normal problem-solving techniques, to resolve the difficulty with which he is faced, the critical situation is emotionally hazardous and he may rapidly move toward a state of crisis. Because the person views the situation as critical, he mobilizes and utilizes all of his abilities and brings them to bear on the problem, for the situation as he sees it demands resolution. A crisis then, is an intolerable situation which must be resolved, for it has the potential to cause the psychosocial deterioration of the person. It is important to remember that a crisis does not mean an individual is confronted with a totally new situation, rather, a crisis is more likely to be a situation in which a previously tolerable set of circumstances is suddenly, by the addition of one other factor, rendered wholly intolerable. One new event sets a whole new set of events into motion.

The crisis, however, is not the situation itself, but the person's response to the situation.) And the person's response is initially ambivalence and uncertainty, not knowing where he is relative to the problem or what he needs to do or can do to solve the problem and return to a point of equilibrium or homeostasis. As a result, the crisis has in it both a danger and an opportunity. It can move the individual to regression, disintegration of personality or resolution, learning and growth. Because of his ambivalence and uncertainty and his need to reach out for assistance, the person is usually open to suggestions, modifications and directions from other individuals to help him solve his problem. Therefore, the crisis provides an opportunity for rapid changes in the personality structure of the individual if the suggestions are seen by him as helpful in the process of reintegration and resolution of his problem.

To summarize, a critical situation is a series of events which take place in a person's life and which together form a hazardous situation in which a crisis can develop. A crisis is the person's response to a hazardous situation, which by the inclusion of one additional event has created an imbalance in his life to the degree that resolution is required. The process of resolution may and often does affect a whole class of events rather than just the one that precipitated the crisis situation.

Regardless of the problem at the moment, which may include suicide, incarceration, personality disintegration, drug-related problems or any other situation defined by the individual as intolerable, all of them share the common characteristic of the need to do something immediate to prevent further deterioration of the personality or injury of the person to himself or to others in his environment.

A crisis, then, implies an emergency or serious situation. The criticalness of the crisis depends on a number of factors: (1) the life style and character structure of the individual; (2) the quality and nature of previous situations with which the individual was confronted; (3) the amount of support that is given to the individual during the crisis; and (4) the person's ability to respond to the crisis situations without disintegration.

Most crises fall into one of two categories: developmental

or incidental. Developmental crises are those which are expected in the normal movement of the individual from birth to death. They are predictable; we know that they will arise in the individual's lifetime. Many of them cannot be changed, for they are necessary for the individual's movement to maturity; for example, the crisis of adolescence. But all of them can be modified, made less hurtful or having less potential for the disintegration of the individual's personality. Incidential crises are of a different variety. These can be prevented or at least substantially influenced. Most crises that occur in the individual's life and result in disintegration of personality are in this category. These crises are precipitated by various events in the individual's life through a set of circumstances which appear to be accidental and arbitrary but in most cases, under careful evaluation, are often specific, predictable and modifiable. These include such incidents as loss of a job, marriage, illness, accidents, moving, death, raising children. They are the predictable stresses in each individual's life. Their effects can be modified by psychological immunization or through utilizng the crtical event as a problem-solving or growth-producing situation. The two crises which account for a major portion of the serious calls received by a suicide and crisis service are included in this category. These are the crises related to suicidal behavior and to drug abuse.

The person's response to the crisis situation can be understood as a process which has contiguous or sometimes overlapping units. Caplan sees the crisis period as having four elements. The first is characterized by the person's response to the critical situation and the resulting increase in activity, tension and disorganization of the individual as he attempts to utilize his normal problem-solving techniques as a means of dealing with the problem with the hope of returning to a point of equilibrium. The second stage is characterized by a lack of success through the use of the normal mechanisms and therefore a continuation of the problem. This results in an exacerbation of the state of disorganization and tension in the individual. In the third stage the tensions developed by the critical situation reach the point where the individual is forced to use additional resources, both external and internal, in his attempt to resolve the problem. As a result of this move the problem may decrease in intensity, and the person may use emergency problem-solving methods; he may see the problem in a new way and solve it or he may give up and withdraw from the situation, seeing it as impossible or the goal as unattainable. In the fourth stage, if the problem remains and it cannot be solved by the techniques available to the individual or if the problem cannot be avoided by him, major personality disorganization occurs and the individual may become psychotic, withdraw, suicide or just give up.

The person in crisis has a number of specific personality characteristics, among these are the following (1) A lowered span of attention, focusing on the foreground images with a restricting of the background or setting within which the problem occurs. (2) A ruminative, introspective stance. He looks inside of himself for possible reasons for the occurrence of the crisis situation or explanations as to how he can resolve it. At the same time he shows a great deal of anguish, fear and both internal and external distress. (3) An emotional reaching out for help and support and a seeming inability to control his emotional responses. (4) A great deal of testing behavior, much of which is impulsive and unproductive. (5) A change in his relationship to people. His social network shows many changes; initially he is involved with people; later, he becomes less aware of his surroundings as he begins to see all individuals in terms of their ability to help him solve his problem. (6) Reduction in orienting attitudes and a lack of perspective about himself as a person in time, space and the community. (7) A great deal of searching behavior in an attempt to solve his problem by looking for usable features of his environment which may help in the resolution. (8) Having a large fund of information available to him relative to the problem with which he is confronted, but this is usually in a very disorganized state and therefore not useful to him.

It is obvious that a crisis is a very serious situation both in terms of its process and its potential effect on the individual's personality structure. Yet, most of these features can be seen positively and the crisis can be a very useful learning and therapeutic tool. The reasons for this are as follows: (1) The individual is in a state of disequilibrium and tension and as a result considerable change is possible for him in a relatively short period of time. His normal pattern of behavior has been broken, his defenses are now open and he is more susceptible to new ideas. If he can find a relationship with someone who can give him an opportunity to work on the problem he has, a minimum amount of effort on the part of a therapist can result in considerable change on the part of the patient since there is so much motivation to solve the problem and an openness and willingness to obtain assistance. (2) If the crisis resolution utilizes the individual's strengths and mobilizes them in reference to the problem, emphasis is placed on the positive aspects of the patient's personality and upon his ability to work through the problems that he is having in a positive way, the result can be an increased sense of self-enhancement and self-regard. (3) Through the process of crisis intervention, the patient can learn to symbolize his problem in verbal terms and to deal with the problem both verbally and behaviorally. This allows him to separate himself from the problem and look at it more objectively and symbolically. It also gives him an opportunity to try his means of solving a problem symbolically and to test it with another individual before using it in the problem situation. (4) Handled appropriately, the resolution of the problem in the crisis situation can result in the individual developing a different, more appropriate way of approaching a crisis—a new way of problem solving and a better way of resolving the crisis situation. This may transfer to other areas of his life and help him deal with subsequent situations in a competent, appropriate and more eloquent manner. (5) Through resolving the crisis, the person may establish a position for himself at a higher point on the mental health continuum (that is, at a point at which he is utilizing less of his energy to deal with problems and therefore has more energy available for living). With his everyday functioning improved and with more energy available for living, his psychosocial view of himself may be enhanced.

THE PROCESS OF CRISIS INTERVENTION

Crisis intervention as a unique therapeutic process began as a technique for dealing with people in disaster situations. It was developed into a system by amalgamating ideas from diverse areas. As I see it, three streams of thought have gone into this development: (1) Through military psychiatry, especially as exemplified in the works of Glass (1965), Tyhurst (1957), and Hausman and Rioch (1967), the basic concepts of responding to crisis and the development of the major elements necessary to deal with the crisis situation were developed. (2) The development of the short-term ego and teaching therapies beginning with Bellock and Small (1965), Ellis (1962), and others. With the emphasis on the here and now and on the positive elements of the patient being emphasized, therapeutic intervention took on a new dimension. (3) The development of the community mental health perspective with situational (rather than office) involvement with the patient and with the development of community emergency services. This concept was developed initially by Caplan, reorganized by Jacobsen (1965) and systematized recently by Hansell *et al.* (1970). Out of these a system of intervention, which I call a social behavior crisis counseling, has been developed. This type of counseling, regardless of its name, differs from the normal psychiatric therapeutic view of people and problems in that (1) There is no concept of mental illness or classification of people into the abstractions of illness or health. (2) It views people in terms of their ability to cope, their strengths and their potentials and their problem-solving abilities. (3) It emphasizes the healthy aspects, not the pathological or sick aspects of the personality. (4) It uses the environment, the social structure of the individual and the community, not just the dynamics of the individual personality for determining disposition. (5) It assumes that patients will make the right response if given information in a setting in which they can use information and that a person's behavior will tend to move toward desirable ends or outcomes. (6) It emphasizes the active, directive role of the care giver in the process of assisting individuals to move out of a crisis situation.

Crisis intervention, then, is an active, cognitively oriented process. It focuses on the individual's thinking process and on both the rational and irrational aspects of his behavior. At the same time it is problem oriented. The helping person directs all of his energies to the solving of the problem that the person has, helping the individual to organize his life in a way which will be useful to him in solving his problem. It is a cross-sectional approach, dealing with an aspect of the individual at one point in time. It is not a genetically determined viewpoint nor does it concern itself with the individual's previous problems; rather, it deals with the situation now and focuses all the energy upon helping the person to resolve his present conflict. To do this it uses the turmoil and upset of the crisis situation to help the person establish new cognitive approaches to working with his problem in a more rational and more appropriate way. Through the use of the person's social network and by tapping individuals within this network or life space to give support to the person in a crisis and thereby helping him to maintain a level of functioning, the process of crisis intervention helps to reintegrate the person into the community. Through this process it attempts to develop a more effective, affectional relationship between the person in crisis and significant people in his environment. By utilizing all of the above, crisis intervention, as a technique, changes the personalty patterns of the individual and helps him move to a more competent life style; yet, the focus is on the here and the now and the present problem with which the individual is confronted. Through working with the problem the individual has at this time, the person often completes previously incompleted or unresolved situations in the past and develops competencies for working with problems he will face in the future.

Effective crisis intervention uses the five basic concepts enunciated by Hausman and Rioch (1967), immediacy, proximity, concurrence, commitment and expectancy. Each of these concepts will be developed individually. In the following discussion I will draw heavily on the works by Hansell (1970) and his concept of crisis counseling.

Immediacy

Effective crisis intervention work depends upon the immediacy of the treatment program. We know that any problem, whether with drugs, suicide, mental health or in any other behavioral area, tends to get rigid with time. In the crisis period, the person is open to change; the sooner we can work with him the more likely we are to minimize the possible deterioration of the personality and to develop an effective solution which will improve the personality functioning of the individual. The potential for positive growth through immediacy of treatment cannot be overemphasized. Immediacy of treatment also gives value to the individual, for there is a sense of importance in not being placed on a waiting list but rather being given assistance when one needs it.

Proximity

Given the setting where the problem has occurred, the closer to the setting we can develop a solution to the problem, the more effective that solution will be. When we can deal with the problem the person has within the setting in which the problem occurred, the person does not need to be removed from the setting to a new location and the solution can develop from the pertinent, positive social aspects of his environment. Therefore, it will be appropriate to that environment and more likely to be used by the individual. At the same time, by developing a solution in this way, the person's identity and role value in his environment is not lost. Because of the difficulty he is having, his role value may be suspended, but since he is not removed from the environment he can reintegrate himself quite easily again.*

Commitment

One of the essential elements of working with a crisis situation and probably one of the most easily achieved, is the concept of commitment. The person in the crisis must be able to commit

---

* This point certainly emphasizes the value of the telephone in working with people in crisis.

himself to working with the helper in the solution of the problem. This is usually quite easy to obtain because the individual in crisis is usually in a state of pain and anxiety and wants resolution to the problem he is having. The conscious commitment on his part to working with a solution is, however, most essential for he needs to take responsibility for his actions and for his part in the crisis situation. Committing himself to working on the problem means to take an active role rather than a passive role in the interaction with the helping person. It means that the person is not acted on, but acting in concert with the therapist. The adequacy and correctness of the solution which is developed will then be one which is developed by the two individuals; not one that is decided by the therapist and given to the person as a prescription or treatment plan.

Concurrence

One of the most critical elements in crisis intervention is to link the person in crisis to the significant people in his life space who will support him and help him develop the skill and competence he needs to maintain himself. The person in crisis is an individual who in essence has lost his mooring or his anchor point. One of our tasks is to help him find within his life space or his neighborhood the links which he needs to maintain himself; those links which will give him support, self- and social esteem. To accomplish this we need to develop a set of caring relationships for him, individuals who are willing to embrace the client; people who expect him to get well. It is important that the helper become a type of transitional social object, focusing the person on those social elements that have a permanent place in his life space. By doing this, we emphasize that the social network of the individual is important and critical. If we can channel and direct this environment we can prevent deterioration and create a climate for improvement. By doing this we powerfully effect the outcome of the crisis; for we say that we expect the person to regain a position of status in his community by using events which will help him to stabilize himself in that community. Further, by using his environment as a support, feedback and expectation base, we use the concurrence from the environment and emphasize to the individual that he is important and of value and that we expect him to return to a position of value in the community. By keeping the person in crisis in touch with his social, cultural community, we forecast for him an outcome whereby he will regain status in that community. We show him that we see in him the capacity to be a functioning member of his community.

Expectancy

By the type and quality of his interaction with the person in crisis, the helping person effectively forecasts for the individual the course of his problem and its eventual outcome. Emphasis must be given to the potential that the person has, to the positive, healthy aspects of his personality and to the possibility that he can again obtain family, social, self- and community esteem. The person in crisis is usually only aware of his anguish and pain and often does not define himself well nor understand his relationship with other people. The view of himself is either fluid or deteriorating. Often he expects an outcome which is negative. The expectancy of the counselor can cut through some of these problems and help the person see that the end can be positive. He can destroy the self-fulfilling negative prophecies of the individual and replace them with neutral or positive concepts. To do this, he must be selective and attentive to certain attitudes and characteristics of the individual in crisis. As Hansell (1968) points out, it is critical that the therapist sees something good, positive, lovable or of value in the patient. Expectancy of the staff is also important in helping individuals to relate to his environment and the environment to relate to him (concurrence). If the helper views the person in crisis in a positive way, the family and the peer group usually see him in the same way. By this process we help the social group to embrace rather than to reject the individual and help them to focus on the potential that the person has for growth, rather than on the initial deterioration that may have taken place during the first stages of the crisis situation.

CRISIS INTERVENTION BY TELEPHONE

To assist the telephone counselor to effectively work with people in crisis, the Suicide Prevention Center in Los Angeles (Farberow *et al.*, undated), has developed a technique for helping individuals through the suicidal crisis. This technique is largely based on the concepts stated above. Although this plan has been developed for working with the suicidal person, with slight modification it is appropriate for use in most crisis situations. The plan which follows is based on their concepts although it has been substantially modified to include ideas which evolved at the Buffalo Suicide Prevention Center.

When taking any crisis call we suggest that the following five, contiguous and overlapping guidelines be used. (1) *Making an initial evaluation regarding the severity of the crisis situation.* One of the first questions that any crisis worker should ask himself whenever he picks up a telephone in a crisis center is, "How much time do I have before I must make a decision regarding this person?" I believe this question is necessary to reduce the anxiety of working with people in crisis, for in most cases one will have sufficient time to work with the person, since most crises do not include the emergency of life or death.* Through the question we place the crisis into the perspective of time, reduce the anxiety of the telephone worker and more objectively deal with the person. (2) *Developing a relationship with the crisis person.* The initial step of the crisis worker is to establish a relationship with the person who is calling. Trust is an essential element of this relationship and will be characterized by the free flow of information from the patient to the therapist. Also in the relationship is the feeling of interest, concern and a nonjudgmental attitude which the therapist will transmit to the crisis person. It is often asumed that a relationship is best established through a sensing and reflecting of the emotional components in the individual's life. By doing this, it is assumed that the person in crisis will feel that here is a person

---

* At the Buffalo Suicide Prevention Center between eight and nine calls out of 100 are now emergency situations where a decision must be made within a relatively short period of time or the possibility of death may occur. In the other ninety plus cases, time is not a critical element.

who cares or is concerned about him. This process is called "tuning in" to the feelings of the person in crisis. In my experience, I have found that (the more severe the crisis situation is, the less necessary it is to focus in on the emotion and the more desirable it is to focus cognitively on the problem the individual is having and helping the person develop a means of working out of the problem situation he has. Concern for the individual can be transmitted as effectively through interested involvement with the problem he has as it can through focusing in on the emotions related to that problem.) In the more severe crisis, there is an assumption of trust in the helping individual and a willingness on the part of the client to give the trust that is necessary to obtain the assistance he needs to resolve the crisis. The less severe the crisis is, the more we will need to focus in on the noncognitive, nonproblem, affective element, to help the person establish a basis for trust and for the free flow of information. (3) *Assist the person to identify the specific problem he has.* The person in crisis is usually confused and disorganized and has difficulty in defining his problems. Care must be taken to explore the individual's total field of interaction before focusing on an individual problem, as the person in crisis is often confused and his desire to work toward an immediate solution of his problem may lead the helper astray. When the problem is specified and placed into perspective, the patient will often feel relieved. At this point, with the suicidal individual, it is important to evaluate the potential for suicide. If the potential is high, immediate intervention or hospitalization may be needed, although this may sometimes be averted through step four. (4) *Assessing and mobilizing the patient's strength and resources.* Individuals who are in crisis often feel they have no resources on which to draw and no friends to give them assistance. In their confusion and disorganization, they often overlook people who would be willing to help. By examining the crisis situation and exploring with the person in crisis individuals in his life space who may be able to help him, the telephone therapist often locates resources that the person has forgotten—resources which can be crucial to his recovery. At the same time, the therapist explores with the person means by which these resources can be mobilized and used as a support network for the patient during the time of crisis. In general, the patient should be encouraged to do this as much as possible for himself. However, the therapist must be willing to accept the responsibility to assist the patient in this activity, especially during the initial stages when confusion and disorganization may be great. (5) *Development of an action plan.* A crisis is a call for action, for decision. It is important to include the caller in making this plan so that he develops a commitment to this plan, senses its appropriateness in terms of himself and his environment and makes it succeed. The plan, of course, may include hospitalization, psychotherapy or other alternatives such as contacting community agencies or organizations. We feel that as much as possible the resources that are used by the patient should be those in his environment or his neighborhood. Our general rule is that if a plan can be made that does not include the involvement or dependence on community, welfare or mental health agencies, the plan is usually of higher quality and has more chance of succeeding than those plans which include dependence upon these agencies.

In working with a person in crisis, especially in a suicidal crisis, the ultimate focus must always be on keeping the individual alive. The telephone worker must be willing to take any action necessary to accomplish this, including an active role in helping the patient or the caller to mobilize resources in the community which can prevent his suicide. Although he cannot take responsibility for the crisis situation, he can allow the caller to use his ego as a means of shoring up his own weak defenses. By emphasizing the present situation and the positive elements available in the patient's personality or life space, the telephone worker helps the caller to see a different perspective on the reality of his crisis and thereby increases his potential to solve it.

CRISIS AND THE TELEPHONE WORKER

Working in a crisis center with individuals who are in various types of problem situations is emotionally very difficult and taxing for the telephone therapist. The elements of meaning, purpose and existence, death and dying, which are normally only tangential to the interactions he has with individuals, now come to the foreground and are essential in his relationship with the caller. It is critical that he examine his own attitudes about these issues; specifically he should come to an awareness that one of the individuals that he talks to may end his crisis with death. Competence, especially technical competence, is in itself no guarantee that the strain of working with individuals who are suicidal will not develop conflicts in the worker. Because of the critical, essential role that he plays in the situation it is easy for him to fall into a Jehovah complex in which he thinks of himself as being all powerful in the life of the caller. When the telephone worker plays this role, it is not only difficult for the patient to get well, but it is also hard for him to accept the possibility that the patient will not resolve his crisis or that the patient may die.

Working with individuals in crisis requires much emotional strength. The telephone worker must remain calm, exhibit clear thinking, maintain a sense of balance while knowing that the caller may impulsively act out and that from the caller's point of view, it may take less courage to face death than to face life. He must recognize that he is probably one of the few stable elements in the caller's life. His work with the person in crisis requires a difficult art of attempting to balance the weaknesses of the individual and his need for external support, with the freedom which is essential in working through the crisis situation. As I mentioned before, in this process the telephone worker must be able to accept the responsibility for a tragic error in which the person, for sometimes unknown reason, takes his own life.

In summary, the telephone worker needs to be secure in himself to work in a crisis service. He must be able to put himself wholeheartedly and unflinchingly into the therapeutic relationship. He must be able to give of himself to satisfy the caller's dependency needs. He must be careful not to get so involved that he loses his own perspective. To be involved with people and not get all mixed up requires real maturity. Finally, he must also be able to sever the relationship with his client, a relationship in which the emotional ties develop very rapidly and intensively, a relationship in which a life may depend on the slender thread of a meaningful communication.

REFERENCES

Bellak, L. and Small, L.: *Emergency Psychotherapy and Brief Psychotherapy.* New York, Grune & Stratton, 1965.

Caplan, G.: *Principles of Preventative Psychiatry.* New York, Basic, 1954.

Caplan, G.: Practical steps for the family physician in the prevention of emotional disorder. *JAMA, 170:*1497, 1970.

Ellis, A.: *Reason and Emotion in Psychotherapy.* New York, Lyle & Stewart, 1962.

Farberow, N. L.; Heilig, S., and Litman, R. E.: Training manual for telephone evaluation and emergency management of suicidal persons. Unpublished, undated.

Glass, A. J.: Principles of combat psychiatry. *Milit. Med., 117:*27-33, 1965.

Hansell, N.: Casualty management method. *Arch. Gen. Psychiatr., 19:*281-289, 1968.

Hansell, N.: Introduction to the screening-linking-planning conference method. Unpublished, 1970.

Hansell, N.; Wodarczyk, M., and Hardlen-Lathrop, B.: Decision counseling method. *Arch. Gen. Psychiatr., 22:*462-467, 1970.

Hausman, W., and Rioch, D. M.: Military psychiatry. *Arch. Gen. Psychiat., 16:*727-739, 1967.

Jacobsen, G. F.: Crisis theory and treatment strategy. *J. Nerv. Ment. Dis., 141:*209-218, 1965.

Lindemann, E.: Symptomatology and management of acute grief. *Am. J. Psychiatr., 101:*141-148, 1944.

Tyhurst, J. S.: The role of transition states. *Symposium on Preventative and Social Psychiatry.* U.S. Government Printing Office, 1957.

Wolberg, L. R.: *Short-term Psychotherapy.* New York, Grune & Stratton, 1965.

Chapter 7

TELEPHONE THERAPY: SOME COMMON ERRORS AND FALLACIES

CHARLES W. LAMB

T HE SUICIDE PREVENTION and Crisis Service of Erie County (SPCS) is a new agency providing twenty-four-hour telephone contact for persons "in crisis." The definition of crisis is left up to the caller—radio, TV, and newspaper advertisements refer to the availability of interested and helpful listeners, and the more than 500 calls per month range from seriously suicidal individuals (10% of all calls) to such problems as the panic-stricken elderly woman who called when her basement filled with water. This program is supported by a short-term counseling service of up to six office interviews, but approximately 70 percent of the callers are handled exclusively by phone. The "night-watchers" to whom I shall be referring are the professionals and graduate students from various disciplines who are responsible for "telephone therapy" from 9 P.M. until 7:30 A.M. weekdays and all day Saturday and Sunday. Full-time nonprofessional counselors, trained in the agency, do the phone work during the day.

This paper attempts a quasi-facetious summary of some of the common problems encountered in learning and teaching telephone therapy. It is not intended to prevent others from making the same mistakes, which may constitute a kind of initiation to the work. It may, however, aid in early recognition of the afflictions when they strike.

Reprinted from *Voices*, 5(4):42-46, 1969-1970, by permission of the author and the American Academy of Psychotherapists.

FANTASIES

Fantasies of Omnipotence (the "we have to do something" error)

You pick up the phone and suddenly you are on the spot. There is a crisis, and it seems up to you to provide an instant, expert, final, once-and-for-all answer. Interesting variations to this delusion are the following:

But all I'm doing is listening! This may be quite all right. At least it's the first thing to do; until you've listened, you have no business even trying to be omnipotent! And the caller may not even want an answer—he may only want an ear. Or he may prefer to find his own answers; your best calls may be those where all you do is let this happen.

If I talk about it, it may happen (the "power of positive thinking" error). People in trouble are not nearly so fragile as we make them out to be. In fact, to have survived some of the stresses they have been through, quite the reverse may be true of our callers. If you think the caller might be suicidal, ask him. Don't pussyfoot, and forget all the euphemisms you know about death. If you, the counselor, are too anxious to talk about such matters, how is the caller to deal realistically with them?

But he's manipulating me (the "who's in charge here" error). When dealing with desperate people, it may be all right to be manipulated. Even though your need might be to play the part of the miraculous therapist, the caller's need is what counts. Perhaps all he wants is someone to acknowledge his existence; perhaps he wants someone to attack. We're here to get him through the crisis. A recent caller said, "Whatever you do, don't call my brother-in-law Henry Smith who lives at 410 Maple street, because I know if he came down here he'd talk me out of killing myself." Shades of Br'er Rabbit and the briar patch. But we called the brother-in-law. Obviously we were manipulated, but the brother-in-law's visit to the caller that night set in motion a benign cycle and great improvement in the plight of the caller. This does not mean that you should not strive to be aware of being manipulated; quite the contrary. But in dealing with crisis you don't have time for character analysis;

you work to put things back together and start benign cycles.
Fantasies of the Good Mother (the all-loving error)

Callers are all lovable human beings (and I am warm, accepting, and tolerant). One cannot be loving for ten straight hours when dealing with crisis. Callers are human and being human, may often be hateful. They are boring, frustrating, abusive, and often downright nasty. Perhaps for many of them one of their biggest problems is that they are not lovable. This leads to a corollary.

We are all of us human. Nightwatchers as well as callers. Some of the people who call have tried the patience of every agency in town to the point of rejection—usually well rationalized, but rejection in fact. If you find yourself hating a caller, and you know yourself fairly well, the chances are good that you hate him because he behaves hatefully. This is not a response for you to eliminate, it is part of the caller's problem and can help you understand his plight. It helps you understand why others reject him; it helps you anticipate what reception he'll get if you make a referral; and awareness of your response helps you avoid getting drawn into the vicious cycle of demand and rejection he may enact with everyone.

Fantasies of Omniscience (the "if only I knew about . . ., I could help" error)

If only I were a (psychiatrist, psychologist, social worker, medicine man) *then I could . . .* Your therapeutic tool is yourself, and the relationship you establish over the wire. A fancy diploma hanging on the wall is of no use at such moments. Corollaries are

If only I had read . . ., or

Why the hell didn't someone tell me . . .

The key to this is the delusion that there is some specific bit of information which, if fed properly and with tender loving care, will transform your caller into a paragon of mental health. Forget it. By the same token, watch out for the following traps:

How can they (Welfare, VA, private practitioners) be so incompetent? Just wait—the caller will demonstrate just how they can, with a deft rendering of "Why don't you, Yes but" or some other carefully polished game.

What if someone asks me for my credentials? or its corollary, "But I'm only a . . ." Look at this question more closely. What is the caller asking? Is he asking "Can you understand me?" or "Can I trust you?" If so, respond to *that* message. Instead of becoming defensive, respond to the caller's need. For example: "I am an associate here at the center. I think you're wondering if I can understand and help you. Why don't you tell me the problem and we'll see?" John Priebe, one of the more experienced nightwatchers, has pointed out that almost any caller who wants to can pick you apart. His suggestion is to not get caught up on explaining yourself (which chances are, you cannot do), but to turn the conversation with a remark such as "I don't think this is what you called to talk about."

Fantasies of Infallibility/Fallibility (the delusion of fixed alternatives)

If it's all I can think of, it must be the answer.

If I can't think of one, there must be no answer (and now what do I do?).

Variant: I'll call the consultant; he'll think of something.

This kind of thinking stops a conversation dead in its tracks; it implies that if neither participant knows the answer, there is nothing more to do. Remember that answers are created not discovered, which leads to the next category involving a failure to use the interpersonal process to solve problems.

Fantasies of the Ultimate Answer (the delusion of wisdom)

There is an answer somewhere out there (the trick is to find it). This leads to either an immediate paralysis of the creative apparatus or a frantic search for wisdom of another sort: The fantasy of the perfect referral.

There is an answer somewhere in here (or "let me consult my Muse"). This response also paralyzes the interpersonal process; it could be referred to as the fantasy of Soul. It occasionally tends to lead to the phenomenon of preciousness, or I'm the one with the answers for you, baby (the "I'll be here on Tuesday night if you need to call me" error). The philosophy of the SPCS is that we are all to some degree interchangeable on the phone. Avoid preciousness; tell the caller he may call again anytime, and that someone is always here to talk with him.

Fantasies of the Benevolent Caretakers (the "Yes, Virginia, there is a Santa Claus" error)

"The police will help" (or, "Lady, what do you think we're running here, a nursery school?"). In fact, the police have been most helpful. To make the most of this help, however, you must learn what is an appropriate problem to pose for them. Our early encounters with this reality were embarrassing.

Agencies are set up to help people (the altruism error). Being made up of humans, agencies are complexly motivated. They do reject people, often those most in need of help and most difficult to help, but whose problems are not framed in terms which open doors to them. Eventually you will learn what you can expect from various agencies in the city and how to make referrals in such a way as to maximize benefit. Until then, it is best to do all you can on the phone and refer conservatively. Other agencies are to be used as a valuable and scarce resource, keeping in mind that if you simply dump the problem, so will they.

ON THE POSITIVE SIDE

At this point, the question usually arises, "What *can* I do, then?" The above is not meant to sound cynical, for there is a tremendous lot that can be done. The above discussion is to suggest that you should keep your expectations realistic. You are limited only by your ingenuity in this kind of work. Within this limit you can do the following:

You can listen. It may be a rare experience for the caller; he may learn something just from having the opportunity to talk freely. Part of the answer for him may lie in learning to ask a better question.

You can be yourself. You are selected on the assumption that you are a good human being, and that relationships with good human beings promote growth. People in a jam need other people.

You can mobilize resources, both in others and for others. The caller often possesses the answer, or the wherewithal to create it, but cannot see it. You can help him find his own answer, by helping focus the question to be answered, for example. You can also mobilize resources for him, in the sense of making referrals, making contacts with other agencies, calling a friend or minister to the rescue, sending police, setting up an appointment in the morning, and so on.

You can learn your own limits and know when it is necessary to mobilize resources for yourself—when to yell for help. Always err on the generous side in using your consultants; we'd rather be awakened for nothing than to read of a suicide in the paper the next day. Or to feel that you don't dare call us simply to share your feelings. We know powerful feelings are aroused by this work.

You can provide feedback. You will learn from the phone work. Share it. Leave notes. Come to the meetings and talk about your experience. Force the agency to take note of its faults. Be involved.

You can sympathize,
  question,
  clarify,
  suggest,
  inform,
  just plain be there!

SUMMARY

This paper presents some of the recurrent difficulties experienced and observed by the author in training volunteers for telephone therapy with callers to a suicide prevention and crisis service. The therapist is warned against a number of potential traps, such as the pressure for instant answers, the fear of being manipulated, the need to achieve closure and provide ultimate answers, and the tendency to rely too heavily upon referrals. The author is convinced that a great deal of truly therapeutic work can be done on the phone with persons in crisis, and that such services are valuable as more than mental health clearinghouses or stop-gap measures.

Chapter 8

THE TELEPHONE CALL: CONVERSATION
OR THERAPY

Gene W. Brockopp

W̲H̲E̲N̲ ̲W̲O̲R̲K̲I̲N̲G̲ ̲O̲N̲ the telephone at a crisis center, it is important to differentiate sharply between the conversational telephone call and the call that requires therapeutic or crisis intervention procedures. Most training programs emphasize the need for the worker at the Suicide Prevention Center to develop a crisis intervention or problem-solving orientation whereby the worker takes an active, sometimes direct role in responding to the caller. Some centers emphasize a therapeutic orientation which is usually defined as being a supportive relationship through which we help the caller to organize himself or his life in a more effective way so that he can deal with the problems he is having. However, it is very easy for the worker to move back into his former habit patterns of using the telephone to obtain and maintain a conversation relationship, a relationship based on the interactions of the two personalities. As a result, the therapeutic or crisis intervention process is minimized, distorted or possibly even entirely eliminated. This is especially true when taking a call from a chronic caller or from an individual with whom the telephone worker has talked previously. It is my opinion that in a center which has the designation (defined as such by the patient community and the staff) of being a crisis intervention or therapeutic unit, a conversational telephone call with a patient is worse than none at all, for it sets up certain expectations on the part of the patient regarding his relationship with the telephone worker and defines the relationship and the center in ways that tend to be unproductive and non-helpful. More explicitly, I feel that a conversational telephone call does

111

the following: (1) It virtually eliminates the possibility that the telephone therapist can be objective or therapeutic in his function for he is cast in the role of a friend rather than a role of a counselor. (2) It minimizes any confrontation except that which occurs in terms of the personalities of the individuals and their ideas and opinions (which is basically not therapeutic). In contradistinction, a therapeutic or crisis intervention confrontation takes place when the thought processes and the behaviors of the caller are used as a basis for the interaction; (3) It may reduce the anxiety of the individual caller to the point where he does not feel a need to work on the problem he is having. In this way it may give him a false sense of security, and he may end up feeling better but not being better. (4) It develops expectations that what is taking place is the process of therapy. Since the caller is calling a place which is designated as being a helping agency, he may feel that the way in which help is given help there is the way help should be given, when in actuality it may only be a conversation. If later he moves into a therapeutic situation, he may have the same expectations, thereby making it difficult for a therapist to engage with him on a therapeutic or crisis intervention process.

The therapeutic or crisis intervention aspect of a telephone call decreases dramatically if the caller makes subsequent calls to a center. This relationship is formulated more specifically by the statement, "An inverse relationship exists between the number of calls an individual makes to a Suicide or Crisis Center and the amount of therapeutic or crisis intervention process taking place within the call." A corollary to this, is that, "When the patient requests to talk to one individual and only one individual at a crisis telephone service, the interaction between the two parties has usually moved to a conversational level." The factors underlying these statements are seen by looking at the type of training counselors receive to work on the telephone. In the short-term intensive training program, emphasis is usually given to helping them become effective crisis interveners, focusing on problems people have that can be dealt with in a very direct, confrontive way, without a detailed understanding of the personality dynamics involved or the process of therapy as traditionally defined. The telephone therapist is trained to be an expert in the process of problem solving. He is usually not qualified or capable of undertaking and following through with a therapeutic plan in terms of treatment goals relative to the interpersonal functioning of the individual. Therefore, when the chronic caller calls the center, the telephone therapist has very few tools available to work with him since the chronic caller usually does not have a problem which can be dealt with in the crisis intervention model (and is usually a "yes, but" person) so the interaction tends to float along in terms of the "things of the moment" rather than being directed toward a problem-solving goal or toward termination. When the caller requests the same person, the communication that takes place is usually of a personal nature, having little overt therapeutic quality even though the patient may use the rationalization that he wishes to talk to a particular person because he has given this person information on himself and does not want to reiterate the information to another individual.* The emotional envolvement between the two people without the corresponding competence on the part of the telephone therapist to deal with this transference or to work with the involved personality dynamics inherent in this situation results in the helpfulness of the call being limited to a friendly conversation.

This process is very seductive. One of the difficulties in working at a suicide and crisis service as a telephone therapist is that one is constantly responding to individual problems without having much feedback as to results of one's interactions. Therefore, when a patient requests to talk to an individual therapist, the amount of reinforcement that this gives to the person is often overwhelming. The result is that the telephone therapist, having a sense of competence and sometimes believing that he is able to work with a patient with whom everyone else has failed, develops a relationship in which he is "over his head" and begins to act like a therapist rather than a crisis intervener or a

---

* See Chapter 17.

supportive counselor. This relationship usually continues for a period of time until the telephone therapist begins to recognize that he is unable to deal with the problems the patient has as he does not have the appropriate tools. His sense of guilt usually overtakes him at this point and he covertly attempts to "dump" the patient without overtly rejecting him. The patient often picks up these signals, views the center and the worker as being incompetent and rejects the center and its help before it rejects him. The end result is a frustrated phone worker.

As I stated previously, to minimize the occurrence of these problems we need to analyze the interaction in the telephone calls. In a conversation telephone call, the relationship between the two individuals is a social one based on the interactions between the two personalities. In a therapeutic or a crisis intervention orientation, the relationship between the telephone therapist and the patient is neither social or antisocial but asocial in orientation and content. This permits the telephone therapist to be objective and to view the problem the caller has in terms of his behavior and his social relationships. The therapist can then engage the patient in discussion of his behavior and problems with the goal of assisting him to improve his situation or modifying the effect of the problem that he has. With the relationship being asocial, the telephone therapist is able to relate to the individual emotionally, while at the same time assisting the person to confront his own behavior and make any changes he feels are necessary. The relationship then does not become one of friendly equality or one of dominance and submission but one in which the primary function of the telephone therapist is to understand the person and the problem which disturbs him (a problem for which the telephone therapist assumes a responsibility to assist the individual) and through the process of self-confrontation or suggestion, effects a change in the caller's life pattern. This requires a great deal of finesse and skill on the part of telephone therapists. We must listen very carefully to what is going on in the relationship, not just in terms of his personal relationship to the patient, but in terms of the way the patient is relating himself and his ways of interacting with people through his contact with the therapist. Changes in the direction of the conversation, emphasis on aspects of the conversation, changes in mood or omissions, all will be used as a basis for understanding the person. The therapist through his objective yet emotional involvement with the person must be able to look past the content into the patterns of behavior through which the person has found himself in difficulty which he is not able to work out for himself.

Within this asocial setting and orientation the telephone therapist works with the problem the person brings to him in an objective, communicative way. By probing into the problem, the emotional reactions the person has to the problem and the assumptions the person has made about himself relative to the problem, the therapist begins to point out directions by which the individual can marshal his resources, both inter and intrapersonally, into a pattern which will sustain him and hopefully move him to a point of satisfaction or equilibrium.

In summary, I want to emphasize that in my opinion a suicide and crisis telephone service is not a social telephone line nor is its primary purpose that of providing social interaction for individuals. We cannot assume that if the therapist is doing no harm by being conversational, he can continue being conversational because he may be doing some good. A crisis intervention or therapeutic relationship seldom takes place in a social setting, and when it does it is achieved only because the therapist is skilled in being able to separate the social elements from the therapeutic ones. It is unlikely that the average telephone therapist has either the insight or the skill to achieve this. Nor should he be expected to have this expertise. Therefore, it is necessary that we clearly differentiate between the crisis intervention, supportive, therapeutic relationship and the social, conversational relationship and train individuals who work on a telephone service to be involved in the former and not in the latter.

A service which provides social interaction for lonely people may be advantageous and useful. However, when a service which is classified as being therapeutic or crisis intervention provides a conversational social relationship, it is both distorting its purpose and setting up assumptions in the patient's mind which often preclude his obtaining therapeutic help. To allow for the advantages of a conversational relationship, it may be necessary for suicide prevention centers to differentiate their telephone services by providing a Care-ring, call-out, conversational phone service for the chronic, disabled, isolated individual and a suicide and crisis line for crisis intervention or supportive therapeutic services. To do less would be to confuse both the public and the telephone therapist and result in the fragmentation of a valuable community service.

Chapter 9

LEGAL AND PROCEDURAL ASPECTS OF TELEPHONE EMERGENCY SERVICES

GENE W. BROCKOPP AND ELLOEEN D. OUGHTERSON

A<small>NY ORGANIZATION HAVING</small> direct contact with the public or indirect contact through a telephone develops methods and procedures by which the interaction with the public is defined or specified. These procedures usually have legal implications in statutory law or in precedents set by cases tried in courts.

Telephone emergency services, especially those developing out of a volunteer orientation, often assume that what they are doing, since they are a telephone service and nonprofessional, will not be legally questioned. Services take the point of view that they are a client-centered operation, are there for the purpose of helping the client, and that they will do what will therefore be in the best interests of the client. Who, they ask, would bring a service of this nature to court for trying to be helpful? Legal issues are often not considered in the development of the service or its operation, and procedures for working with people develop pragmatically out of the service operation without much thought for the legal implications or the ultimate effects that may occur.

While it is true that the types of the activities of centers throughout the country vary widely, and that each center has to develop guidelines through the day-to-day involvement with the population it serves, this type of thinking often means that the accepted procedure is what the center feels it can "get away with" at any particular period of time. The result is that what is done at a specific center will vary, depending upon who is answering the telephone, not on accepted rules or procedures. This usually means a lack of consistency in the service which the

117

agency is attempting to perform in the community and a good probability that what it is doing may have negative legal implications.

While we would agree that emergency services must act in the spirit of the situation posed to them and not within the letter of the procedure when responding to an individual who is in great difficulty, it is critical that centers develop procedures based on the appropriate legal requirements and on the appropriateness of the act of intervention. This is necessary to allow for the varying types of involvement which the volunteer will have with the person at the other end of the telephone, while giving him a basic set of legal or procedural rules to use in making a decision in a "sticky" situation.

In this chapter we will look at some of the procedural and legal aspects of operating an emergency telephone service, attempt to sharpen some of the issues that are to be considered, and define the basis on which decisions can be made. In this endeavor we are using our experience at the Suicide Prevention and Crisis Service in Buffalo as our guideline and the laws of New York State as they pertain to the issues raised as our "rule book." We would emphasize that before another agency applies this information to their telephone emergency service, they should check into both the local and state laws that may refer to the issues being raised.

CIVIL RIGHTS AND INTERVENTION

A basic question posed by the very purpose of the emergency telephone service is whether intervention is a deprivation of the civil rights of the person on whose behalf such intervention is being made. Although the question is an appropriate one regardless of the situation the person is in, it is probably brought into sharpest focus when dealing with the issue of the suicidal person calling on the telephone. The legal question is, Is the right to take one's own life a civil right?

In the historic sense, within the law, suicide was once considered a crime, although punishment of a successful act could only be the escheat of his property to the Church or to the state.

However, suicide has not been included in the criminal law for centuries. In New York State even attempting suicide has not been a crime since 1919. This is also true in most other jurisdictions. However, under the provisions of the Penal Law of the State of New York, one who aids, abets or assists in the commission of a suicide can be tried for first degree murder or varying degrees of lesser homicide or manslaughter.* Aiding an attempted suicide may bring criminal charges from attempted murder to lower degrees of assault.† On the other hand, force in an appropriate degree, may be used to prevent a suicide, where the intervenor is acting in the reasonable belief that a person is about to commit suicide or inflict serious physical injury upon himself.‡ This permitted force would secure the intervenor from charges of assault or false imprisonment.

Since the law specifically allows as a defense for the serious use of force the prevention of suicide, the person who is called upon for aid must exercise his means and capacities to try to save the suicidal person. The question of whether a person by failing to act to prevent a suicide could be considered assisting or aiding a person commit or attempt to commit suicide is really the question of difference between malfeasance and nonfeasance. The law has never enforced as severe penalties in the case of nonfeasance, or failure to act, as in malfeasance, the wrongful act. Certainly the negative implication of these statutes would mitigate against any concept that suicide is one of the elusive civil rights of man.

Furthermore, it is also a premise of law that life is "sacred" and may not be taken by another without legal consequence, to the ultimate nonsequitur of the death penalty being used as a deterrant. When exceptions are allowed, such as self-defense or war, they are carefully spelled out and strictly interpreted. It is assumed legally that taking one's own life is an irrational act and is evidence per se that the person attempting it is mentally ill. If a person is mentally ill, then he is not competent to make

---

* New York Penal Law, § 125 et seq.
† New York Penal Law, § 120 et seq.
‡ New York Penal Law, § 33.10.

any decision for himself, and other individuals should do all that can be done to save his life. This too would be sufficient to allow intervention without any liability for invasion of privacy or interference with civil rights. For example, a peace officer in New York State may act under the Mental Hygiene Law to take into custody any person who appears to be mentally ill or is conducting himself in a manner which in a sane person would be disorderly, and he may remove the person to a hospital or temporarily detain the person in a safe and comfortable place pending examination or removal to a hospital.*

Relating the above concepts to the operation of a telephone emergency service, one fact is paramount: Since the caller has initiated the intervention of the service, he has by implication requested that service help him within the framework of its greater experience and resources. This means that all methods of help and assistance which can be brought to bear on the problem or difficulty the individual has are also implicitly requested. All the activities of the service, ranging from continuing the conversation in counseling and dissuading to tracing the call to requesting assistance from the police or sending outreach workers to the callers, are appropriate. If the service is to err in making a decision of how involved it will become in this area, it should err in the direction of trying to maintain the individual's life. In doing this it will often overstep the bounds of what more traditional community agencies would do.

Conversely, we want to make it clear that a telephone emergency service, and for that matter any individual, cannot take ultimate responsibility for another person's life, nor should it presume to do so. In a relationship with a suicidal individual some clear specification of areas of responsibility will need to be stated, for unless they are stated the person in difficulty can use and build on the manipulative aspects of suicide to his own detriment or can become so dependent on the helping individual that he is unable to function by himself and thereby loses his own life in the process of being "helped." It is also necessary from another point of view that the telephone volunteer specify

_____

* New York Mental Hygiene Law, § 78 (3).

this relationship. The more clearly he can specify his area of responsibility, his abilities and inabilities, the more he can reduce the sense of anguish, anxiety and guilt that will develop when a person that he is working with commits suicide or injures himself. If the helping person accepts the fact that a client may commit suicide and that he cannot be ultimately responsible for this act, he can usually approach the relationship in a much more objective way and actually be much more helpful to the person than if he presumes to accept full responsibility for the individual's life and thereby becomes emotionally involved to the point of being unable to act with objectivity and perspective.

MALPRACTICE AND LIABILITY

If the service has a duty to help the individual requesting intervention, what is its responsibility if it should experience failure to save the person from death or injury? This question opens up the whole problem of malpractice, which generally speaking is a question of concern to everyone whose actions affect another individual. It is doubtful if any claims for damages by a caller, his estate or representative would be successful against the emergency telephone service. However, as the specifics of the intervention become more active, liability would rest upon the same grounds as in any action for negligence.

It should be remembered that malpractice is limited to professional persons, and other staff and volunteers are not involved in actions in malpractice, except as they are extension or aides of the professional and are therefore liable as part of *his* professional actions rather than being personally liable. The staff psychiatrist, physician, and psychologist should also be aware that he might be liable personally, as an independent contractor, if he is a part-time staff member and might not be covered by any insurance secured by the agency.

The basis of a malpractice action is that the injury is presumed to result from a lack of requisite knowledge or skill, or an omission to use reasonable care and diligence, or a failure to exercise best judgment in performing professional service for a patient or client. Further, the damage which could be suffered by a patient or client would vary greatly, depending upon the service to be offered by the professional person ranging from counseling to plastic surgery.

Defenses available to defendants in malpractice actions include requirements that the plaintiff or injured person be free of contributory negligence, that he has given consent to the treatment, or that he has personally assumed the risk of his own actions. The obvious difference between a patient anesthetized on an operating table under a surgeon's knife and an anonymous caller on the other end of a telephone line who has previously taken an overlose would indicate that the greater defenses would be available in malpractice claims against an emergency telephone service. Moreover, emergency treatment has always been judged on a lesser standard of care unless there has been gross negligence on the part of the professional. Where the patient or client is in control of the circumstances surrounding his action, the agency is unable to take responsibility for treatment; it rests with the person himself.

The presumption of having acted properly and with care is extended by the law in favor of the practitioner, so that a poor or unsuccessful result in treatment does not create an inference of malpractice. The burden of proof in each case is upon the one who is bringing the claim and must include expert testimony to show that the facts of the case do evidence the lack of professional skills; it is difficult to secure expert witnesses who could state with any degree of professional certainty that the practitioner had not acted with reasonable care or had failed to exercise his best judgment. These are subjective matters, and the jury could not impute unreasonable objective standards to measure them.

Further, the public good being promoted by the offering of a telephone service to save lives, a jury would hesitate to assess damages against any agency for its zeal in performing that service it is organized to provide; successful law suits would result in the withdrawal of such service and a greater harm to a greater number of persons.

Generally, civil liability for suicide where damages are awarded in substantial amounts would not involve the service whose function is prevention. Workmen's compensation benefits have been made payable to dependents of persons whose suicidal death arose out of the employment or a traumatic experience within it. Patients who have been admitted to hospitals or institutions with a known history of suicidal behavior and who are successful in committing or attempting to commit suicide because of the failure of the staff to exercise due care, have created successful causes of action against these institutions. All of these cases must be carefully proved, with substantial evidence, to overcome the basic fact that suicide is the personal, deliberate act of the person committing it.

There are two primary reasons why a suicide crisis or drug hotline service should secure malpractice insurance. The first is that even though a suit is unlikely to occur (and if it does occur, it is not likely to be successful),* the legal services to defend the suit would be expensive and would be provided by the insurance company. The second is that it reduces anxiety and gives a sense of security to the workers at the center to know that they are covered by an insurance policy as they engage in a life and death conversation with a caller. It is an effective statement to them that the agency respects them and will stand behind their work and their expertise.

Obtaining malpractice insurance for these services is difficult as few companies write this type of policy and those that do have little expertise with volunteer services and therefore no history of risk involved on which to base their premium. Unless a service has professional staff in some supervisory capacity it may find it impossible to obtain a policy.†

Finally, it must be accepted that malpractice insurance will not cover all of the possible contingencies that may arise in the

---

* In the history of emergency telephone services only a few legal suits have been brought against them. To our knowledge none of them have been successful.

† At the Suicide Prevention and Crisis Service in Buffalo we have been able to obtain a 100,000-300,000 dollar policy which covers both the volunteer and professional in their telephone and face-to-face contact with clients. The agent informs us that the policy is based on their experience with our agency and that the company may not write similar policies with other agencies.

course of the helper-client interaction and that the telephone service cannot be bound to do only those things that are covered by insurance. To do it would become a very staid, rigid agency, unresponsive to people's problems for it would respond more by the "book" than to the person in difficulty.

TREATMENT OF THE UNDER-AGED INDIVIDUAL

One of the concerns of the professional person is the treatment of the under-aged individual. Although it is often assumed that there are legal or statutory regulations regarding this situation, in reality, there are no stringent rules to be followed, other than the exercise of care and good judgment. While there are strong limitations which would mitigate against an operation on an infant in the absence of an emergency without the consent of the parent, the reverse of these elements would imply that an emergency treatment, not constituting surgical procedures, would be available for minors, particularly where the involvement of their parents would further alienate them and minimize the potential positive effects of the treatment itself.

The reasons for securing consent of parent or guardians include the need to obtain this consent to be assured of collecting professional fees. In the case of an emergency telephone service, this is not a serious problem; if later professional counseling (with fees) are deemed necessary, parents would be liable for them as necessities provided to their children even without their consent. Minors themselves can be held liable for necessary services though they might not be held to other types of contracts made while they were under twenty-one years of age. The age of consent for various legal rights and responsibilities is not a single one; it varies, depending on the issue, from legal ages of driving, use of alcohol, voting, marrying, committing crimes, owning property and many more relationships and activities. As to negligence, which includes contributory negligence and assumption of risk, there is no age limit within the law, since it is dependent on capacity to act and understand the consequences of such action. Also while parents have responsibility for children, they may be relieved of it and may not exercise authority over their children who have been emancipated, that is, those who are self-supporting or self-controlling.

The staff of an emergency agency should not presume to prejudge the status of the child within the law by refusing him service. Even if the decision were favorable in any suit brought by the parents for treatment without consent, the measure of actual damages would still be established by the same considerations affecting malpractice and other claims and would in all likelihood be nominal if assessed at all. The possibility of being sued should not deter the service from offering assistance to any who call or from limiting such service to those who have attained their majority. The ultimate of absurdity would be to try to secure proof of age in a telephone conversation before giving the requested assistance.

PRIVACY AND CONFIDENTIALITY

The major problem in this area is that most individuals have no understanding, from a legal point of view, of the principles and concepts of privilege, confidentiality and secrecy. In speaking to a telephone client, an unidentified volunteer may imply to an equally unknown caller that his statements will be held in confidence. What he really means is that, "I will keep your secret, except as to the fact that I am taping this call, and that the tape can be replayed by my supervisor and may be used for group discussion or training; that I am making a record which will go into your permanent files, identifying as far as possible all the facts I have gleaned from this conversation; that I will not tell anyone in authority about the call, except that I'm not sure if I could refuse to answer were I subpoenaed to a legal proceeding." In essence he is saying, "I will not wilfully give this information to anyone I feel does not need to know or who may hurt you."

Confidentiality is a special legal concept which gives a person immunity from legal pressures to reveal information secured because of the particular relationships of the parties. It can be evoked by both or either party and in some respects cannot even be waived. Once privilege is established or invoked, it is so powerful that if the person is called as a witness he can refuse to answer without the fear of being cited for contempt of court. Traditionally, confidentiality within the law was limited to certain professional and personal relationships wherein full disclosure between the parties, without fear of violation of the secrecy of the confidence voluntarily or by court order, was necessary for the fullest development of the relationship. These were husband-wife communications, and three professions whose practitioners needed the full cooperation of the layman they attempt to assist; the doctor-patient, lawyer-client and clergyman-penitent relationships.

In New York State, as in other specific states and countries, these confidential relationships, traditional under the Common Law, are reinforced by Statutory prohibitions against disclosure of confidential communications. Inevitably, of course, many cases interpret the specific application of the statutes and the relationships of the parties and nature of the communications.*

The attorney-client privilege includes the employee of the attorney;* disclosure by a file clerk to the authorities of the knowledge of a crime committed by the client gained through his work solely as an employee of the lawyer would not only prevent testimony to this effect by the clerk, but taint any proof secured through this source. The same information overheard by the file clerk in listening to a casual conversation between the lawyer and the client in a public place where the possibility of public knowledge was apparent and should have been anticipated would open the door completely to disclosure of that information.

By New York Statute, a person authorized to practice medicine, dentistry and registered professional nursing or licensed practical nursing is included in the physician-patient privilege (except a dentist is required by the same law to disclose information to identify a patient, and all three are required to disclose information indicating that a patient under the age of sixteen

---

* New York Civil Practice Law and Rules, § 4502.
* New York Civil Practice Law and Rules § 4503.

years has been the victim of a crime).† Under the peculiar exigencies of the profit and loss motive the same laws that permit physicians to incorporate for tax purposes extend the privilege to medical corporations,‡ a corporation being a fictitious person, or entity, which was certainly never contemplated under the old Common Law as a special person whose personal relationships needed protecting. When the priest was the only clergyman who could be involved in relating to a penitent in the confessional, this relationship was easy to define, but now it must be expanded to any clergyman, including a Christian Science practitioner, and the confession must be made in his professional character as a spiritual advisor.§ Thus a Roman Catholic speaking to a Jewish Rabbi in such a capacity would still be protected by the "seal of the confessional" even though both parties might otherwise consider their religions as incompatible.

New professions have begun to secure certain privileges of confidentiality, motivated perhaps by the need to recognize that these younger professions, not contemplated in a less complex society, should have the same protections to fulfill their responsibilities as the older professions. Thus, New York law extends this same privilege to a psychologist who is registered under the State Education Law and places the communication between the "registered psychologist" and his client on the same basis as those provided by law between attorney and client.*

The strangest of the new privileges is the granting by the State of New York of certification under specific statutory qualifications and procedures to a social worker under the Education Law, and thereafter a duly certified social worker

shall not be required to disclose a communication made by his client to him, or his advice given thereon, in the course of his professional employment, nor shall any clerk, stenographer or other person working for the same employer as the certified social worker or for the certified social worker be allowed to disclose any such com-

---

† New York Civil Practice Law and Rules § 4504.
‡ New York Public Health Law § 4400 to 4403.
§ New York Civil Practice Law and Rules § 4504.
* New York Civil Practice Law and Rules, § 4507.

munication or advice given thereon; "except" that the client may authorize disclosure; or a certified social worker shall not be required to treat as confidential a communication which reveals the contemplation of a crime or harmful act; or where the client is under the age of sixteen years, and the information indicates that such child has been the victim or subject of a crime the certified social worker may be required to testify fully in relation thereto on examination, trial or other legal proceeding where such crime is the subject of inquiry; and if the client brings charges of professional misconduct against the certified social worker involving the confidential communication, he waives the privilege.†

Since the cloak of the certified social worker depends upon the hiring by an agency of such a professional qualified person, this privilege is limited, indeed.*

Since the door has been opened under the recent amendments in New York State law to extend confidentiality to corporations, the telephone emergency service, which duly incorporates itself, might consider that it has created at least the first step in seeking legal privilege for itself, its employees and its clients. However, a medical corporation is one which must be very carefully established under the law for all the tax and other benefits accruing thereunder to apply, and it is unlikely that a twenty-four-hour emergency service, even with a physician on staff, could qualify as such a corporation and obtain the confidential doctor-patient relationship. While the cloak of a certified social worker might be dropped over such an agency, the confidential relationship of any other employee, such as a volunteer, to the client would certainly not be stretched by any court to cover

---

† New York Civil Practice Law and Rules, § 4508.

* Interestingly, the only interpretations of this new law have been negative; a certified social worker, who was a parole officer, was required to report his full findings to the board of parole, since he was an employee of the board, whose duties included interviewing prisoners or parolees, and these persons could not invoke the privilege. In the only law suit involving the statute, an agency protested the attempt of the mother of a child within the care of the agency to invoke the privilege as to her communications to the certified social worker and agency personnel being used to prove her an unfit mother; the court agreed that the prime consideration was the child and that the communications between mother and agency were not within the privilege protected by the statute. (In Re Clear (1969), 58 Misc. 2d 699, 296 N.Y.S. 2d 184, Rev. on other grounds. 32 A.D. 2d 915. 302 N.Y.S. 2d 418.)

any communication not involving the certified social worker. The specifics of the social worker statute would directly mitigate against the promise of confidentiality made to the client, if the contemplation of a criminal or harmful act is the basis of the call for help.

The extension of the privilege of a physician (including specifically a psychiatrist), an attorney, a clergyman, or registered psychologist on the staff of the telephone service, to the other staff, including volunteers, is problematical, in that their position has not been determined by legal or statutory procedures.

From a practical point of view, we question whether the concept of privilege is an appropriate one for use in the emergency telephone service. It is much more appropriate to base relationship with the caller on the concept of trust—the trust that the caller is being honest in regard to his problem and his concerns as he sees them at this time, and the trust that the person answering the telephone will do nothing wilfully to hurt the caller or betray the trust which has been given to him by the caller. We feel this type of relationship gives a great deal more latitude than the concept of privilege and is also more appropriate for a service in which what is done may be in the best interest of the client, although not what he wishes in a given situation.

TAPING AND TRACING CALLS

Contrary to common belief, taping of telephone conversations is not against the law in most states; it is a violation only of the telephone company tariffs. These are agreements which the Federal government has with the telephone company which prohibit taping of a call without an audible beep every fifteen seconds. To tape without this beep, however, is not illegal. The worst that can happen is that the telephone company can remove the telephones from the premise. The question of taping, then, becomes a procedural one. Is it appropriate for a service to tape the call from the caller without his knowledge, even though his best interests may be a major concern? The arguments for taping are many, ranging from a need to supervise the telephone therapist to the need to pick up critical information which may be necessary to save the caller's life. Furthermore, it is not a violation of the individual's rights to privacy to tape a call which has been placed with an agency for the purpose of seeking help with a problem he is having. If a trust relationship has been established between the patient and the service, the taping of the call is incidental to it and is nothing more than an extension of the notes which the worker is making. Neither will be used to the detriment of the client. We have found in our work at Buffalo that once a trust relationship is established with the client, it matters little to him whether or not the call is being taped. If the person calling should inquire if the call is being taped, he should be told honestly that it is. To do less would destroy the confidence of the caller in the center. At the same time, however, the unspoken question, though implied, should also be dealt with; whether the client and his problems will be exposed to the world. When both questions are handled directly, with the assurance that the call and information will be kept confidential and not be used to the patient's detriment, most individuals do not object to the taping of the call.*

The legal status of taping of calls will be changing as both Federal and state laws become more specific. However, at the present time the question is primarily a procedural one, and there are no compelling reasons why a telephone call should not be taped.

KEEPING RECORDS

The continuity and quality of the telephone service depends in part on completeness of the records that are kept on individuals who call the center. Adequacy of information on the record forms provides an appropriate basis for the making of referrals to agencies and for checking back to see if the referral was appropriate. Furthermore, the proper implementation of the corporate purposes of the agency as imposed by the community include keeping of the proper records and may include the

---

* If the person still objects, the tape machine should be turned off for the clinical relationship always should take precedence over the procedural.

conducting of research for the treatment and prevention of the conditions under observation.

Yet the keeping of records can be a serious hindrance to a telephone emergency's service. The anonymity of a person's contacts on the telephone service may be the basis on which he makes the contact. To insist on knowledge of the individual, which could identify him, may keep him from calling the center and obtain the service that he needs.

We feel, however, that to hesitate to keep records because of their potential negative value would itself be unprofessional. That records may be subpoenaed should never be a reason for failure to keep them. The person who seeks help opens the door to an invasion of his privacy. If the service is trustworthy, the records it has would never deliberately be used in any but the client's best interest.

CONCLUSION

It is clear from the information presented in this chapter that many of the issues in this area and the answers to them are not precise. The variations in the emergency telephone services and the dearth of laws or legal precedents on the issues faced by them result in opinions rather than clear guidelines. Yet appropriate methods and procedures are needed for we are working in an activity in which death is possible—one in which emotions are intense, the risks are high, and the possibility of error is great.

Prudence would require that each center carefully evaluate its procedures with a competent attorney in view of state and local laws, community expectations and ongoing purposes. From these perspectives the risk the agency wishes to accept should be specified as precisely as possible to give guidelines to the volunteers and staff. Constant review of these guidelines in the light of changing laws and problem cases will be the best protection to helping the agency involved with people and yet appropriate in its decisions.

Chapter 10

BEYOND THE TELEPHONE CONTACT

Lee Ann Hoff

S *ituation 1.* Telephone call to SPCS, wrist-cutting in process, rescue operation, medical treatment, return home, repeat call to SPCS, wrist cutting in process, and so on.

Situation 2. Telephone call to SPCS, threat of overdose, face-to-face treatment at SPCS, failure to involve significant other, overdose of barbiturates, medical treatment, family treatment, broken appointments, repeat calls to SPCS.

Situation 3. Telephone call to SPCS, impending plan of carbon monoxide poisoning, acceptance of treatment opportunity at SPCS, no further calls.

Situation 4. Completed overdose of lethal dose, telephone call to SPCS, rescue operation, intensive medical treatment followed by long-term comprehensive psychological treatment, no further calls.

Each of these situations includes elements of self-destructive behavior in the patient which are more or less lethal. Which patient represents a high suicidal risk? Who is manipulative as well as suicidal? What steps can be taken to prevent chronicity among callers? The intent in what follows is not to answer these questions as such, but highlight the importance of three questions as they influence what happened after a call. That is, following a call, what are the implications for the caller himself, the significant other, the counselor, and the community at large?

From these brief descriptions above, it is already evident

This chapter focuses upon the patient in a suicidal crisis. The concepts and possibilities outlined can, however, easily be extended to patients in nonsuicidal crises.

that a vicious cycle can occur in relation to telephone calls from would-be suicides. Alternatively, emergency telephone counseling can function as the focal event launching a network of interaction among persons and agencies: the caller, the counselor, significant other(s), rescue squad, crisis clinic, and so on. Everything that happens after the call is significantly related to the counselor's knowledge of the caller and his psychosocial pattern of behavior and how this pattern influences the counselor, the significant other and the community at large. The relationship of these variables and how they affect the outcome of calls to a suicide prevention center will be explored in what follows. Also, there will be an attempt to delineate some of the problems and limitations intrinsic to the telephone service, as these pertain to the outcome of calls. Illustrative case examples will be cited.

THE CALLER, WHO IS HE?

The importance of this question can hardly be overemphasized. The identity of callers and their social-psychological patterns of behavior frequently remain ambiguous to the telephone counselor. If this occurs, a vicious cycle can result: call, rescue, symptomatic treatment, discharge, call. Once this cycle develops, the negative effects for the caller himself, significant other, counselor and agencies are difficult to counteract. Identity of callers, then, along with fine discrimination and understanding regarding their overt and covert needs constitutes the first necessity for developing adequate follow-through after a telephone call. The failure to identify callers and discriminate between their differing needs and levels of lethality can result not only in a possible suicide, which might have been averted, but also in a barrage of undesired results for the significant other, counselor, and various agencies.

Several kinds of callers must be distinguished in order to discuss the outcomes of calls:

1. The caller who is a high suicidal risk, low suicidal risk, manipulative, self-mutilative, or a repeater.
2. The unidentified caller and the identified caller.
3. A significant other calling on behalf of a suicidal person.

The characteristics of callers may often overlap; for example, a highly suicidal person may also be manipulative.

Outcome of anonymous calls may vary considerably from those in which the caller is known. The lack of identification for a caller may be a result of the caller, the counselor or a combination of factors. Some callers who are highly suicidal refuse to give their name until they have tested the counselor's degree of caring and ability to help him discover alternatives to suicide. In most instances this testing is accomplished in the first few minutes of the call, during which the average counselor is able to establish rapport with the caller. The relative ease of this interaction is heavily influenced by the suicidal person's ambivalence about dying which he frequently manifests by initiating the call and responding positively to the rescue process. The rescue operation resulting from these calls represents the first step in what should constitute a comprehensive service to the suicidal person. Callers who are less highly lethal, manipulative and/or self-mutilative demand different responses from the counselors as compared to highly lethal callers. Thus, the counselor's ability to discriminate and assess the lethality of callers is a most critical factor affecting outcomes of calls.

Factors relative to identity of callers merit research attention: for example, what is the therapeutic potential in remaining anonymous? Does the caller remain anonymous for his own unexplained reasons or because of the counselor's inattention to identity factors? What are the treatment implications for the caller who uses several names? Are there intrinsic liabilities in a telephone service such as indefinite availability of instant gratification for repeat callers not in crisis? Does the value of important emergency services for persons in crisis outweigh these liabilities? Are there other systems in the community which can provide crisis services without these liabilities?

SUPPORTIVE SERVICES

Regardless of who the caller is, adequate follow-up of the call can not be accomplished without supportive services functioning interchangeably among the counselor, the SPCS itself, the significant other, as well as the community at large.

Once a person has made contact with the SPCS and his lethality has been assessed several things may occur, but in any case the interaction should not end with the telephone contact, which ideally is only the beginning of a comprehensive program of service to the caller and others surrounding him. The suicidal or self-mutilative person is asking for response not only from the counselor but from the significant others in his life which may include agencies he is already in contact with.

In the event that the person has made a potentially lethal suicide attempt, the rescue procedure is fairly obvious and is carried out usually in a straightforward manner with few complications. Medical treatment and/or hospitalization are frequently indicated. This first stage of treatment should be followed by a long-range program focusing not only on the client himself but on the underlying causes and life circumstances influencing his self-destructive behavior. For example, individual psychotherapy and psychotropic drug treatment may be helpful for the depressed person; but if factors such as repeated job failure, inability to develop and sustain satisfying relationships, substandard housing, marital strife and a family scapegoat role are present, a broader treatment approach is indicated. Examples would be family, marital or group therapy, vocational rehabilitation and social action input to alter a social system which is more destructive than nurturing to the individual. Such a comprehensive program is widely used in many community mental health programs and its inclusion here may appear to be a statement of the obvious. This is true. However, there are special difficulties in implementing a comprehensive program for the suicidal person, particularly the repeat attemptor. Several factors surrounding the repeat attemptor seem to militate against the treatment process. These will be examined in some detail as they comprise central issues influencing outcomes of calls from repeat suicide attemptors or self mutilators.

The self-mutilative person's social psychological history is often characterized by family turmoil, sexual trauma, deficient interpersonal skills, identity problems, social deviancy and stigmatization. His interpersonal responses are generally inadequate to satisfy his needs. Ordinary communication patterns have been unsuccessful. He often fails to gain the sustained attention of significant others, including treatment agencies, except through some kind of deviant behavior, such as self-mutilation. Even in the absence of social deviance and history of overt family turmoil the self-mutilator has for some reason been unable to communicate his needs to those around him. After his first suicide attempt, he experiences a different response from significant others, not necessarily a positive response, but different. His lethality at this point may be low: he has made no prior attempts, the method is nonlethal, he has clearly provided for rescue, his ambivalence is high and his self-mutilative action appears to be directed toward change of his interpersonal field rather than toward death. However, since the self-mutilative behavior is nonlethal, it is easy for significant others and treatment agencies to miss the message of the self-mutilator's behavior. Sometimes out of shame and stigma families will shield the attemptor and take the risk of omitting medical treatment. More typically there is a response of concern mixed with resentment, anger and confusion about the meaning of the behavior. The response, however, often remains focused on the symptom itself, namely, self-mutilative behavior, either because the family is unwilling or unmotivated to deal with underlying social and psychological factors, or because treatment personnel likewise miss the meaning of the behavior and focus on a symptomatic approach. When this occurs, the client is almost inevitably left with the option of repeating his self-mutilative behavior. Successive suicide attempts generally increase in lethality inasmuch as prior attempts fail to accomplish a change in the interpersonal field. Significant others and treatment agencies at the same time become more inured to the attemptor's self-mutilative behavior, which in turn perpetuates the behavior. In addition to these factors, the self-mutilator often has personality features which seem to naturally elicit rejection from others. Or his interpersonal experience includes predominantly a pattern of rejection from others so that he is unable to deal with a response of caring and acceptance without extreme testing behavior. This can result in impatience on the part of counselors, which, if not dealt with constructively, can increase further the attemptor's feelings of rejection. The counselor, on the other hand, can be left with feelings of helplessness, failure, resentment, guilt and general discouragement in working with this group of clients. These feelings are often shared by agencies as well.

What happens to a client after a call depends then not only on who the caller is and what his needs are but also on the counselor's ability to assess these needs, mobilize client and community resources and initiate follow-up activity appropriate to the individual situation.

Among these functions, follow-up is perhaps the most challenging. This includes several facets which will be explored especially as they pertain to the function of a suicide prevention center. For the client requiring medical and/or hospital treatment following a suicide attempt, a comprehensive treatment program may be initiated in the hospital if there is a psychiatric service. If the suicide prevention center is administratively a part of a comprehensive psychiatric service, such as in a community mental health center, there is a natural framework in which to facilitate continuity of treatment between the telephone contact and other services indicated by the client's needs. When this is not the case, it is important for suicide prevention centers to establish and maintain relationships with the various community agencies necessary to support a total program for the client following his call. Effective interagency communication and coordination is of critical importance in follow-up work with the self-mutilator who has a history of repeat behavior of this kind. Given the difficulties of responding therapeutically to these clients, it is readily apparent why this kind of person is often an active client with several agencies simultaneously. If this is the case, the client's suicide potential may increase by virtue of his repeated experience of failure to respond to treatment and/or inadvertant rejection by the agencies due to the factors described above. When this occurs the client will usually increase his calls to the suicide prevention center where essentially the same result can occur if follow-up and interagency comprehensive treatment planning are lacking. Potentially, then, a vicious cycle can develop: call to suicide prevention center, rescue operation, symptomatic treatment, client's approach to another agency, treatment with little result, feelings of failure by the client, counselor and agencies, return call to suicide prevention center, and so on.

Effective intervention in this cycle is one of the most challenging problems facing not only suicide prevention centers but other helping agencies as well. A comprehensive follow-up program is perhaps the most basic element in such intervention. Suicide prevention centers have a responsibility not only to initiate, implement and evaluate follow-up programs themselves but also can offer consultation and education services to other agencies working with suicidal persons and the chronic self-mutilator.

THE SIGNIFICANT OTHER

How does the significant other influence the outcome of a call; how is the significant other influenced by the outcome of the call? And, how is the outcome influenced by the apparent lack of a significant other in the life of the caller? If a suicide attempt has already been made and a straightforward rescue operation is accomplished by the suicide prevention center, usually the significant other is not on the immediate scene. Depending on the urgency of physical rescue needs, the counselor may or may not have obtained information about the significant others in the caller's life. If such data are not obtained by the telephone counselor, it is, of course, highly important that the significant other be appropriately included in comprehensive follow-up programs. Failure to do so can contribute to perpetuating the cycle of "call, rescue, failure, call" cited above. In other cases successful involvement of the significant other necessitates a sensitive, skilled approach by the counselor to a situation in which latent content and the message of suicide behavior must be understood and dealt with. Sometimes suicidal behavior is a response to the lack of significant others. For callers like this who either lack resources or are cut off from communication with them, the counselor may become the most significant other. Hopefully the outcome of calls from such persons will result in the mutual discovery of new resources—even if limited at first to a meaningful link with the agency and a counselor—and alternatives to the choice of suicide. Callers may make the manifest plea to the counselor not to involve the significant other or may threaten to carry out suicidal plans if the significant other is called. When suicidal behavior constitutes a covert message of some kind to the significant other, the counselor is faced with the task of helping the caller communicate with significant others at a cost less than the price of his life and not alienating the caller in the process. This is a delicate task involving a clear and secure understanding of confidentiality, the purpose of which is lost, of course, if the counselor colludes with the caller's suicidal plan by dealing only with the manifest plea or threat and promising not to involve significant others.

Most counselors and therapists handle this by a frank explanation of the fact that confidentiality does not apply to information which if kept confidential can potentially contribute to the client's death, for example a lethal suicidal plan. Skillful involvement of significant others by the telephone counselor can lay the groundwork for a comprehensive follow-up program. As noted above, when significant others are not included in the treatment program, not only is self-destructive behavior likely to continue, but opportunities are lost for working educationally with the problem of taboo. Also, significant others are an important supportive avenue for suicide prevention workers to address themselves to the social and community problems contributing to self-destructive behavior, such as housing, economic and sexual oppression, racism.

Significant others are, of course, profoundly affected by self-destructive or self-mutilative behavior, whether this be in the form of disgust, confusion, fear, resentment, concern or a combination of these feelings. Positive outcomes of calls hopefully will include positive results for significant others as well as for the callers themselves. Ideally this will occur whether the call is from the suicidal person himself or from a significant other on behalf of another. In short, significant others are vital facets in the network of interaction between the caller, the counselor and supportive treatment and social action agencies in the community. If they are excluded either as potential helpers or as persons to be helped, the self-destructive person will be served less well both during and after the call.

THE COUNSELOR

Helping self-destructive persons via the telephone is fraught with difficulties, potential complications and uncertainties which are much less prevalent in the face-to-face counseling situation. In lieu of this and the fact that the greater portion of telephone counseling in suicide prevention centers is done by lay volunteers, implications for volunteers after the call deserves serious consideration. Any therapist who has worked with suicidal persons is familiar with the emotional energy that can be exacted in the process. He also knows the importance of sharing responsibility for these clients with other therapists as well as with significant others. As a matter of fact, in the case of a client whose suicidal motivation focuses on otherwise unexpressed anger and revenge toward a significant other and the significant other is a therapist, assumption of therapeutic responsibility by a single therapist can inadvertently increase suicidal potential. During stages of therapy when the client's suicide potential is higher, the therapist often assumes a more active role with the client than is indicated in other therapeutic interactions. This can be both time-consuming and exhausting, and unless colleague and team support is forthcoming, can readily become a source of discouragement and eventual disinclination to work with suicidal persons.

If this is true for the professional therapist, it is doubly so for the volunteer telephone counselor, who is frequently less trained and experienced and also works in physical isolation during the most critical hours of the night. After a call from a self-destructive person the counselor can be left with feelings of isolation, confusion, failure, insecurity, resentment, guilt or he may experience a sense of satisfaction in responding effectively to persons in critical need. The counselor's feelings after a call are inevitably affected by the outcome of the call for the client and significant other. If an adequate treatment program does not follow upon initiation of the rescue and treatment process by the client and telephone counselor, the counselor begins to experience a sense of futility of effort as the client continues to call the telephone service with little or no change in the social and interpersonal field. Also he senses vaguely that somehow he is contributing to the perpetuation of dependency on the telephone service which is a less than adequate substitute for a planned treatment program. This is particularly true if the telephone service focuses on emergency and crisis intervention and there is no built-in provision for or expectation of continuity of treatment by telephone. Follow-up treatment generally includes availability of emergency telephone service for a client who is highly suicidal. In these instances the therapist may advise telephone counselors of factors which would facilitate emergency counseling on the phone. This is particularly important in the case of self-mutilative callers who are also manipulative. Most emergency telephone services are manned by volunteers who work a limited number of hours which complicates the possibility of providing continuity of service via the telephone. In view of these factors, direction and support of the telephone counselor becomes increasingly important. In fact, the outcome of calls is significantly influenced by the consistency of support to the telephone worker. In instances where the caller's suicide potential is difficult to assess, the counselor needs ready access to consultants who can assist with this task in a skilled manner. When the counselor cannot obtain the identity of the caller and the risk of suicide is high, the counselor will probably experience a sense of failure and insecurity regarding the adequacy of his approach to and management of the situation. Also, when a caller has made a suicide attempt before calling and then lapses into unconsciousness and drops the phone, the counselor often experiences a sense of helplessness or an unrealistic degree of responsibility for the life of the client. In all of these instances the counselor should have easy access to a consultant on both an immediate and long-range basis. This provides not only reassurance but the opportunity to work through feelings of excessive responsibility or neurotically tinged guilt associated with centuries-old societal attitudes regarding suicide and his own possibly unresolved feelings about suicide and death. The consultation and supervisory process also affords the telephone counselor a medium for constant evaluation and improvement of his work with suicidal persons. Obviously, as the telephone counselor becomes more proficient in his role the client and significant others will be favorably affected following a call to a suicide prevention center. Telephone counseling is an exacting and demanding ingredient in the network of services available for persons in suicidal crisis. The emergency telephone service is regarded by many suicide prevention centers as "the heart of the agency" or front line in a complex of services to persons in suicidal crisis. To maintain this difficult facet of suicide prevention work at a quality level, supportive services must be elicited on behalf of the counselor as well as the caller. This is especially urgent when the counseling is done by volunteers. It is strangely paradoxical that suicide prevention centers have developed a work division pattern in which the workers with least preparation, namely, the volunteers, have responsibility for dealing with the client when his suicidal crisis is potentially most critical, and that this same group of workers are frequently barred from participating in face-to-face counseling with suicidal persons, presumably because they lack sufficient skill for this. Yet counseling of a person in suicidal crisis on a face-to-face basis is considerably less trying and fraught with uncertainty and risk than is the telephone situation. This fact merits exploration and evaluation by suicide prevention workers.

SUMMARY

Factors influencing the outcome of calls from self-destructive persons have been discussed as they pertain to the caller, supportive agencies, the significant other and the telephone counselor. Difficulties and problems hindering favorable results are cited. Apropos of these problems, it appears that telephone emergency service to potentially self-destructive persons seeking help is a valuable and unduplicated service in most communities. However, suicide prevention workers might address themselves to the question of whether the problems associated with providing such a service are inherent in working with suicidal persons, or whether they are related to organizational and manpower factors such as excessive reliance on nonprofessional workers for the most critical facet of the work. At a time when the manpower shortage in service agencies is more acute than ever, suicide prevention centers have been unique in their extensive and creative use of nonprofessionals. However, it is a well-established fact that while volunteers offer a distinctive quality that speaks for its own value, the success of their efforts depends on supportive services in whatever setting they work. If and when volunteer counselors work in relative isolation from other facets of the helping network the outcome of telephone counseling can be seriously jeopardized.

The case examples which follow will be illustrative of the factors, issues and problems inherent in determining what happens "after the call."

Case Situation 1

John Kone, age thirty-one, called SPCS at 4 A.M. Sunday of a holiday weekend. John was in the process of cutting his wrists when he called. His general message to the counselor was one of desperate loneliness, isolation, helplessness, physical illness, bitterness about past rejections and extreme dependence on someone to relieve him of his misery. Among the rejection experiences cited, he revealed that the last time he called presenting a similar picture, the counselor had called John's therapist who advised use of the rescue squad. According to John, the rescue squad as well as the psychiatric resident at the local hospital spurned his suicide attempts and left him feeling that they could care less if he killed himself. He was given medical first aid and sent home.

Attempts by the counselor to ascertain the degree of physical injury and need for emergency medical treatment again resulted in evasiveness on John's part. In spite of the counselor's attempt to dissuade John from cutting his wrists and focus on underlying problems, John continued with his wrist-cutting behavior. When the counselor discussed rescue possibilities, utilizing the local rescue squad, John announced that he had a gun and would shoot anyone who came to the house. John also stated that his therapist (from a psychiatric outpatient department of a local hospital) "really doesn't understand" and rejects him at times, and that he wanted to speak with the telephone counselor on a face-to-face basis at 4:30 A.M. When the counselor proposed the possibility of seeing the consultant on a face-to-face emergency basis, John insisted that he would talk with no one but the telephone consultant. The interaction between John and the counselor left the counselor with a strong sense of responsibility for John. John had asked for rescue but refused ordinary rescue operations and managed to elicit guilt feelings in the counselor when she explained that she could not see him in person while manning the telephone service.

At this point the volunteer terminated the call temporarily and advised John that she would call him back after seeking assistance in her efforts to help him. She called the consultant who discussed with her the lethality factors and apparent manipulative elements of the situation. The consultant and counselor agreed to propose to John a crisis home visit by the consultant which would be preceded by the consultant's direct telephone conversation with John. John responded to this plan by stating he would not answer the phone when the consultant called.

After one-half hour of busy signals or no answer, the consultant notified the telephone counselor of the results, having decided not to make the home visit, based on her judgment that the lethality elements were outweighed by manipulative factors. In the event that John called back he would be told of attempts to reach him. As anticipated, John called back shortly thereafter and was persuaded by the counselor to answer the consultant's call, which he did.

During a forty-minute session, John and the consultant discussed all the foregoing interaction in a very straightforward manner. John's manipulative behavior became more clear as well as less rewarding in interaction with the consultant than with the counselor, at which point it was possible to talk with John about his underlying problems instead of remaining focused on the wrist-cutting behavior. John denied his threats about shooting would-be rescuers and stated he had only scratched his wrists and did not need medical attention. The consultant and John finally agreed on the following plan. Since it was a Sunday night of a holiday weekend, the consultant would call him Monday evening because of the increased anxiety and loneliness he experiences at bedtime, and the following Tuesday a joint conference would be arranged with his therapist, the consultant and the telephone counselor.

During the ensuing conference, therapy goals were clarified among which were attempts to reduce John's extreme dependency needs and help him meet his attention needs in more satisfying ways than by self-mutilative behavior.

Following the conference, John continued to call the suicide prevention center with a presenting behavior pattern similar to that cited above. Telephone counselors, however, were in a more knowledgeable position to respond to him therapeutically, as they had been advised of approaches which led to more positive results and complemented the overall treatment program directed by his regular therapist. In instances when John's manipulative behavior became extreme, often when talking with a less experienced volunteer, the problem was dealt with by the staff consultant's direct conversation with John. Periodic conferences continued between the therapist and SPCS staff. Eventually John's physical problems improved with ongoing medical treatment, he became involved in a program of vocational rehabilitation, began to reestablish himself in the community socially, saw his therapist on a gradually decreasing basis and called the SPCS only rarely. Totally John was in treatment about one year.

Case Situation 2

Karen Brown, age fifteen, called the SPCS at 8 P.M. threatening to take an overdose of her mother's sleeping pills which were readily available to her. Her presenting difficulty as told to the telephone counselor was a sense of total misunderstanding and unacceptance by her parents. Karen felt unable to communicate her distress to her parents; in fact, she was calling from a local drugstore telephone booth at a shopping center near her suburban home.

After a half-hour discussion with the telephone counselor, Karen was relieved of some of her abhorence of returning home, said she felt she could control herself from taking the pills though she still could not tell her parents how distressed she was. She felt encouraged by the possibilities of help available the next day on a face-to-face basis at the SPCS. Karen refused to give her last name, parents' name, address or telephone number out of fear that the counselor would involve her parents without her consent.

Karen kept her appointment the next day and after the third session continued to resist all efforts of the therapist to involve her parents, refusing to give necessary identifying data.*

The day following the third session Karen took an overdose of twenty of her mother's sleeping pills (barbiturates) in school and informed her close girlfriend and a teacher she trusted, who took her to a nearby hospital emergency room. Her parents were, of course, identified and involved at this point. During the course of brief hospitalization Karen was seen by a psychiatrist. Karen resisted therapy from the psychiatrist, requesting a return to SPCS. Following this, joint treatment planning ensued between the psychiatrist, Karen and her parents and the SPCS. Family therapy was decided on with an apparently positive beginning. After three sessions, however, Karen's parents broke the appointments and Karen in the meantime began using the telephone service threatening suicide again.

The SPCS family therapist attempted by telephone contact to reengage the parents in therapy with no results and Karen continued to call. Eventually a home visit was made and the parents finally began to cooperate in the therapy process after gaining a better understanding of the meaning and seriousness

---

* SPCS has a policy of not treating minors (under age 18) without parental consent. In the case of high suicide potential treatment is continued on an exceptional basis with therapy including a focus on eventual involvement of significant others.

of Karen's suicidal behavior. Among the paradoxes and problems encountered with the parents was their resentment of Karen's use of the telephone, on the one hand, and their refusal to deal with underlying causes on the other. The therapy program included family sessions as well as intermittent individual sessions with Karen over an eight-week period. As treatment proceeded Karen stopped using the telephone service and was no longer suicidal. Termination included referral and coordinating efforts with Karen's favorite teacher and the counseling service of her private school.

Case Situation 3

Mr. Philip Jones, age fifty-two, called the SPCS at 9 P.M. presenting a picture of an acutely suicidal individual. As a Ph.D. engineer he had recently been laid off his job because of the company's economic straits (a first-time experience for him), was dependent on his wife, an executive secretary, for support, had been told by his wife of her plan to divorce him, was experiencing acute clinical depression with crying bouts, anorexia and sleeplessness, and felt the strong urge to kill himself by carbon monoxide poisoning.

After a fifty-minute session with the telephone counselor, Mr. Jones decided against carrying out his suicidal intentions and was willing to work on discovering alternatives to suicide through face-to-face counselng at SPCS. Two hours after the call the counselor called Mr. Jones in an effort to strengthen his link to the SPCS as a resource since he was considered quite highly suicidal. Mr. Jones was feeling less suicidal at this time and was able to share with his wife that he would be seeing a therapist the next day. Mr. Jones was seen in therapy three times a week for four weeks and less frequently for three more weeks. During this time he was able to redirect his energies into developing new job potentials, changed his way of relating to his wife but could not deal with the reality of the impending divorce. He continued to blame himself for the apparent failure of the marriage and was obsessed about the thought of suicide which he visualized as the only solution when the divorce eventually was to take place.

He continued treatment very enthusiastically for another six months during which time the divorce was finalized. By this time he had experienced some success in a new job as well as stronger relationships with his two grown children. Upon termination of therapy at the end of eight months he was still having occasional suicidal ideation but was generally relieved of severe depression and felt a positive link with SPCS and his therapist in the event of a future suicidal crisis.

Case Situation 4

Susan Black, age twenty-three, called the SPCS stating she had taken forty Thorazine® tablets one-half hour earlier. She was beginning to experience drowsiness but in general presented a picture of great panic about what would happen to her if she were taken to the hospital. She was alone at the time of the call, her two roommates having gone out of town for the weekend. The counselor's attempt to alleviate her fears about the rescue squad were met by a hysterical response mingled with crying and irrational objections to rescue while at the same time pleading to be saved. Susan gave her address to the counselor but said she would jump out the window if the Fire Department rescue squad* came. A telephone counseling colleague called the consultant who arranged to go to Susan's home with the telephone counselor she talked with. This plan was acceptable to Susan, who also consented to be taken to a private hospital of her choice for medical treatment. There she was admitted to the Intensive Care Unit. Following medical recovery, a comprehensive treatment plan was developed in collaboration with Susan's medical doctor prior to her discharge from the general hospital. Susan's parents and her roommates were included in various facets of the treatment from time to time. Susan had made three prior suicide attempts, all less lethal than this one, but had always received only emergency medical treatment and was discharged with psychotherapy. After five sessions at SPCS Susan was referred for longer-term treatment to the counseling center of a local university where she was a graduate student. She made no further calls to SPCS.

---

* The rescue resource used by SPCS.

Chapter 11

CARE TEAM: AN ANSWER TO NEED FOR SUICIDE PREVENTION CENTER OUTREACH PROGRAM

WAYNE C. RICHARD AND RICHARD K. McGEE

DURING RECENT YEARS suicide prevention centers have proliferated across this country and many others. The model of crisis intervention used in the development of these centers has followed the theory and sometimes the practice of the Los Angeles S.P.C. under the direction of Shneidman, Farberow, Litman and others. Most services utilize the telephone answering crisis system with some centers supplementing that procedure with office interviews in the central crisis center location. There has been one important extension of telephone crisis work, namely, the outreach program, that needs to be identified, articulated and, hopefully, fully developed with the guidance of badly needed research information. Louis Dublin, noted suicide theorist, made reference to this need at the 1968 A.A.S. meeting in Chicago with the phrase *"Put content into the contact . . ."* by sending people from the S.P.C. out into the community to intervene during crisis situations which need face-to-face contact in order to enhance the efficiency of crisis intervention. A few experimental programs of this nature are currently in use: In addition to our program at Gainesville, Florida, at least two other programs exist—one in Atlanta, Georgia, which utilizes a team of mental health professionals in the emergency room at Grady Memorial Hospital and one in Vermont which has a team of public health nurses in the field at all times during the day ready to respond immediately to crisis calls. Others have been tried and failed, while still others are being planned. Some outreach programs probably exist which have not yet come to the attention of the present authors This paper will focus on the organization and functions of the CARE team in Gainesville, Florida.

RATIONALE AND ORGANIZATION OF OUTREACH PROGRAM

As the Gainesville Suicide and Crisis Intervention Service (SCIS) was being developed by Richard McGee, Judy Hoffman, Joyce Rowe, Barbara Beardsley, and others, it became apparent that an opportunity was available to develop a unique feature of crisis intervention. Capitalizing on Dublin's plea, the public health model of health service delivery, community psychology theory, and the availability of crisis work-trained graduate students in clinical psychology, at the University of Florida, McGee and associates created the CARE team. During daytime work hours, the center staff, supplemented by psychology interns and practicum students from the University (and more recently by paraprofessionals from Santa Fe Community College), are available and expected to respond to serious life-threatening or other crises which cannot be totally managed by telephone intervention alone. During the evening and nighttime hours (4 P.M. to 7 A.M.) a special volunteer team of at least two people is on call to respond to serious situations. Examples of such situations include

1. Suicide attempts—in progress, threatened, suspected, or treatment of (follow-up of every suicide attempt is *imperative*).

2. Drug crises—bad trips, friends who need help in managing others, transporation to drug treatment center, and so on.

3. Runaways—transportation, crisis counseling.

4. Marital or family conflict—resource identification, crisis counseling.

5. Alcoholism—transportation, remove harmful objects.

6. Help police or other agency—police are not adequately trained to deal effectively with suicide and many other types of crisis situations.*

---

* We have found that police intervention is limited in certain respects because of legal restrictions and stereotypic responses by threatened clients. Crisis center workers when accompanying police do not further inflame situations, can remove lethal objects easier than uniformed officers and are free to break and enter without search warrants when life or death is at stake. Police frequently call us to accompany them in cases where the above needs prevail.

7. Completed suicides—psychological autopsy, family bereavement, managing last business affairs of deceased.

During the first year of SCIS operation over 500 CARE team calls were made to houses, businesses, police departments, hospital emergency rooms, parks, laudramats, motels, schools, and other places. At this time a total of approximately thirty people serve on CARE team. A goal which is being realized now is to supplement the professionals and professionals-in-training with lay volunteers who are experienced telephone workers and who have exhibited superior talent in their telephone work. At present, about six lay persons are on CARE team. It should be emphasized that we now have enough knowledge and experience in CARE team work to train lay persons who may or may not be telephone crisis workers. We are preparing to offer this training service to other communities in close geographical range.

FUNCTION OF CARE TEAM

The criteria for sending the two-member CARE team out on a call depends on many factors, some objective and some subjective. The most explicit situations, which account for approximately half the calls, include suicide attempts in progress or in treatment in emergency rooms and hospitals, bad drug trips where transportation to treatment facility is needed, walk-in cases to crisis centers during off duty hours, and requests by police for immediate aid. Generally, the telephone crisis worker will get in touch with the CARE team members when high lethality is suspected. Together, the telephone worker and the CARE team will assess the availability of other appropriate resources, extent to which telephone contact is not being effective in reducing the stress and the need for additional information before adequate assessment of the lethality can be determined. The word CARE has special significance beyond the demonstration of the overall meaning of the word itself:

Contacting
Assessing
Relieving
Engaging

Contacting implies the need in some situations and with some people for more intimate relations in time of emergency than just a phone conversation. Most of the time clients can go somewhere to meet this need. At other times, however, they may be too disorganized or distraught, physically unable, simply have no transportation available to go anywhere. Going to the client satisfies this need and presents an opportunity for the crisis worker to gather more data about the immediate and overall situations. Mobilization of community resources to help with managing a person through the current crisis and toward prevention of future crises may be initiated by this contact.

Assessing alludes to the opportunity for the crisis worker to determine more about a situation than it is possible to do with telephone contact alone. He has the opportunity to discreetly (or not so discreetly) search the premises for lethal weapons, pills, sharp objects, alcoholic beverages. He may also learn about present living conditions and appraise attitudes of spouses, children, parents, friends, who may be present or close by. He will have the opportunity to assess the psychological and physical ramifications of the present situation.

Relieving exemplifies response to "the cry for help—a summons for relief." Often times we are amazed at the power of the presence of another person (even a stranger) who "goes out of his way" to respond to a person who has lost all of the usual personal resources that have been helpful to him in the past— they usually get positive results in the form of receptiveness to help and relief from distress. The ambivalence of a crisis can usually be resolved when a crisis worker agrees to help with the management of affairs that have resulted from the client's response to crisis. A frightened runaway teenager is usually relieved to learn that the crisis team will not turn him over to the police, but will try to help his parents understand his needs to escape an intolerable home situation. A frightened young person who got some "bad acid" is usually relieved when we tell him he is not going to be picked up or turned over to the police. These are examples of the relief that is felt by a person in distress who needs a life-manager temporarily until a serious crisis passes.

Engaging. One of the primary functions of crisis center work is to effect a linkup between the client and community resources to relieve the cause of his distress. The "transfer" nature of the operation depends on accurate assessment of the individual's needs and knowledge of resources available for problem solution. The crisis worker's job is not complete until the relationship between client and helper is solidified. The CARE team frequently bring the helper and helpee together during the crisis period or immediately following some stress relief period in order that the problem solution process can be set in motion. The team members do not disengage themselves until they are confident a helping relationship has been established and both parties are *mutually committed* to resolving the issues which led to the present crisis. This type of activity might take this form of (1) getting a friend to agree to spend the remainder of the night with a moderately suicidal person; (2) getting an estranged husband and wife together (one of whom may be threatening suicide) and obtaining a commitment to begin marital counseling tomorrow; (3) taking an indigent person under high stress to the welfare department or employment agency to obtain money or job prospects; (4) helping stranded travelers obtain emergency funds to continue their journey; or (5) helping a seriously mentally ill person obtain inpatient or outpatient psychiatric care immediately or the very next day. *It is the first duty of the CARE team members to pass on to the SCIS staff and volunteer telephone workers who come on to duty the next day well-formulated and very explicit action plans for the clients seen last night so that continuity of management can be maintained.* Nothing is more disappointing to a client than an unfulfilled promise of a phone call or visit from the SCIS in a few hours. This condition may prevail if communication between crisis worker groups is not at a highly efficient level.

It can readily be seen from the descriptive and clinical nature of this report that several major issues involving CARE team work have not been quantified or answered with any objective degree of certainty. A research program into CARE team operation is just beginning to be formulated, with this paper being the initial effort to organize our thoughts. A thorough investigation of the CARE team log, case reports, clients' responses, team member and community agency reports, and other information will be forthcoming. Hopefully we will be able to answer conclusively such important questions as (1) What constitutes the actual criteria for a CARE team visit? (2) What comprises a successful visit? (3) Are some team members more successful than others? (4) What skills make a CARE team member competent? (5) What should the training consist of? (6) Are we more successful with some clients than others? (7) Are some types of cases more amenable to successful personal intervention than others? These are but a few of the questions that deserve to be answered about Outreach Programs via CARE team model.

PART III
PROBLEM CALLERS

INTRODUCTION

ALL CALLERS HAVE some problem. Most crisis intervention centers assume that by choosing to call, all callers are in a crisis state. The aim of the chapters in this section, however, is not to discuss the treatment of particular kinds of problems or crises. Rather, the problem callers discussed in this section pose special problems for the telephone counseling service. This is best illustrated by the following example.

The individual who calls a telephone counseling service in order to masturbate while a female talks to him has a problem. This problem can be handled much as the counselor would handle other problems presented to her. However, the masturbator presents a special problem to the service because of the fact that he tends to produce panic, anxiety, and distress in the counselor which disrupts the whole service temporarily. Occasionally, the entire female staff of a telephone counseling service can become uncontrollably agitated through the continued calling of a masturbator.

Every counselor may have some areas in which he is vulnerable and unable to act as a counselor. This can occur whether a counselor is treating patients in face-to-face therapy or via telephone therapy. The chapters in this section do not attempt to help the counselor with all the problem patients he may face, but rather with those that are unique to telephone counseling services.

The problem callers discussed in this section are the obscene caller (in particular, the masturbator), the chronic caller (who may call the center up to 5 times a day every day of the year), the silent caller (who calls but refuses to speak), the prank or nuisance caller, and the caller who wants to speak only to one of the many volunteers who work at the center.

Chapter 12

THE OBSCENE CALLER

RESPONDING TO THE MASTURBATOR

Gene W. Brockopp and David Lester

After a few days of working at a Suicide and Crisis Service, answering calls from people in various types of difficulties and crises, the telephone therapist learns to respond to most problems with a type of "concerned objectivity." Yet some problems seem to tap a system of responses which generally is not therapeutic and leaves the therapist with a feeling of hurt, anger, or uselessness. One of the situations which probably does this more than any other is the call from a male who seems to use the services of the center for the sole purpose of masturbating to the voice of a female. For example, a few months ago, the following note was entered into our case file:

> A man masturbating while saying: "talk to me. Don't leave me."
> I was not able to locate the file but felt he had called before. As he became more excited he became more verbal with remarks like "Open your legs." I terminated the call by suggesting he call back when he had finished to discuss why he needs a stranger rather than a friend at this time.

In checking our case file we noted that over the past few months, this type of phone call has been received about three times a week.

The problems associated with this type of call can be divided into three categories: (1) how to develop an appropriate treatment plan for this type of caller; (2) how to deal with the feelings of the telephone therapist who receives the call; and (3) the effect of this type of call on the service the agency is to perform in the community at large. It should be noted that these

157

problems are not unique to calls from masturbators, but are associated with any type of difficult call that a telephone service receives. For example, females may call the center and act seductively to a male counselor, callers may arouse hostility and anger in counselors by the difficult problems they present, or callers may, by their unwillingness to work with the telephone therapist, evoke feelings of inadequacy in the therapist. Certainly the call from a person who is actively suicidal will raise the anxiety of the telephone therapist and may make it more difficult for him to react appropriately to the crisis situation.

Yet the masturbator does, perhaps, require special attention because his calls have a very disrupting effect on counselors by arousing very strong negative emotions in them which may result in their inadequate handling of this call. They also have a "fall out" which affects the effectiveness of the counselor on calls made by individuals with other types of problems.

From our analysis of the calls received at the center, there appear to be two types of masturbating callers. One type will discuss a problem which may or may not be fictional, and either the counselor may suspect that the caller is masturbating and confront him with this, or the patient himself will state that he is masturbating. In working with this type of person, the counselors have reported feeling "useless" or "ineffectual" and "furious at putting in hard work to no end."* The second type of caller merely breathes heavily and says words like, "Talk to me," "Don't leave me," "Please let me finish," and so on. He frequently may hang up and then call back immediately.† To this type of person, who does not allow the counselor to establish a relationship that can be seen by her as possibly therapeutic, the counselor reports feeling used, sexually exploited, angry, uptight, or disgusted. These feelings are intensified if the counselor is alone at the center and if the call comes in at night. Often the counselor feels that she can handle the situation intellectually, but not emotionally.

---

* These are the responses of female phone therapists. Our experience with this type of caller is that he will hang up whenever a male answers the phone.

† On one occasion as many as twenty calls have been received from such an individual in the space of two hours.

Without question, the therapist's feelings of anger, hostility, or disgust interfere with the appropriate handling of this type of call. In most cases the counselor is responding to her own feelings rather than to the patient's problem. It appears that this may be a result of the counselor's attitudes toward deviant sexual behavior, her inability to know what a therapeutic response would be, or a combination of both. If the problem is the result of the counselor's attitude toward this type of behavior, it should be dealt with on an individual basis between her and her supervisor. The discussion would, of course, extend beyond the particular case of the masturbator to cover such issues as the counselor's attitudes towards sexual behavior in general and the feelings aroused when the counselor feels inadequate in handling any patient call. From our discussion with the telephone counselors, it appears that their inability to respond therapeutically to the masturbator is a result of a lack of specific knowledge on the handling of this type of call combined with the intense emotional feelings of being used inappropriately by the caller. It is to these two issues that we would like to address ourselves.

Before discussing the possible methods of working with the masturbator, it might be well to discuss the philosophy of the telephone service. The unique feature of telephone therapy is its ability to respond immediately to individuals in difficulty on their own basis, with anonymity, and with the control remaining with the patient. In this type of therapy situation more than any other, the therapist is at a distinct disadvantage in that he does not have personal face-to-face knowledge of his patient. He has minimal clues with which to work and he must accept the fact that the patient has as much (possibly more) control of the situation as he does. It is therefore necessary for him to move into the problem situation on the patient's basis, and only on the patient's basis.* If he does not do this, he may lose the patient, probably irretrievably, since in many cases he has no knowledge of the person's name, address, or phone number. It would, therefore, seem imperative that the axiom of meeting

---

* We would like to emphasize that we are speaking here about the development of a relationship and not about the subsequent therapeutic movements.

patients "where they are" would become the basic guideline for working with all types of difficult calls.

With this as a background we would like to list five possible approaches to responding to the masturbator, in the hope that these suggestions would aid the counselor in a practical way when receiving such a call by also making alternative behaviors available to her so that she may feel more adequate in handling this type of caller.

1. The counselor can respond by saying nothing or with controlled silence.

2. The counselor can communicate her disgust to the caller and/or hang up.

3. The counselor can try to be accepting, point out that the caller has a problem and that he could benefit from seeing someone in a therapeutic relationship, and then hang up.

4. The counselor can establish a minimal relationship with the masturbator, refuse to stay on the phone while he is masturbating, but urge him to call her back after he has finished masturbating.

5. The counselor can stay with the caller, allow herself to be used if necessary, with the hope that the relationship can move from this level to one in which she can be more therapeutic to the person calling.

It appears to us that the first two approaches are at odds with the concept of a telephone service devoted to rendering therapeutic assistance to individuals in the community. Both of them either reject the patient overtly or communicate non-acceptance of the patient by the therapist. Without acceptance of the patient, regardless of his behavior or feelings, a therapeutic relationship is most difficult, if not impossible to establish. It could be argued, however, that a strong negative response on the part of the counselor might negatively reinforce the behavior and cause it to extinguish. In a controlled therapy situation, this may take place. On the telephone, however, a more likely occurrence would be the calling of another person by the masturbator until he had obtained the verbal assistance of a female to satisfy his need. Mere rejection of the behavior by the therapist would appear to be of value only in allaying some of the therapist's feelings.

Response 3 is better, but since many of the callers do not see masturbation as a problem, they may not see any reason for coming in for a face-to-face discussion. Indeed, it is most unlikely that this type of exchange will take place, for this person is unlikely to make himself known to the therapist. Also, this approach rejects, but to a lesser extent, the use of a telephone as a means of aiding the individual. However, if the counselor has personal concerns in handling such a call, this approach is probably the best for her to take.

Response 4 requires more acceptance of the patient by the counselor, but the chances of the person calling back after he has finished masturbating are probably slight. An extension of this approach would be for the counselor to suggest other stimuli for the masturbator to use to achieve sexual gratification in a more private manner, such as television, radio, or records. This may reduce the negative social aspects of the patient's behavior, but it is also likely to decrease the possibility of his receiving appropriate help.

Response 5 is clearly the best, in that the therapist is responding in a way that will maximize the chances for developing a relationship with the patient which may be used later for therapeutic purposes. It should be emphasized here that acceptance of the person does not imply the reinforcing of the behavior or the condoning of it. It means tolerating the condition while attempting to develop a more honest, trusting relationship with the patient to achieve this balance; the counselor, of course, must be careful not to be too seductive or encouraging.

Conversely, she also must not be too confrontative to the patient. To ask the person why he is masturbating may be too difficult a question for him to answer and impose too much distance between him, the counselor and his present behavior. The focus of the counselor should be on the affective relationship and the value of it for the patient. Perhaps the patient is lonely and depressed or is having difficulty in developing socially desirable relationships. Focusing on these areas may facilitate establishment of a more sustained and positive therapeutic relationship and may facilitate the patient's visit to a therapist if the relationship moves to a point where trust can be established between the patient and the counselor. Also, focusing on the purpose or goal of the behavior seems to be more appropriate and less threatening than an attempt to discover the underlying genesis of the behavior. The patient can be asked what he feels his behavior is achieving for him, how he feels that calling achieves this end for him, and how he sees his own behavior.

To use this last approach, the counselor must be aware of her own feelings in responding to this type of patient but keep them in the background. She must recognize that her approach to him must be one that meets him at the level of his needs, with the covert intent that if a relationship of trust can be established, the patient may look at his behavior in a more positive and therapeutic manner. Recognition must be given to the fact that this may never be achieved—the patient may simply use the therapist for his own end without any therapeutic movement on his part. Even though this may take place, and the therapeutic relationship is misused, we feel that the counselor on the telephone cannot set demands which might be appropriate when counseling a person on a face-to-face basis. Therefore, we feel that if a person can only relate on the telephone through masturbating, it is necessary to meet the person at this level, not to demand that he change his behavior, but hope that in the process of being used by him in this way in the present a therapeutic movement can be made in the future.

❀ ❀ ❀

THE OBSCENE CALLER

DAVID LESTER

In the previous section, we discussed the problems associated with the caller to a twenty-four-hour telephone service whose purpose in calling is to masturbate while being stimulated by a female voice. We discussed the emotional reactions of counselors handling this kind of caller and possible approaches that they can take in dealing therapeutically with him. There is nothing written in the psychiatric literature about such men, but there is some documentation of other kinds of obscene callers.

I want to present here some data on the prevalence of obscene calls received by the general public and on the psychodynamics of the obscene caller.

The Prevalence of Obscene Calls

Murray (1967) questioned 396 female undergraduates enrolled in introductory psychology courses and of these 183 (47%) indicated that they had received an obscene phone call: sixty-nine had received one, thirty-five had received two, and seventy-nine had received three or more. Among the calls received, 70 percent involved sexual suggestion and lewd language from the caller, while the remaining calls were humorous or threatening. Relatively few of the calls were reported to the police or the telephone company (only 32%). There was a tendency for more nuisance calls to be received in the warm months than in the cold months, which suggests that a large proportion of calls may be made to people known to and recently seen by the caller (assuming that people go out more in public in the summer than in the winter).

Murray interviewed thirty-four of the girls and classified the calls they had received into five kinds:

1. The prank, nuisance call which is made by teenagers of either sex to either friends or people selected randomly from the phone directory. An example is, "Is your refrigerator running? Then you'd better catch it before it gets away."

2. One kind of obscene call has implicit sexual propositions. There is no lewd or foul language in these calls, but they have reference to sexual behavior. The caller often seems to know the daily routine of the callee. An example is, "How about going with me to some place dark and quiet and we'll really make love?"

3. Another kind of obscene call has explicit sexual propositions and employs lewd and foul language. The caller may know the callee; for example, the calls are often received immediately after the callee arrives home from a social engagement. Many

obscene callers, however, do select names at random from the phone directory or from the news media.

4. The vicious or threatening call may consist merely of silence and breathing but be received frequently. One callee received about eighteen a day over a six-month period. An example of a spoken vicious call is, "Is this . . .? I am going to kill you because your father cheated me."

5. Other nuisance calls use particular ruses such as surveys or quizzes: "A friend recommended you . . .," and so on.

Murray and Beran (1968) surveyed more students in introductory psychology courses and found that in this survey 90 percent of the females and 73 percent of the males had received nuisance calls. Thirty-nine percent of the males and 75 percent of the females had received obscene calls. It appears, therefore, that males also receive obscene calls.

Nadler (1968) noted that in a nine-month period in New York City in 1966, the business office received 65,500 complaints of which 5 percent concerned threats, 19 percent obscene calls, 66 percent harassments and 10 percent mechanical difficulties in the telephone service.

The Psychodynamics of the Obscene Caller

What kind of person makes obscene calls? If we could describe these individuals, then we might be better able to devise particular kinds of therapeutic approaches for dealing with them.

Nadler (1968) noted that in the past, the obscene call has been categorized as a scoptophilic act (deriving pleasure from contemplation or looking) and as an exhibitionistic act (deriving pleasure from the reactions of another person by exposing them to sexual stimuli). Nadler presented three case reports of men who had made obscene calls.

1. A sixteen-year-old white male started making obscene calls to his friends and moved to calling at random. His calls became more threatening with time. His need to call ebbed at times—when he had a job, when he was in camp, and when he was hospitalized. His frequency of calling increased when he

was tense or fearful about his adequacy or performance in almost any area. He would become increasingly tense until eventually he telephoned. After the call, the tension went away without any genital activity. While telephoning, he was fearful and felt as though he had no control over what he might say. He was not close to his parents or his sister and did not fraternize much with boys of his own age.

2. A white graduate student in his mid-twenties came into therapy for impotence. Whenever he felt particularly unworthy because of schoolwork or after an argument with his mother he would try to demean a woman in a sexual way. For example, he would pick up a black prostitute while dressed impeccably himself and would insult her with lewd expressions. Occasionally he would engage in sexual activity with her. He then began masturbating (while not exposed) in subways, seeking to contrast the crudity of his action with his appearance. Finally, he began making obscene calls. He had always been a lonely youngster, unable to get close to anyone, and seemed to be defending against a sense of inferiority.

3. A twenty-five-year-old white male was referred by a court for exhibitionism. He began making obscene calls to telephone operators after his release from military service when other sexual activity became less easy to obtain.

Nadler noted the low self-esteem and the dependence upon others for reassurance in these men. In each case there was evidence of anger toward women which perhaps stemmed from their relationships with the mother. Their mothers were described as bossy, overprotective, and dominating. The fathers tended to be meek with regard to the mother and uninterested in the sons. From a psychopathological point of view, Nadler noted schizoid and depressive tendencies. Nadler noted that the use of the telephone for exhibitionism eliminated the anxiety felt in face-to-face confrontation. He feels safer from retribution and he is less likely to be laughed at. It prevents him from getting too involved with the person and protects him from the danger of physically acting out his rage and murderous fantasies.

The use of telephone calls in order to gain a sense of mastery and power through the reactions of others was seen by Nadler as similar to the behavior of the exhibitionist. It is likely, however, that the obscene caller is more timid and scared than the exhibitionist since he lacks the courage to physically confront another but would prefer to interpose the telephone.

Kisker (1964) also saw the obscene caller as similar psychodynamically to the exhibitionist, but a case report of a sixteen-year-old boy describes a boy with gross sexual confusion and lack of awareness of appropriateness. This boy was apprehended for patting coeds on the rear in a park and he had formerly made sexual advances to his teacher and an older friend's wife. Kisker diagnosed the boy as having strong, but latent homosexual inclinations. Although Kisker does not report on the boy's social relationships, it appears that they were poor and minimal. Again, we have a relatively lonely and isolated individual, perhaps with feelings of inferiority, trying to find a sexual outlet and master his feelings of inadequacy.

Therapy for the Obscene Caller

We have seen how the obscene caller is frequently seen as similar to the exhibitionist. Ideas for the therapeutic handling of the obscene caller may be obtained, therefore, from experiences with the therapy of exhibitionists. Mathis and Collins (1970) have reported upon their experiences with group therapy with exhibitionists and their conclusions have some relevance for the obscene caller.

Their group work was with exhibitionists forced into a therapy situation by legal authorities. All had been arrested at least once. Of the forty-five men treated, fifteen were able to escape the legal pressure, and all but two of these quit treatment. It appears, therefore, that legal pressure is essential initially to keep the men in treatment.

In the course of the group therapy, Mathis and Collins noted six distinct phases.

1. Initially, the men used denial extensively. They usually felt remorse, shame, and guilt after the first few exhibiting episodes, but these uncomfortable feelings were quickly denied

access to awareness. The men remained convinced that treatment was unnecessary since the problem no longer existed. Occasionally, the abnormality of the act is denied. This use of denial permeated the whole life style of the exhibitionist. They had low tolerance for anxiety and little awareness of emotional aspects of life, which in turn led to a poverty of relationships. They frequently denied the need for the group. Mathis and Collins felt that it takes up to six months for this pattern of behavior to break down and for the exhibitionist to face reality and to continue treatment voluntarily. The presence of confrontations from exhibitionists who have passed through this phase is necessary to breakthrough the denial. Interpretations and explanations by the group leaders have little effect here.

2. There follows a period of acceptance that he is emotionally immature and the exhibitionist begins to talk and recognize emotions. The group is now overidealized by him.

3. Anger is most frightening to the exhibitionist, probably because he fears being overwhelmed by his infantile-like rage if he allows it expression (rather than fearing retaliation). Eventually, anger begins to be expressed in the group and in other situations.

4. There follows a phase of disappointment resulting from the overidealization in the second phase and fright encountered during the phase of anger. He becomes disappointed at his lack of progress and improvement.

5. After about a year of group participation, the patients, who are usually underachievers, begin to make changes that promote upward mobility and promote feelings of mastery. For example, one of the patients in Mathis and Collins' group returned to college while maintaining his job as a laborer and managing to stay independent from his parents.

6. Finally, the phase of separation must be faced.

Mathis and Collins noted that these phases may not be unique to the exhibitionist and may be characteristic of many kinds of groups. Furthermore, the phases are rarely as distinct as implied by a formal presentation and description. However, their findings have many implications for the treatment of the obscene caller.

If the obscene caller is motivated by psychodynamics similar to those of the exhibitionist, then there are several clear implications. First, the obscene caller is very likely to use denial as a defense mechanism. He may deny that he has a problem or that he needs treatment. He may resist ordinary counseling because of his avoidance of talk and consideration of emotions. It is notable that no obscene caller to the Erie County SPCS has ever been successfully referred in for therapy. This may mean that if we want to treat the obscene caller meaningfully, we must identify him and have him forced into therapy by legal pressure. To generalize from the experience with exhibitionists, this pressure must be maintained for a long period of time—up to six months or more—or he will terminate treatment. This entails tracing the obscene caller and instituting legal procedures to commit him to treatment. Clearly, this may conflict with the values and policies of many counselors. However, not to do so may mean that successful therapy with the obscene caller is impossible.

The necessity for legal pressure in the case of the obscene caller is perhaps even greater due to the fact that he is possibly even more timid and anxious than the exhibitionist, who can at least face open confrontation with his "viewer."

It may not be feasible, in terms of whether a center feels that it is ethical for such callers to be traced and threatened with legal action, for such calls to be traced and for the callers to be referred in for therapy by a court. However, if there is no reason to suppose that telephone counseling can assist the obscene caller therapeutically, then perhaps centers should give up trying to be therapeutic toward these callers. Trying to be therapeutic may merely result in the telephone counselors providing sexual stimulation for such callers with no therapeutic movement, and, thus, they may be merely reinforcing the behavior of these men. It may be more appropriate to discourage such callers from using the telephone service for sexual stimulation. To discourage callers is against the policy of many crisis centers and many counselors might feel that to do so is inappropriate for a telephone crisis service where the aim is to help people with any kind of problem. Occasionally, however, when a crisis service realizes that it is ineffective in dealing with particular types of callers, it may be legitimate to discourage such callers from using the service.

Secondly, Mathis and Collins argue for the use of group therapy for such men. They note that other men who are in a later stage of therapy are more useful in building up the ability of the patient to face reality and admit his problems than is the therapist. However, since exhibitionists are more common than obscene callers, it may prove difficult to form a group of obscene callers for therapy. One possibility is to integrate the obscene caller into a group of exhibitionists.

References

Kisker, G. W.: *The Disorganized Personality.* New York, McGraw-Hill, 1964.

Mathis, J. L. and Collins, M.: Progressive phases in the group therapy of exhibitionists. *Int. J. Group Psychother., 20*:163-169, 1970.

Murray, F. S.: A preliminary investigation of anonymous nuisance telephone calls to females. *Psycho. Rec., 17*:395-400, 1967.

Murray, F. S. and Beran, L. C.: A survey of nuisance calls received by males and females. *Psychol. Rec., 18*:107-109, 1968.

Nadler, R. P.: Approach to psychodynamics of obscene telephone calls. *N.Y. State J. Med., 68*:521-526, 1968.

WORKING WITH THE OBSCENE CALLER

Gene W. Brockopp

In a previous section on working with the person who masturbates while making a call to an emergency telephone service, we stated that when a caller uses any verbal aspect of sexuality in his relationship with the telephone therapist he usually puts the helping person at a distinct disadvantage. This is, in part, due to the usual "up-tightness" one has when confronted in this area and also by the lack of experience the average telephone therapist has in working with this type of problem. The tendency to blame, moralize or punish the caller by hanging up the phone is almost automatic and the superego pat-on-the-back that we receive when we do these things helps to assuage any feelings of guilt that we may not have helped the caller by our actions.

Some of the information in the previous section by Lester can be very useful in dealing with this type of caller. However, to transpose the concepts and therapeutic approaches that he develops to this type of caller would result in a grave error. To place the information he reports on in the context of emergency telephone service. I feel three points must be emphasized:

1. There is very little basis for assuming that the motivational pattern and personality structure of the obscene caller and the exhibitionist are similar enough to assume that a treatment program which works for one will work for the other.

2. It is much easier to obtain legal sanctions against and treatment for the exhibitionist than for the obscene caller.

3. It is important to recognize that the obscene call to a telephone therapy service differs from an obscene call to the general public, for the standards of "acceptable" behavior are much broader at such a center and the level of tolerance should be much greater. Also, the purpose of the center is to be responsive to individuals with all types of difficulties, even those who use the ticket of obscenity.

I believe it follows from the above statements that an emergency telephone service must differ both from the way the public would respond to this type of individual and from the way that this individual would be responded to in a normal psychiatric or clinical setting. If, for example, the center attempted to trace every obscene caller and obtain legal sanctions against them, it is questionable whether they could remain an effective agent in the community for the word would quickly spread throughout the area that a call to the emergency service, which was not made in a way which was appropriate to the center's standards of behavior in the community, would result in the individual's incarceration. Generalizations would automatically take place on the part of the individual who has any type of paranoid streak in his personality. Certainly calls from drug users would begin to decline. In no way can the center serve as a policeman or an arm of the legal agencies in the community if it is to maintain an open-door policy for individuals in crisis or problem situations, nor can the center simply be an arm of the mental health agencies in the community. If necessary, even at the price of not getting a person into therapy or not getting a person who has violated the law into the courts, the integrity of the telephone service as a place where any person can call with any type of problem and receive interested, concerned and therapeutically appropriate responses must be maintained.

Even with this philosophical concept in mind, what is a therapeutically appropriate response to the obscene caller at a telephone emergency service? It would appear to me that it is necessary to make an arbitrary grouping of the obscene caller into two categories: (1) the one-time or occasional obscene caller, and (2) the chronic obscene caller. Each of these types of callers will be dealt with separately.

The One-time or Occasional Obscene Caller

From a theoretical point of view, the individual who calls a telephone emergency service and uses obscene language or other overt sexual material should be dealt with in a similar way to the person who calls the center and masturbates while on the telephone—that is, the telephone counselor should respond to both the overt and covert messages in the telephone call and not merely to the words or the content of the telephone call. Usually the covert message is, "I am very angry" or, "Can you accept me as I really feel I am" or, "Can I embarrass, unnerve or frustrate you with my language (and my problems)." By responding to both messages, the telephone emergency service gives the individual a chance to use the service to meet his own needs in the hope that through the accepting attitude of the telephone therapist he will develop a trust relationship with the center, move past the overt sexual aspects of this call into the problems or areas or concerns that he is covering up through his aggressive approach. The telephone counselor must clearly keep in mind the concept that she is and must be a transitional, social object for this type of call and recognize that to be a pipeline for this individual to a unit in the community that is more appropriate for his treatment she will need to accept his frustration, irritation and obscene language. If this can be done, then either through a continuous telephone contact with the center or by taking a referral to an appropriate mental health agency, the caller may move past the overt, obscene language into an appropriate therapeutic relationship.

For this type of caller no trace should be initiated nor should any threat of police or legal action be used. To do so is to help him achieve his covert goal of being rejected or wishing to be rejected and thereby confirm his feelings about himself and about other people in his environment. This caller is usually ambivalent about dealing directly with his problem and therefore uses a method which usually has resulted in his being rejected in the past in order to assure him that nobody really cares about helping him. By threatening a trace on his call or police or legal action, the telephone therapist is dealing only with the overt behavior. By refusing to do this, she is passing his test for acceptance. Only by getting past this test of self-rejection can the telephone counselor or any other therapist give him the help he is asking for in his ambivalent yet aggressive way.

The Chronic Obscene Caller

The chronic obscene caller must be handled in a different type of way for the dynamics behind his call are usually quite different. Even though anger at a world may be an essential part of his personality structure, the intensity of the anger and his pervasive character in his way of living is much greater. By flaunting his problem at the telephone service, he may be asking for direct assistance with this problem which he cannot consciously control, even though he would be the first to deny either that it is a problem or that he is asking for help. Yet through his continual calling (of an obscene nature) to an emergency service which advertises itself to be a helping agency in the community, he is covertly asking for this assistance. If this were not so, he could be making these types of calls to any other person or agency in the community. This type of call requires a different method of approach. Initially, the response of a telephone service to this type of caller would be the same as to the occasional obscene caller. Only after the pattern is clearly established that this person can only relate in an obscene way should a more intensive method be approached. The following steps would be recommended in developing that approach. First, a conference should be called between individuals who have worked with this obscene caller and with a consultant who has dealt with people having this type of problem. In the conference a case history including a summarization of the patient's contacts with the center should be presented. If they are available, tape recordings of his calls might be very appropriately used to clarify whether the obscene calls are made in response to some of the latent, nonverbal messages of the staff or as a result of the manifestation of the pathology of the individual. The staff should then explore what type of help he is requesting through his continued obscene calls to the center and develop some recommendations regarding what type of treatment program would be most appropriate for him. If it is felt that an appropriate treatment program can be developed for him either at the center or at any agency in the community, a decision may be made at this point to trace the call so as to obtain the person's name and address so a legal sanction can be obtained against this individual. Before this is done, however, the center should clearly examine the probable legal results of this action. If the individual is apprehended for placing obscene calls, will he be given an opportunity for treatment or will he be turned loose because of lack of evidence or because the telephone company, police agencies or legal community do not wish to deal with this type of problem situation. In some communities it is also important to know whether or not this individual will be simply placed on probation or incarcerated for a period of time rather than given appropriate psychiatric attention. If it is determined that he would be given the opportunity for therapeutic treatment, it is necessary to determine whether or not this type of therapy is available in the community. As was emphasized in the section by Lester, at least one year of intensive therapy is necessary in order to effectively treat a person with this type of problem. If the center is going to attempt to get help for the individual by using the legal sanctions of the community, we must be willing to completely and thoroughly follow this recommendation so that the individual who is placing the obscene call can obtain the type of help which will assist him in overcoming the problem which he has. If this does not occur, tracing the call can simply result in his going to jail for a period of time, being given a fine or placed on probation. This type of treatment would simply reaffirm to him that the community really does not care about him or about assisting him with the problems that he has.

It is necessary to emphasize that for most obscene callers, the tracing of the call and the use of legal sanctions will be the exception rather than the rule for a telephone emergency service. The results of having individuals of this type in therapy are not sufficiently clear that this method can be unequivocally recommended. It is my feeling that a trusting, accepting, understanding relationship with this person which deals both with the covert and the overt messages he is giving would result in a better final outcome. To achieve this goal is extremely difficult, for in any encounter the telephone therapist will find that this type of caller is one of the most difficult to relate to for he stimulates our fantasies while at the same time affront our sense of modesty and our moral standards. The telephone therapist who can work with this type of caller without being seduced through the titilations of his sexual fantasies or conversely responding with anger because of the negative countertransference is an unusual person. Yet it is within these two bounds that probably the most effective work with this type of person can be accomplished.

Chapter 13

THE CHRONIC CALLER

CHRONIC CALLERS TO A SUICIDE PREVENTION CENTER*

DAVID LESTER AND GENE W. BROCKOPP

T HE OPENING OF twenty-four-hour telephone services by suicide prevention centers has made available to the communities served by them a means to obtain help and support during times of crisis. Only a small proportion of calls to suicide prevention centers are from people who are suicidal (at the Suicide Prevention and Crisis Service of Erie County the proportion is about 20%). The majority of calls come from people who are lonely, depressed, or in conflict with a significant other but who do not claim to be potential suicides.

One group of people who do make use of twenty-four-hour telephone services is characterized by the fact that they make numerous calls to the center. The Suicide Prevention and Crisis Service of Erie County, which opened on October 31, 1968, had received 3,910 calls by June 30, 1969, from 2,128 separate patients. In this population of callers, there were twenty-four individuals who had called more than ten times. The number of calls made by these twenty-four individuals is shown in Table 13-I. As can be seen, the most frequent caller had called the center on 173 occasions at the time the data were analyzed.

It is frequently thought that these chronic callers are not suicidal risks and that they merely tie up the staff operating suicide prevention centers. One consequence of this point of view is the suggestion that chronic callers should be discouraged from using the center. An alternative viewpoint is that a suicide

---

* Reprinted from the *Community Mental Health Journal*, 6:246-250, 1970, by permission of Behavior Publications.

TABLE 13-I

CHARACTERISTICS OF 24 CHRONIC CALLERS TO THE
SUICIDE PREVENTION CENTER

Age	Sex	Marital Status	Treatment of Status	No. of Calls
25	male	divorced	seeking treatment	10
29	female	married	seeking treatment	10
37	female	married	seeing psychiatrist	10
44	female	married	former patient	11
54	female	widowed	no indication	12
43	male	single	seeing psychiatrist	12
41	female	married	former patient	12
23	male	single	seeking treatment	13
39	female	married	no indication	13
20	male	single	former patient	14
55	male	widowed	no indication	15
56	male	married	former patient	15
?*	female	?	no indication	17
25	female	single	no indication	18
37	female	married	no indication	18
42	female	widowed	former patient	18
35	female	single	former patient	18
55	female	single	former patient	19
25	female	single	former patient	21
30-40	female	married	seeing psychiatrist	42
23	female	single	seeing psychiatrist	42
36	male	single	seeing psychiatrist	47
44	male	single	former patient	69
52	female	married	seeing psychiatrist	173

* This patient claimed to be a 33- or 21-year-old married female, but the staff believed her to be a young girl aged 10 to 15.

prevention center can help these individuals lead an adequate life in society by providing them with periodic help and support. To do this costs very little (both in expense and time) compared to the cost of long-term treatment and custodial care.

The aim of the present chapter is to describe these chronic callers and to investigate the types of problems that they have and the ways in which a suicide prevention service can help them.

General Characteristics of Chronic Callers

The twenty-four chronic callers were compared with a sample of callers to the Suicide Prevention and Crisis Service of Erie County who called only once. The chronic callers (n = 24) did not differ from the one-time callers (n = 378) in sex ($\chi^2 = 0.00$, df = 1), age, marital status, possession of children ($\chi^2 = 3.23$, df = 1), number of children, race, living arrangements (alone or with others), suicidal history, rated suicidal risk on the first call, or the presenting problem. They were significantly less likely to be anonymous callers ($\chi^2 = 4.51$, df = 1, $p < 0.05$) but this may result from the fact that after many calls the chronic caller was more likely to identify himself than the individual who called only once.

It appears, therefore, that the chronic caller did not differ in general characteristics from the individual who called only once.

Some Categories of Chronic Callers

The chronic callers fall into four categories with regard to their aims in calling the center. These categories were defined in terms of the treatment status of the caller.

1. Seven of the chronic callers were seeing an additional therapist during the time that they were calling the center. They often used the center to voice anxieties about therapy and criticisms of their present therapist. In a few cases, it appeared that the visits to the therapist were not felt to be sufficient by the caller and the center was used as an additional source of support.

Case 1: A depressed lonely man, aged forty-three and single. After being healthy all his life, he was now suffering from several illnesses. He came to the center for short-term treatment, but his therapist suggested that the treatment plan should be to urge him to use his therapist rather than the center. He continued to call and express hostility toward the therapist and to assert that the center was more useful. He attempted suicide and subsequently obtained a different therapist. (12 calls.)

2. Two callers were seeking treatment of some kind and used the center to help them.

Case 2. A twenty-three-year-old single male. His family had been killed in a car accident and he appeared to feel guilty. He was temporarily employed through the use of labor pools. He was hostile and looking for someone to take care of him.

He tried to get himself admitted to several psychiatric hospitals but was not admitted. He came to the center once and demanded that the center negotiate with his landlady the sale of a television to him. (13 calls.)

3. Six callers gave no indication of having received psychiatric treatment in the past or of being in therapy at the present time. They called the center merely to "ventilate" their feelings.

Case 3: A fifty-four-year-old female who had survived two husbands. She had been alone now for twelve years. She had two children who had left home and she had stopped working. She would not leave the house and drank and smoked a lot. She tried to cover her loneliness with jokes but she had broken down once and cried. She was understanding if the counselor was busy and she had to hang up. She thanked the center for allowing her to call and talk. (12 calls.)

4. Nine callers had been in treatment in the past and appeared to be disturbed people who called to ventilate their emotions and pursue their delusions.

Case 4: A thirty-five-year-old single female living with parents. She was parnoid and delusional and had been hospitalized three times. She called to ventilate especially when her customary listeners got irritated with her. She was concerned with body deformations and her revelations from God. (18 calls.)

Reactions of the Staff to Chronic Callers

The staff at the center responded to chronic callers in a way that depended upon the characteristics of the callers (and the staff). The staff became quite concerned about many of the callers and were often fond of them. The callers were discussed and their continued calling was followed by most of the counseling staff. This reaction was shown in the extreme by their reactions to the fifty-two-year-old married female who called 173 times. This woman was seeing a psychiatrist and she called both him and the center about once a day. She rarely talked for more than a few minutes. She was depressed but was always interrupted, supposedly by her employer or her husband. She appeared to find no help in being questioned by the counselor or by discussions of her problem. All she appeared to want was to reiterate her problem. At one point she was hospitalized for shock treatment for a few weeks and did not call. When she finally called again, the counselor who answered the telephone expressed her pleasure that she had called again and how the staff had missed her. Eventually, her husband and she moved to another state. In her last few calls she said how much better she felt and how much she had appreciated the staff at the center. Her departure coincided with the departure of one of the counselors who had been at the center since its opening and much was made of this coincidence. She wrote from her new home to express her gratitude and to tell of her activities. In a sense, by virtue of her frequent calls, this chronic caller had become as much a part of the center as the staff.

How Suicidal Are the Chronic Callers?

Of twenty-four chronic callers, eleven gave no indication of current or past suicidal ideation. Four of them threatened suicide and one of these claimed to have attempted suicide but called back later to say that she had only tried to scare her husband. Five of the callers reported having attempted suicide and three attempted suicide during the period that they were in contact with the center. Thus, these chronic callers were equally as likely to be suicidal cases as those who were not chronic callers. Furthermore, since they called the center frequently, there was more opportunity for the staff to intervene and to prevent their suicidal actions.

Discussion

With some chronic callers there is no problem in deciding how the center is going to deal with them. They call with specific problems, will accept referrals to other community resources, and will visit the center so that more adequate evaluation and diagnosis can be made. There is a feeling on the part of the staff that some improvement is possible for such a caller.

In other cases, where the caller is already in treatment, the center can coordinate with the psychiatrist or therapist with whom the caller is in treatment. In some cases this can mean simply urging the caller to use his present therapist rather than the center. In some cases, this can entail providing support for the caller in addition to that received from the therapist.

Problems arise mainly with those chronic callers who call the center frequently, who avoid questions put to them by the counselor, who refuse to focus upon and to discuss their problems, and who seem to want someone merely to listen to them talk. These callers often arouse a great deal of resentment on the part of the staff. The staff feels ineffective and frustrated in their attempts to help the caller. They feel that their time is being occupied and wasted by these callers when there are more important things to do.

Four approaches are possible with such callers, two of which seem to be useful.

1. The callers could be discouraged from calling the center. This approach seems unacceptable because it is against the whole concept of a twenty-four-hour telephone service. A center that provides such a telephone service is obligated to accept calls. The image of a center might be seriously impaired if calls were refused. From a clinical point of view, it may well be argued that repetitive and unfocussed support can serve only to reinforce maladaptive behavior when no valid treatment is operative as a corrective. Even if this were the case, the center's position is a difficult one if it proposes to take all calls. In a therapeutic relationship, within a longer-term and face-to-face situation, one may choose to allow dependency, seductiveness, demands, projection, and so forth in the beginning months of treatment with a plan to help the patient in the course of time to understand and then to relinquish those aspects of his personality. Perhaps the very nature of telephone contact acts as a limit in this regard and also limits effective treatment with chronic callers, short of real help by merely listening.

2. A second approach is just to listen to the caller. The counselor can listen to chronic callers for as long as there is time and there are not other individuals calling into the center.

Perhaps this is not harmful to the caller but it may lead to hostility on the part of the counselor and a feeling that his time is being wasted. Thus, the counselor's functioning is impaired.

3. One constructive approach is for the counselor to limit the call of the chronic caller from the outset. The counselor can say that it is a very busy time and that he can spend only ten minutes with the caller. Many chronic callers understand this and will offer to hang up when they hear another line ring. Those who do not respond appropriately have at least been warned at the beginning of their call that their conversation may be terminated. They can also be told to call back in a few hours.

4. The most constructive approach is to keep a list of chronic callers and to have the professional staff formulate a plan, however limited in scope, for dealing with the caller. For example, it may be decided with a patient that the counselor should try to encourage self-disclosure. Thus, the counselor has a plan of action when dealing with the caller and can feel that therapeutic intervention has not been abandoned for this particular caller. If, to pursue our example, a particular chronic caller begins to make more self-disclosures, then the professional staff can reformulate their plan. The next stage may require the counselor to reinforce self-disclosures of a particular type, and so on. In this way, over the course of many calls, a caller may be helped to some small extent along a path that is recognizable to the counselor as focussed, therapeutic, and useful. Not only does this approach fit in with the concept of a twenty-four-hour telephone service available to all, but it also serves to reduce the feelings of hostility on the part of the counselor and to give him a sense of task involvement.

Summary

Individuals who called a suicide prevention center a large number of times (chronic callers) were found to be very similar in general characteristics to the general population of callers. They were just as likely to be suicidal risks as the average caller. Several types of chronic callers are described and possible approaches are outlined for dealing with those who reject therapeutic counsel and who appear to need merely to ventilate their emotions.

* * *

THE THERAPEUTIC MANAGEMENT OF THE CHRONIC CALLER

GENE W. BROCKOPP

With the chronic caller, the emergency telephone service is faced with an unusual problem. As the number of calls the individual makes to the center increase, factual data about the person (his history, background, home and life experiences) develop into an impressive case history. With this amount of material, it would seem that it would be easier to develop an effective treatment program for this caller than for most other callers. This, however, is not the case. Here is a caller who very likely has been to most of the social agencies in the community and has not received the assistance he has desired. But he still may continue to contact them, possibly out of the remote possibility that someone, somewhere may have the magic answer to solve his problem. So, in most instances, the chronic caller is being heard not only by the center but by many other agencies and organizations in the community. The center, because it is limited to verbal contact with the chronic caller, often has little influence over the range of the person's therapeutic and personal experiences. Therefore, it has little basis to assume that any behavior change on the part of the individual is a result of the contact with the center. Often these individuals call regardless of the nature of their most recent relationship with the center. This may indicate that they are receiving some therapeutic aid from the counselors, or it may indicate that they are calling to maintain contact in case one of the other sources of help begins to fail.

With the chronic caller, it is therefore very difficult to know which treatment method is therapeutic and almost impossible to isolate a single, most effective treatment approach for them. From an analysis of this type of caller at the Erie County Suicide Prevention Center, certain principles appear to be appropriate for use as guidelines when dealing with this type of caller:

1. The center must develop a consistent method of respond-

ing to this type of caller. This is quite difficult to achieve since most telephone emergency services use a large number of volunteers, each of whom has his own particular approach and therapeutic style in working with individuals in crisis situations. In working with this type of caller, the individualism of the counselor must be minimized and the patterned response of the center maximized in order to formulate and implement a reasoned, consistent, therapeutic response. Every effort must be made by the volunteers to keep their response to the chronic caller in agreement with the approved program, for differences between the telephone therapists will often be taken by the chronic caller as signs of weakness or lack of knowledge. Consistency in telephone work allows for the person-to-person concern to come through by minimizing the hostility and frustration that the counselor may feel when working with the patient who has called the center many times. The therapeutic plan also helps the counselor to develop more of a sense of sureness which is transmitted to the client in the noncognitive aspects of the communication.

2. Determine the scope of the reaching out behavior. With the chronic caller it is important to be aware that the individual may be seeing a therapist, calling other mental health services in the community and possibly being a patient of one or more physicians. An attempt should be made by the staff to determine what organizations and groups in the community the chronic caller is contacting. If the person is seeing a therapist on a regular basis, it is important that the center obtain permission from the client to talk with this therapist and together with him develop a consistent approach of working with this individual. If it is determined that other agencies and organizations are also being contacted by this person, it is necessary to work with them to determine the appropriate area of help each of the agencies will provide. Sometimes it is useful to call the members of the agencies together with the chronic caller to work out a plan how each of them will work with the problems the person is presenting.

3. Suicidal risk must be continually evaluated. Chronic callers, especially if they have had any suicidal ideation in the

past or have evidenced suicidal behavior, are very prone to make suicide attempts to underline the critical nature of their chronic condition and to "prove" their need for help. As a result, they may (accidentally or eventually) kill themselves. With the natural habituation a telephone emergency service makes to the continual threats of the chronic caller, unless it is very alert, it will miss the cues that this caller will give out before making a serious suicide attempt. These missed cues, covert as they may be, are often seen by the chronic caller as a direct rejection of their being. Care must be taken therefore not to underestimate the seriousness of any life threatening behavior mentioned by the chronic caller. Many times the mentioning of this behavior is a type of test by them to determine whether or not the center still cares. Although the chronic caller is a low risk at any particular time, even though he makes suicide threats (since this person tends to live in a continual upset state) he is a high suicidal risk over a lifetime and may end his life through suicide.

4. The telephone therapy with the chronic caller should emphasize the person-to-person relationship. The chronic caller is usually operating at a very basic level in his relationships with other individuals. Often he is lonely, has a sense of separation and isolation from other beings and feels no one cares for him or is willing to take him seriously. Unsureness, both in his inter-action with people and in his feeling of self-value, result in his being convinced that no one is interested enough in him to make a caring response. The focus of the telephone therapy should, therefore, emphasize trust, support and confidence. Confrontation should be used sparingly and no attempt should be made to develop insight on the part of the caller regarding the basis for his problems. If confrontation with the individual is necessary in order to develop and maintain an appropriate treatment program, the confrontation should be made on the content of the telephone conversation rather than on an emotional aspect of the relationship. Even if the confrontation is used in this way, it is difficult for the chronic patient not to seize on the confrontation as evidence of their rejection by the telephone counselor. When confrontations are used, they are best stated in terms of

open-ended nonpejorative statements, which allow the individual to accept and define the confrontations at a level which is not too threatening to his psychological integrity. This will give the counselor a good idea of whether or not it is appropriate to move ahead with any further confrontation.

5. Develop neighborhood support systems for the chronic caller. While it is necessary to allow the chronic caller to maintain some dependency on the center and on persons at the center, the emphasis in all the contacts should be to direct the person back to those systems in his home or neighborhood which would give him support. Help must be given so that he will see the center and its personnel as a transitional social object, which he can use, but one which must be supplanted by relationships that are more fixed and permanent in his environment. The direction of all the contacts should be on assisting the individual to make better use of himself and of his own environment and of developing embrace systems in the environment rather than focusing on the center and the telephone contact for sustenance and support. It is important to note in this regard that with some chronic callers, the telephone therapist gives the caller clues which imply that he or the center has a desire to maintain contact with the caller and to continue the dependency relationship. This is especially true if the chronic caller is a young person and presents a seductive set of problems or involves the therapist in a personal way.

6. Focus on specific reality oriented problems. The chronic caller usually presents a plethora of problems, each one more involved than the last, and each one adding to the difficulty in understanding the condition that the individual is in, and/or developing a solution for the condition. With each additional problem that the caller elucidates, his anxiety increases and his ability to cope decreases. Our experience with the chronic caller indicates that when we help the patient to focus on specific life-problem situations, we not only reduce the length of the calls and his anxiety but also maximize his ability to work with his problems and develop appropriate solutions. To achieve this, it is necessary for the telephone therapist to become quite

selective and direct with the material the patient presents. Statements summarizing the problem the patient has are important. Through this type of teaching approach to the chronic patient we are helping to develop a method of approaching and solving problems which he can use on his own. By refusing to focus on the emotional aspects of the call and emphasizing the content or rational aspects of the patient's life, we are helping him to become more objective about his concern and feel a sense of being able to deal with his life problems in a more appropriate way than simply emoting about the hardness of his life and the many difficulties with which he is burdened.

Chronic callers are extremely taxing on the emotional energies of staff of an emergency telephone service. In an attempt to work with them more effectively and to utilize our time more efficiently, we have formulated a number of new methods for working with them which may improve their basic condition and minimize the negative effect they have on the center and its personnel.

1. Arrange a liason between the chronic caller and other lonely people in the community who may desire a relationship or who may wish a human contact but be unable to obtain it. As was mentioned previously, the chronic caller is usually a person who is very lonely and who uses his contact with the center to obtain and maintain a relationship with someone who cares. Through a careful analysis of the phone calls received by the center a number of people can usually be found who also need a human contact and who could profit from listening to the hurts and problems of another person and be able to respond to them on a feeling level. Although the chronic caller may call throughout the day, he usually makes his calls at night and in early hours of the morning when the loneliness of his existence is compounded by his inability to sleep. To develop relationships that may be useful to him at these times, the center may need to enlist the help of people who tend to be awake at night or who for one reason or another do not go to sleep until early in the morning, for example, the wives of men who work on a swing shift. The center can sometimes enlist their help and support to take telephone calls at night. Of course, the center must maintain

a liason with people who take these calls and must provide them with the needed backup services of consultation, counseling, and referral.

2. Enlist the assistance of former telephone therapists. Every center has a list of individuals who have volunteered their time at the center and who have dropped out of active volunteer service. Some of these maintain a high interest in the work of the center and recognize the value of the service the center is performing in the community. Although they may not be willing to continue to work a regular shift at the center, they might be willing to have their name and their telephone number given out to some chronic caller. The chronic callers could then call them for support and friendship rather than calling the center. The use of former telephone therapists, of course, would help to assure the center that appropriate types of decisions would be made regarding the problems that the chronic caller is bringing up.

3. Use community groups for support relationships. Since the chronic callers tend to be older individuals or individuals who demand a great deal of support and succorance, groups of individuals in the community who can give time can sometimes be tapped to work with the chronic caller. For example, Golden Age Club members could talk with these individuals either by telephone or in person. Even individuals who are bedridden (for example, individuals in nursing homes) could be utilized for this purpose and while giving help could be obtaining desirable outside contacts for themselves.

4. Group therapy for chronic callers. By bringing together a group of individuals who are chronic callers at the center for a period of time each week and allowing them to interact with each other, the amount of time they spend calling the center could be substantially reduced. At the same time the approach could help them develop additional personal contacts in the community, see the way other people are handling their problems, and provide a support base for them when they try out new behaviors. During the group therapy period, discussions could be initiated as to the value of the phone service for them and the ways in which they could make more effective use of this service.

5. Use writing therapy. We have found it is sometimes useful to have a chronic caller write to a center rather than calling the center. Some individuals communicate their difficulties much more precisely and carefully through the written word rather than through the telephone, and the real needs, which they cover up through a large amount of verbiage, may become clear when they are asked to put them in writing. This process also allows the center to give a more thoughtful type of response to the chronic caller and, thereby, to deal with the problem in a less demanding and time-consuming method. Letter writing also effectively moves the person into a more objective relationship which may allow the client caller to deal more with the reality-oriented aspects of his problem and less with his feelings.

6. Call the chronic caller. Sometimes the center can best help the chronic caller by showing interest and concern for them through calling them rather than waiting for them to call the center. In this way the telephone therapist can help them to "set their day" in a more positive framework and can help them to plan for the activities of their day. It also allows him to have more control over the conversation, directing it and terminating it without the caller feeling hurt. The call also gives the caller the assurance that the center is interested and concerned about him and often makes it less necessary for him to call the center and be reassured that the agency is still there and available to him.*

The usual, often nonverbal reactions of telephone counselors to another call from a "crock" interfere with the appropriate handling of the caller and destroy any therapeutic relationship which the counselor may have with the caller. To effectively deal with this type of caller, the center must formulate and implement a reasoned and consistent policy of working with this type of patient and develop new and innovative methods of responding to them. If this is not done, the chronic caller will eventually be rejected, either covertly or overtly, by a frustrated telephone counselor.

----

* This is one form of the care-ring service which has been extremely effective in some parts of the country as a means of dealing with lonely people.

THE CHRONIC CALLER TO A SUICIDE PREVENTION CENTER: REPORT OF A CASE

Diane Blum and David Lester

In the previous section we discussed the individual who makes a large number of calls to a suicide prevention center. We described the characteristics of these chronic callers, presented some case illustrations, and discussed possible policies that a center might adopt for the chronic caller.

The present section examines one chronic caller in greater detail and explores some of the approaches that the counselors have taken with her, their reactions to her, and how these reactions affected the counseling process.

Mrs. A was a forty-year-old divorced woman who called the center at least once a day (and often as many as 3 or 4 times a day) for over six months. She usually discussed her feelings of loneliness, depression, and rejection and she expressed hostility toward all the people who have been unwilling to establish relationships with her. Much of her concern centered on why her fifteen-year-old daughter chose to live in a foster home rather than with her. Mrs. A was often hostile and angry but occasionally she was happy and talked to the counselors about cheerful topics.

The problem facing a suicide prevention center in trying to help such a patient is increased by the fact that a caller who calls frequently may speak to anyone of about two or three dozen counselors. Therefore, not only is it difficult to formulate a therapeutic plan that might prove useful in helping the caller, but it is also difficult to implement such a plan. Consequently, the caller experiences a variety of therapeutic approaches. The counselors were able to identify a number of different approaches that they had taken with Mrs. A.

1. Many of the counselors tried to demonstrate their acceptance of Mrs. A and convey warmth and support. This approach was used especially after she had been released from a state hospital and felt very insecure living alone. Counselors employed this approach to encourage Mrs. A to find a job and to support her efforts to succeed in it. The counselors using this approach

assured Mrs. A that they realized how difficult working was for her and they acknowledged her loneliness.

This approach was helpful since Mrs. A had few interpersonal contacts and received very little support from any person in her life. The continued support she received may have helped her find a job and maintain it. The disadvantage of continually expressing acceptance to Mrs. A lay in the reactions of the counselor. When the counselors told Mrs. A that they know how difficult things were for her, she often replied, "How do you know how hard it is? You've never been alone like I am." The counselors felt frustrated when Mrs. A reacted in this way to them.

2. The counselors sometimes focused on particular problems Mrs. A presented and offered interpretations to her as to why she was feeling a certain way.

Concentrating on a particular problem helped to focus Mrs. A's often disorganized conversation. However, interpretations such as, "Are you feeling bad today because your daughter did not call?" and discussing Mrs. A's feelings about her daughter often resulted in her generalizing her feelings about her daughter to everyone else. Her conversation again became a statement of her overwhelming loneliness and unhappiness. Consequently, focusing Mrs. A's thoughts was extremely difficult.

3. The counselors also reacted with hostility to Mrs. A and told her that they were tired of listening to her problems. This approach was used when a particular counselor had had several long conversations with Mrs. A during which Mrs. A had been especially angry.

The counselors all said that at times their only reaction to Mrs. A had been one of hostility. However, usually they controlled their anger and they felt that Mrs. A had sensed their hostile feelings. Anger is an understandable feeling here but may result in guilt on the part of the counselor as it is at odds with their idealized aim of communicating acceptance. It is also very likely that Mrs. A recognized, at some level, the hostility in the counselor and reacted to it. Expression of anger by a counselor to a patient is not necessarily unwise or damaging. However, for a counselor to use such a response to a patient usefully the counselor should, in general, be aware of these feelings and be in control of them (as opposed to being controlled by them).

4. The counselors limited Mrs. A's time to ten or fifteen minutes and permitted her to control the conversation during this time.

This response to Mrs. A often occurred inadvertently as the counselor had to terminate her call to take another call. A time-limited conversation did not seem to upset Mrs. A since she believed that the counselors at the center would talk to her again when she called later.

5. The counselors confronted Mrs. A with the fact that she was not accepting any of their suggestions and demonstrated to her that this was a pattern of behavior for her. The counselors indicated that if she treated her friends and relatives the way she treated the counselors, then it was not surprising that people rebuffed her attempts at friendship.

Confronting Mrs. A with her patterns of behavior might be a valid treatment method if it was utilized consistently by all counselors. On the other hand, the counselor's lack of patience weakened the usefulness of this approach. Several of the counselors expressed the feeling that when they confronted Mrs. A, she merely turned their statement back to them and said they had no idea of what she was going through. This made them frustrated and angry.

6. The counselors concentrated on specific suggestions such as going to Recovery, bingo, or church. It seems as if Mrs. A usually initiated the possibility of some activity and then questioned various counselors about their opinion of it.

This approach was utilized frequently. However, there was no combined effort on the part of the counselors to develop particular plans of activity for Mrs. A and no one was able to determine who initiated a certain suggestion. One counselor suggested that it was Mrs. A who first mentioned an activity and then each counselor reacted to it personally. The danger in this stems from the fact that Mrs. A could have received conflicting opinions from the various counselors with whom she spoke. However, she did receive consistent advice and support for the idea of going to Recovery and bingo and she expressed satisfaction from participating in these activities. Several of the counselors focused on the importance of her medication since Mrs. A was refusing to take her medicine.

It is the general impression of the counselors that Mrs. A improved during the time she called the center. Initially she appeared unable to leave her house alone, whereas later she appeared to have sought and found employment. It is difficult to estimate to what extent her contact with the center was responsible for this change. It is impossible, therefore, to try to evaluate the usefulness of the different approaches utilized by counselors.

Two general points are worth emphasizing here. First, the reactions of counselors to particular types of callers may on occasion interfere with the effective handling of the therapeutic relationship that the counselor must establish with the caller. Secondly, since a suicide prevention center uses a large number of counselors, attempts must be made to formulate and implement a reasoned and consistent policy for particular patients. Both of these problems can be dealt with by means of case conferences centered around particular patients. In such meetings the feelings of the counselors can be expressed and dealt with and a therapeutic intervention policy can be formulated.

Chapter 14

THE COVERT CRY FOR HELP

GENE W. BROCKOPP

THE CRY FOR HELP takes many different forms in a crisis telephone service. When most individuals are in a crisis, they make it quite clear that they are at the end of their resources and in need of assistance. They call for help in a direct and unmistakable way and in so doing obtain the aid of other individuals who have the understanding, background and skills necessary to help them with their problems.

For other individuals the call for help is initially a covert one. To express overtly that they need help is not possible for them for a number of reasons. Some people feel that to call for help is a sign of weakness, others fear the possibility of rejection if it is announced to the world that they are in the vulnerable position of needing help. Some have been rebuffed before by their direct cry for help and are uncertain whether they should try to obtain assistance again. Still other individuals are too proud to call for help in a direct way. Any of the above individuals may use a covert cry for help as a test to see if the service is willing to reach out to them, even though they have not committed themselves to accept the help if it is offered to them. The covert cry for help is often a method by which they hope to make a determination whether or not they can trust the unseen helper with the problems that are upsetting them and putting them in crisis.

Because of the very nature of a telephone emergency service, it must be very careful not to define too precisely the modes and ways it will become involved with people in difficulty. It must be alert to the nuances that individuals use in making a call for help and respond to them with openness and honesty, listening

193

for the covert message while responding to the overt questions or concerns that the individual is raising on the telephone. Each call to a crisis center, no matter what the overt purpose of the call may be, is potentially a call from an individual in crisis.

Probably the most common covert call for help is the call that is made ostensibly for another individual who is in difficulty —one with whom the caller has a close association. At my center, between 14 and 25 percent of the calls are made out of concern for a third party. It is difficult to tell, of course, when the call is in reality about a third party, or when it is about the caller himself. At my center the rules that we use are (1) to always make the assumption that the call is about the person who is on the phone, and (2) never attempt to force the individual to prove that the call is about someone else, but rather take the call as he overtly states it to be. The initial focus with this type of call is to get the caller involved with the person that is supposedly in crisis, by helping him to organize the resources in his neighborhood that he (the person in crisis) can call on for assistance. A secondary focus (which is usually always used) is to give the individual some additional resources that he can use in the community. Often we use our center as one of these resources and tell the person that his friend can come to the center at any time he wishes and can come anonymously, if he so desires. This type of statement, I feel, indicates to the caller that we are more interested in working with him and the problem that he has than in personal information which he is often reluctant to give.

Another set of covert cries come in terms of what I call "checking out the service" calls. These fall into four categories. The most common probably is the call where the individual dials the service, reaches the crisis worker, and then hangs up the phone before making verbal contact. Irritating as this may be to the crisis worker, I believe that this is also a test. The person may be unconsciously sensing acceptance or rejection from such things as whether a male or female voice answers the phone, or whether the tonal qualities or other cues that are present in the voice of the crisis worker indicate acceptance and concern to him. When speaking to individuals who have told us that they have called the service a number of times and have hung up immediately after the phone has been answered, they speak about not having enough courage to go on, of being afraid, or feeling that the problem was not one that they should bother someone else with. Until they found someone who could successfully pass their test, they continued to hang up the phone. Another variation on this theme is the person who calls the center and then responds by saying, "I have the wrong number." At a suicide center it should be axiomatic that there are no wrong numbers. This response on the part of the caller should be greeted with, "May I help you? What number were you calling?" and then followed with a clear statement as to the type of service that they are connected with. We have found that some people will say something like, "Oh, since I have you on the phone, I may as well talk about——," and then go on talking about a problem they have Or others (more often) hang up the phone, possibly evaluate their reception at the center and then decide to either dial again (if they were actually calling the service) or dial the number they want. A third type of "checking out the service" is seen in the person who calls and then does not talk, but rather waits for the crisis worker to make the correct statement or connection before he makes any comment. More than likely, this individual will eventually hang up the phone before making a comment, yet the way that the phone is answered by the crisis worker is critical, in that it will often determine whether or not this person will call back a second time and begin to talk about the problem he is having. The last variation on this theme, we have found, is the person who calls up and then makes a statement in a semi-surprised voice: "Oh, is someone really there? I thought it was probably an answering service, or a recorded message." Again, if the question is answered only on the surface level, the person is not likely to bring up the problem that he has. As in all of these cases, the telephone worker must make himself readily available to the individual calling and facilitate that person's movement into a discussion of the problems he is having.

Often the person who is calling asking for information is

setting himself up to be rejected by the telephone service, through the service answering his question and not responding to the problems that he is having at this particular period of time. To only give the specific information the person is requesting is not to respond to the affective mood that is usually present in the call for information. These affective moods usually convey a message such as the fear of going to a social or mental health agency, the possibility of rejection, the sense of unsureness about oneself, or the need felt to deal with the problem immediately. The crisis worker must be very careful that she is not unknowingly rejecting the person by simply giving the person the information he is asking for and nothing more. The information call is often a call covertly designed to keep the level of conversation on an intellectual plane. With this type of call, the ability to deal with the affective needs of the caller, while giving the information desired, is the crucial test of effectiveness for the crisis worker.

Sometimes the covert cry for help comes in a humorous cloak. The caller is likely to say something like, "You mean there really is a service like that?" or, "I'll bet you hear some real good ones from people who call there," or, "You must be crazy to work in a place like that." Regardless of its form, this type of call usually has a very serious purpose to it, and the caller is often using these phrases as a test to determine how his feelings will be handled by a telepehone service. We find it best to handle this type of call in a very direct and factual way, not responding at all to the humor that may be implied in the message. To respond to the humor is to play directly into the hands of this individual and to fail the test that he is making of the telephone service, which is, "Will you handle my call in a humorous way, or will you be serious about what I want to talk to you about?"

A covert call for help that is handled in exactly the opposite way is the one from a person who cries for help in a hostile, abusive manner. This individual is usually trying to test the possibility that we will be rejected by the crisis worker or by the service through his direct and assaultive manner. Generally, the best way to respond to this type of individual is through a cool, intellectual response in which the abuse that the individual is giving is accepted or tolerated and at the same time met with the controlled anger and personal stability of the telephone worker. This gives the caller a chance to vent his wrath within a stabilized setting and helps him to obtain the clear message that the service is not going to be ruffled by his belligerent and loud-mouthed behavior, but rather is able to tolerate this and still respond to him in a direct helpful and unemotional way.

The intellectual caller is a difficult person to work with. Usually he is very cool and calculating, precise in his manner, knowledgeable in the field, and capable of "unnerving" most of the telephone workers. As he is likely to know more about the subject that he is speaking about than they do and since he usually is a very capable, argumentative person, he is able to win whenever he is challenged on his own grounds. The key to working with this type of caller is not to challenge him. Under the cool, calculating exterior is often an individual who is quite concerned and somewhat unsure of himself. To remain on an intellectual level with this person is to assist him in his process of covering over his unsureness with intellectualizations. Since one of the important factors involved with this type of individual is the question of control, I have found that one of the best ways to work with this type of individual is to allow them to "defeat" me by telling them directly that I will not fight with them and then to talk about the feelings that they have when they have succeeded in controlling the situation. The conversation usually moves into the problems that they have been trying to cover up through the process of intellectualization. The caller can then begin to deal with the problems on an emotional level.

Another type of the covert call for help is the "yes—but" caller. This individual is extremely exasperating to the telephone worker for it seems that no matter what type of answer one gives to the problem that the individual is presenting, he responds with "yes—but" and then proceeds to move to another facet of the problem or to predict the impossibilities of working with the solution as it has been developed by them and the telephone worker. A variation of this type of caller is the person who continually asks the question, "What would you do if I——?"

then completes the statement with a behavior that usually has dire consequences. For both of these types of callers, the best approach is generally one which brings them back to the realities of the situation; one which focuses on the specific problem that they are having at this particular time and gives them reasonable directions for handling the problems that they are presenting. Usually with the "yes—but" caller a summarization by the telephone worker of the concerns that the individual has presented along with directions that the person may take to ameliorate the problem moves the person into an action stage. Getting the "what would you do" caller involved with the solution to his own problem will often help eliminate this type of description which keeps the worker from moving toward any type of closure with the caller.

The exasperated caller, the wrong number, the calls for a third party, the person who is hostile and abusive, the individual who uses humor, intellectualizations, or calls for information are often callers who are making covert cries for help. They are all calls in which the individual caller may speak on one level, while indirectly hoping to receive help and understanding of his problems at another level. If the telephone worker listens to only the overt level of the conversation, he is certain to miss the real message and is likely to turn the caller away from the source of help he is actually seeking.

Chapter 15

THE SILENT CALLER

WORKING WITH THE SILENT CALLER

GENE W. BROCKOPP

ONE OF THE MOST frustrating people to work with either in a face-to-face therapeutic interview or over the telephone is the person who chooses not to engage in a verbal interaction with a therapist. In a face-to-face interview, other nonverbal means of communication can be elicited and utilized by the therapist to engage the client. When the telephone is used as the medium for communication, the therapist is at a distinct disadvantage as most of the usual avenues of nonverbal communication are not available.

In the silent caller we have an excellent example of ambivalence. Here is a person who deliberately made the effort to call a center designed to assist people who have personal problems. When he reaches the source of assistance, he, for any number of reasons, chooses not to engage in verbal communication which may be necessary to ameliorate his problems. This behavior, which appears inconsistent, usually has a basis in his psychological makeup or previous experiences with helping agencies. Many callers to a suicide prevention center have been rejected by other agencies and organizations or by their families and friends and therefore are unsure whether or not they will be accepted and listened to at the suicide prevention center. As a result, they may call in a reluctant manner to reduce the psychological effect of the potential rejection.*

---

* In substance this behavior is quite normal, for in every type of therapeutic situation the patient presents a test to the therapist whereby he, the patient, ascertains whether or not the person he is talking to is one who will understand him or one who is worthy of the trust which he, the patient, has to give. The only real difference is that in this type of caller the test is more ambiguous.

One of the apparent advantages of a telephone conversation is that the caller, from a psychological point of view, is intimately close to the person he is talking to regardless of the physical distance. To the silent caller this may be a disadvantage. With his concern about being accepted by the telephone therapist, the immediacy of this intimate relationship with another individual may become too frightening for him. While he utilizes the telephone in order to gain psychological mobility without a change in his physical environment, the rapidity of the change and the impact of the closeness may frighten him away from beginning a conversation unless the person on the other end of the telephone is aware of his concern and does something to facilitate his talking with a statement that says, "You can trust me," "I want to help," or "I'm here to listen."*

But what does one do when the caller makes no verbal response, yet remains on the line, making his presence known? Faced with this type of caller, the telephone therapist must first overcome his initial tendency (which may be appropriate in other nontherapeutic situations) to hang up the phone assuming that it is a so-called prank or nuisance call. He must remember that his first task as a telephone therapist is to meet the caller at his level of acceptance and to try and remove any impediment which may keep the person from communicating his problem or difficulty.

At our center we have developed the following procedure for working with this type of caller. If upon answering the telephone with "Suicide and Crisis Service, may I help you?" the therapist receives no response from the caller he is to respond to any of the nonverbal cues which he feels may be used at that time. If there are any sighs or heavy breathing he may say,

---

* This type of caller is also one who may use the ploy after the telephone is answered of saying, "Oh, I'm sorry, I must have the wrong number." It is for this reason that the telephone therapist must not accept at face value a "wrong number." Instead of saying "ok," or "I'm sorry," the telephone therapist must respond with a helpful comment such as "What number were you calling?" or "May I be of assistance to you?" Even though this usually will not engage the person in a conversation at that time, it does indicate to him that the people at the center are real, human, and interested in helping him if he needs help. It will be easier for the caller to place his call and to complete it next time.

"Sometimes it's very hard to begin talking about things that trouble you," or if he feels that the person may have hurt himself or be in pain and is unwilling to verbalize this he may say, "Have you hurt yourself? Is there any way in which I can help you?"

If there's no response and he is convinced, based on the minimal cues he has, that the person is not in any desperate situation, the telephone therapist will repeat, "This is the Suicide Prevention Center, may I help you?" and continue to sound reassuring, interested, and willing to wait until the caller is ready to talk. He may, after a few moments of silence, say "I'll be here willing to talk with you as soon as you're ready." Again after a silent period he may respond with "I would like to talk with you. Maybe together we can work out the problem that's bothering you." After a few moments he may say "It's very hard for me to know what's happening to you and what kinds of things are taking place that make you feel you can't talk to me about your problems. If you like, maybe we can talk about something else for a few minutes." If there is still no response he may, after a period of silence, say "I'll be here to listen and talk with you as soon as you're ready." If a minute or so has gone by without any response on the part of the caller (and assuming that the telephone therapist feels that the individual is in no physical danger), the telephone therapist may say, "I'd like to talk to you but I guess you find it very difficult to talk right now, I'll stay on the line for about another minute. If you want to talk I'll be here to listen to you." Again following a period of silence he may say, "I'd like to talk to you but I'll have to hang up the phone in about another half-a-minute, unless we can begin a conversation. I want you to know that I'm interested in talking with you about any problems that you may have and that there is someone here twenty-four hours a day." After a few moments of silence the telephone therapist will terminate the call with a statement like, "I'm sorry you found it difficult to talk at this time. Sometimes it's hard to talk about problems that one feels very deeply. There is someone here at 854-1966, twenty-four hours a day. If you feel we can be of any help to you, please call us. If you would rather talk to someone in person you can come to the center at 560 Main Street any time between 9 in the morning and 9 at night. I have to hang up the phone now. Thank you for calling. Good-bye." He then hangs up the phone, terminating the call.

For some callers the silent call has the special significance of a ritual. We find that a very small number of callers must go through a process of being rejected by the center before they are willing to engage in a verbal relationship with the telephone therapist. These callers will virtually force the center to go through the above routine, wait for the telephone to be hung up and then immediately call back and begin talking, sometimes to the same telephone therapist. We find that these individuals will, after a period of time, give out a cue during their first call that indicates who they are so that the center can "reject" them by hanging up the telephone. They then immediately call the center again and begin to talk about their problem.

We also have noted that some individuals are unable or unwilling to talk over the telephone about things that disturb them or problems that they have. In some cases we have engaged in a therapeutic relationship with these individuals by asking them to write to us at the center (which is an effective way of removing one's self one more step from the intimacy of the telephone relationship). Other individuals want a closer relationship, in which they can see the therapist, and will accept the invitation to come into the center and be seen on a face-to-face basis. (That a person has accepted the invitation is, of course, only known after the patient has been seen at the center and who in the course of therapy may identify himself as a person who did not just "walk-in" to the center, but one to whom it was suggested to come into the center and talk because he was unwilling to converse over the telephone.)

The silent caller presents the center with a problem and a challenge. By refusing to engage with us on a verbal level, he hits the telephone therapy service at its most vulnerable spot. Expecting anger, rejection, or hurt as a response to this "low blow" he waits for the telephone therapist to hang up on him.

By accepting his feelings and concerns and exploring with him the kind of relationship which is acceptable to him, the center reinforces its role as an accepting therapeutic service.

* * *

THE CALLER WHO REMAINS SILENT: REPORT OF AN UNUSUAL CASE

DAVID LESTER

As noted above, suicide prevention centers and crisis services occasionally receive calls in which the caller remains silent. The aim of this section is to describe an unusual solution to this problem.

It is important to note that counselors frequently classify these kinds of calls as nuisance calls or pranks. To do this runs the danger that people in crisis will not be aided by the service. Brockopp discusses the so-called nuisance call in Chapter 16 and noted that no call to a center should be viewed as a nuisance call. The telephone counselor cannot reliably judge a call to be a prank call. As Brockopp notes, to classify a call as a prank call is to set up an arbitrary standard as to the type of problem or situation with which the counselor will work.

If the counselor stays with the person, speaks sympathetically to him, and encourages him, he may eventually overcome his fear or embarrassment. If the caller hangs up without talking, this may reflect upon the counselor's competence rather than the seriousness of the caller.

If the caller initially remains silent, it may later prove to be difficult for him to begin talking to the counselor, to break the silence. In that case, the counselor has several alternatives. He can stay with the caller and continue to encourage him to talk. He can suggest that the caller hang up and call back at another time. He can suggest that the caller write to the center rather than call. The following case report describes a fourth possibility. In this the counselor suggested to the caller that she answer yes or no by code. A sigh represented yes and silence represented no. In this way he was able to elicit a great deal of information from the caller.*

In order to best illustrate how this call proceeded, some extracts from the call are reproduced below.

(1) ... OK. So here's what I know. I know that you are 15. I know that you're a girl. And I know that Tuesday you broke up with your boyfriend. And you've been thinking about it and felt really bad and depressed and you cried a lot since then. And you haven't talked with anybody about it and you cut yourself. You cut your wrists tonight. And they bled a little. Did you call us before you cut your wrists or after?
Did you call after? Sigh.
Did you call before?—
You called after. OK. So I know that about you. That's when I stopped being able to find out things about you. I know that you haven't talked to your parents about it. I know you haven't talked to your girl friends about it or anybody else. And I know you say you want to talk to me and I know you can talk. But you won't. And I don't know why.
Do you know why?—
You don't know why.

(2) ... Do you want to use words to talk with me? Sigh.
You do.
Have you started to talk to me but never been able to begin? Sigh.

(3) ... Do you feel ... I don't know how you feel when you can't talk with me. I know you feel bad and depressed. You feel like it's the end of the world and you can't live without your boyfriend. I know you feel all that but I don't know what it is that won't let you talk.

(4) ... I'm interested in what you do when you're silent. When I don't say anything and you never say anything. When I don't say anything and you don't sigh and everything's just kinda pretty quiet.
Are you thinking? Sigh.
Are you thinking about talking with me? Sigh.

---

* To those readers who feel that the patient here was playing games I would again point out that it is not really essential for the counselor to decide whether the patient is playing a game. A patient may equally well play games during a verbal conversation with the counselor. To prejudge and accuse a caller of playing games may serve to reject the caller and render therapeutic intervention impossible.

A little bit. Are you thinking about your boyfriend? Sigh.
Are you thinking about yourself? Sigh.
A lot? Sigh.
Are you going to hurt yourself tonight? Sigh.
(5) ... Have you told me the truth tonight? Sigh.
Yes? Sigh.
All of it?—
Was all of it the truth?—
Did you lie to me tonight? Sigh.*

It is clear that the counselor here was able to learn a lot about the patient. Although having to ask questions that could be answered "yes" or "no" restricted him, he was able to discuss feelings, events, and assess the lethality of the caller. He was also able to present himself as a sympathetic and understanding person. In doing so, he increased the likelihood that this patient would call back and make use of the service. It is possible that on subsequent calls, her reluctance to talk was less and that this first contact served to reduce her inhibitions about talking to a counselor.

---

* Further questioning revealed that she had lied about the area of the city in which she lived.

Chapter 16

THE NUISANCE CALLER

Gene W. Brockopp

$\mathbf{O}$NE OF THE CONCERNS of a crisis center is how to respond to the nuisance, prank, fake, or hang-up call.* A nuisance call is usually pragmatically defined as a call about a trivial or inappropriate situation or condition. It implies that certain calls can, on the basis of their substance or length, be defined as noncritical, noncrisis, or nonproblem calls, that there is some standard by which we can designate some calls as being nuisance calls, whereas other calls of a similar nature will be designated as being "real" problem calls. I feel it is questionable whether we can categorize calls into real calls and nuisance calls. To define a call as a nuisance call is to set up an arbitrary standard as to the type of problem or situation which an emergency telephone center will accept. It involves making a judgment and setting criteria which the individual must meet before he makes a call to the center. As such it forces an individual to make a decision about the validity or severity of his problem before he attempts to seek help. I feel it is inappropriate to require this of a caller.

---

* It is questionable whether a center can effectively reduce nuisance calls. For example, the suicide prevention center of White Plains, New York, tried to reduce the number of nuisance calls by placing a news item in the local newspaper: "SNARLING A LIFE LINE the emergency suicide prevention service operated by the Mental Health Association (dial a number for professional counseling) is experiencing a number of crank calls for the first time in its history, a spokesman for the association discloses. In view of the fact that someone really needing help might find that the line is kept busy by some prankster tying up the counseling service's phone, the subject could boil down to technical manslaughter." Although the newspaper ran a subsequent item relating how the volume of nuisance calls had decreased, Elaine Feiden, the coordinator of the Suicide Prevention Service, reports that the articles had little impact on the volume of nuisance calls.

206

To do so will eventually be detrimental to the telephone therapy service. Just as a face-to-face therapist needs some kind of communication before he can work on a problem that his client or patient presents (and these communications may come in a variety of ways, many of them nonverbal), the telephone therapist needs calls before he can begin to work on a problem. Any impediment placed in a person's way, which may keep him from making a call, or any movement to force him to predefine the validity of his call before he makes it would seem to be an unnecessary hurdle for the caller and would place the crisis service in the same category as many other helping agencies, that is, a problem of a client is considered to be a real problem only when the agency defines it as such. For example, some agencies only work with sixteen-year-olds and above, or the child, or marriage problems, or psychotics, or individuals with neurotic disorders. The crisis telephone service in contradistinction to these predefined types of agencies should be a source of help which is open to all individuals, regardless of their age, orientation, background or difficulty. A place where anyone through a telephone contact can have a potential therapeutic relationship with a helping individual.

Most people who have a personal or emotional problem feel uncertain whether or not they should attempt to get help for themselves or whether they should be "strong" and live with the problem, hoping it will work itself out. Stated another way, people in crisis are often unsure about the validity of their seeking help with their problem and whether they will be accepted by a helping individual. The center should not force these individuals into a situation where they have to decide whether or not their problem is severe enough before they can call. This will mean that the center must be open to all types of calls, many of which will appear to be trivial and many of which will appear on the surface to be of a nuisance nature. As a result of this orientation, the center may receive a number of calls that might be better described as being incomplete, that is, calls in which substantial interaction with the helping individual is not allowed to take place because the caller decides not to allow the conversation to develop or to terminate the conversation. This type of orientation is in agreement with the kind of therapeutic relationship which the center attempts to develop with each individual, for it lets the caller define his problem in his own way while the center responds with the assumption of honesty on the part of the caller. In essence, it places all the responsibility on the individual calling, for it does not allow the caller to manipulate the telephone therapist into having him make a decision whether or not the call is real. We have found in our center that even the most obvious type of nuisance call, that of a call from teenagers at a party, often can begin to focus on a problem if handled correctly. We have found that the individual who makes a nuisance or incomplete call to a suicide center may not be completely aware of why he is doing this. He may give the impression of being a nonserious caller and in so doing unconsciously sets himself up to be rejected by the center as he has been by other agencies and organizations. Therefore, it seems to be imperative for the center not to make decisions on which calls are real and which are not. It must accept all calls and allow itself to be manipulated by a caller and accept this as part of the price it has to pay to be available to all individuals.

Another point also appears to be important. Any person who makes a call classified as either a nuisance call or as an incomplete call should be considered to have a problem, even though he may not recognize it at the time. To cut off the person by making a statement such as, "One should only call when one has a problem to talk about," would seem to reinforce his not calling because of the possibility of rejection. Conversely, accepting any call as a call from an individual with a problem, regardless of what takes place or how short the call is, will reinforce the individual that a call to the center will be handled in a direct way with full acceptance of the individual and his problem. Stated another way, the person may not be consciously aware that he has a problem at the time he is making the nuisance call, but he will be left with the attitude that the center does not play games with him, and that it will respond to any call in a direct and honest manner. When the anxiety of the caller increases because of the undefined problem he has, the possibility of his making a call to the center is greatly enhanced.

Based on the foregoing considerations, I would like to make the following conclusions and suggestions:

1. There is no such thing as a nuisance call at a twenty-four-hour telephone emergency service. No call being taken at the center should be designated as such, since to do so is to prejudice the telephone counselor against the caller and to preclude, if not eliminate, the possibility of assistance being given to the caller for it gives the telephone therapist a feeling that she can handle the call in a less serious, less considerate, less concerned manner.

2. Calls coming in to the center should be designated as complete or incomplete calls. Complete calls are those in which the termination of the call is made through the mutual agreement of both parties. Incomplete calls are those in which the termination of the call is determined by one of the parties without consideration for the other individual.

3. The telephone therapist should assume that there is no such thing as a wrong number or a mistake in dialing a number. Every effort should be made to engage the person who places this type of call in a conversation by being helpful and concerned about giving assistance to the individual. Persons who make these calls are often giving the telephone therapist a test to determine whether or not they will be accepted before they reveal that they have actually really placed the call to the Suicide and Crisis Service.*

4. The telephone service must allow itself to be used or manipulated (if necessary) by answering all calls in a straightforward, direct and honest way. After a period of time, it is possible for a telephone therapist to begin to hear the "ring" of an honest call or of a dishonest manipulative call. But to make this type of judgment incorrectly can have negative consequences for the care or treatment of the caller and may result in the telephone therapist losing a real emergency call. We have found that when

---

* See Chapter 14 for a development of this point.

we play a call out, even though we may suspect it may be a crank or a manipulative fake call, the individual will sometimes call back after he hangs up the phone and tell us that he is not in danger, and that he is sorry he has placed the call.

5. Each time a person calls the center and obtains a response which is positive and facilitative, regardless of whether the person calling is calling with a real problem, the center is developing the concept in the community that individuals at the center will not "play games" with people on the telephone, but that they will listen to them honestly and directly and respond to them in this manner.

Rather than being detrimental, the number of incomplete calls the center receives can be looked on as being a positive measure of the interest that a community has in the center and as a measure of the increased number of individuals in the community who know about the center and are calling it to see if it is really there.

Chapter 17

THE "ONE COUNSELOR" CALLER

Gene W. Brockopp

Every telephone emergency service, like any service system which deals with a large number of people and has a large diverse staff, eventually must deal with the problem of the client who wishes to relate with only one person on the staff. Unlike large service agencies, for example, welfare or Medicare, which divide clients among various full-time case workers who maintain contact with the client and assume responsibility for helping them obtain the service they need, suicide prevention centers are usually staffed by volunteers who have limited training and only part-time contact with the agency. The kind of client who wants to relate to only one person usually has insistent needs for "distant intimacy" (such as a telephone might permit), a history of rejections by various social and mental health agencies and some feeling of concern that now he is calling a suicide or crisis service. The reason a client states why he wants to talk to the same person as he spoke to before may be one of the following:

1. This person has helped me before. Most clients will automatically return to those individuals who have helped them previously or those with whom they have developed a sense of trust. Their advice, assistance or thoughtful listening has proven useful in reducing the anxiety of the individual or assisting him to work through the problem which he has had. However, the line between obtaining assistance and developing a dependency relationship is very close. Although I am not opposed to the development of the dependency relationship when it is appropriate or needed by the individual for maintaining himself or his life, I do feel that the person who continues to call a telephone service usually is not in this type of condition but

211

rather is a chronic caller who is usually not too lethal. If the person were seriously self-destructive, it is certainly hoped that there would be encouragement by the telephone therapist for professional intervention on a face-to-face basis rather than on the phone service.

2. This person understands me. Again, although this is an important characteristic of a therapeutic relationship and necessary if any help is to be given to the individual, the implicit assumption is that no one else can understand him or give him the help he needs. This attitude often closes off many other areas of help for the individual and makes a referral to an agency improbable and unlikely to be taken by the person.

3. I won't have to repeat myself or begin at the beginning once again, Although some callers delight in telling their story of grief and trouble to various individuals, most individuals would prefer not to go through the details of the problems with another individual unless this is absolutely necessary or unless they are trying to rationalize their feelings or reinforce the correctness of their actions.

4. I like talking to this person. Requests or demands for the same therapist which fall into this category of reasons usually very strongly imply that the relationship between the counselor and the client is one of conversation and friendship rather than one of therapy. In this kind of relationship, there is little chance of confrontation of the individual with his problem or making a movement toward a solution of these problems.

5. I can't or won't talk to anyone else. In this situation, the caller is setting demands on the service or on the individual, which if granted will overtly and covertly place him in a controlling position—one in which the relationship is much more important than the solving of a problem or the working through of the difficulty. The person who sets up this type of condition generally is not hurting very much and usually has more of a friendship relationship than a therapeutic one with the counselor.

These five reasons or variations of them are commonly used by the caller to request talking to the same individual with whom he has spoken before. I feel that the only ones that are justified are the first and the third. The other three indicate that the client has reduced the therapeutic relationship to one of a conversation, thereby making emergency telephone service into an old-fashioned party-line type of operation.

I feel there are decided disadvantages to allowing this type of relationship to develop from the point of view of the service itself:

1. The counselor may not be there or able to take the call from the client at that particular time. If there is a stated or implied agreement that the counselor is going to take calls from this particular individual, the counselor must be available to the individual at all times or deal with the feelings of rejection that the individual may feel as a result of his lack of availability to the client. In addition, since the person working on the telephone must be available to any individual regardless of his previous relationship with a specific client, to develop a relationship with one client which makes this concept difficult to achieve distorts the purpose of the telephone service.

2. Calls of this type tend to become conversational rather than remain therapeutic partly because of the type of training the telephone therapist has had. In most cases the volunteer telephone therapist is able to deal with crisis calls quite well and to work through crisis situations. However, dealing with individuals on a long-term basis is quite different and requires a different type of competency. This skill is usually not available to the telephone therapist, and so the telephone call from the one person caller generally deteriorates into a conversational one. Although talking may give some support to the individual who is calling the center, the function of the telephone therapist is often then limited to merely listening. In a sense he prostitutes his therapeutic function to becoming a conversationalist. This service may be very useful, but it does not appear to me to be a desirable one for a phone operation.

3. Pressure by the client on the counselor may result in covert rejection. Extending the idea expressed above, since the counselor is usually not able to handle this type of call over a long period of time in an appropriate therapeutic way, what often occurs is an initial sense of importance on being requested by the client to work with him with his problems. As the

telephone call deteriorates into a conversational relationship, a sense of inadequacy often develops on the part of the counselor. In a short time, a sense of frustration and covert wishing to get rid of the problem caller develops because nothing seems to work with him. In either case, whether the person is covertly rejected or maintained at a conversational level because of the inadequacy of the telephone therapist, change is unlikely to occur in the caller and eventually neither the caller nor the counselor find the relationship satisfactory.

4. Calls of this type move toward an "owning" of callers by specific counselors. The feeling of importance that each of us has about ourselves and wishes to maintain and enhance is tapped by the single-person caller. What results is that rather than functioning in a cooperative way, a competition develops between phone workers regarding specific callers and each person, in essence, sets up a private practice within the center.

5. The one-person caller may develop more out of the need of the counselor than the needs of the client. Extending point 4 above, we find that some individuals who work in a telephone answering service do so to fulfill deep needs in themselves for developing close personal relationships with other individuals. They use the one-person caller to achieve these ends. Consequently, a symbiotic type of relationship develops in which each person is fulfilling his own pathological needs and the problem that the client has is unattended.

6. Manipulation by the caller is much easier. With a type of dependency relationship developing between the counselor and the client, which taps some of the needs of the counselor for consistency, importance, and value, the one-person caller (who is usually a past master at using his environment to maintain a level of functioning which is neither healthy nor sick) usually is able to keep his psychological "hooks" into the counselor, controlling and manipulating him to his own ends.

At the same time as there are disadvantages to the center in allowing the one-person caller, I feel that there are important advantages that need to be considered in determining whether a telephone service should allow the one-person caller.

1. Consistency in therapeutic approach is enhanced. Clearly, consistency in working with an individual is enhanced when only one therapist maintains the counseling relationship. Each person in the dyad develops some sense of the style of the other individual and is able to work within that style, although as pointed out above, the handling of the call may not be appropriate. It is, however, consistent, and this is an important value to consider with certain types of callers.

2. Calls from the chronic caller can be limited, focused, and evaluated. The chronic caller poses a number of severe problems for the telephone emergency service. Since their life style is usually self-destructive from a long-range perspective, it is critical that an evaluation be made of each call to find out where the individual is at that particular time so that an appropriate response without manipulation can be made. If one person handles the calls from a chronic caller, this can be achieved.

3. The one-person caller gives the counselor a sense of continuity. Probably one of the most difficult aspects of working at a telephone emergency service is the sense of discontinuity in working with people. Each time the phone rings, a crisis is occurring in someone's life, and the individual who answers the phone must be able to respond to that crisis without, in many cases, knowing the disposition of the previous problem to which he has responded. We have found that the professional staff members in a suicide and crisis service need a few long-term patients to maintain a balance for themselves, to see outcomes and maintain a perspective on the work they are doing with crisis clients. The same may be true of the person who works on the telephone service.

4. The patient does not need to repeat himself. I emphasized this point previously and would merely like to add here that the need for an adequate record system is evident if the calls are to be handled properly.

5. The patient has an increased sense of belonging and value. Through the one-person contact, the patient takes on an identity as a person rather than losing his identity and becoming a number or a file folder in the center. Since the individuals

who call a telephone service are often on the peripheral edges of society, the sense of belongingness may be most important to them and may give them a base from which they can move into more involved areas of social life.

6. With the one-person caller, both the level and the extent of the communication may be enhanced if the telephone therapist is adequately trained to respond to this type of caller. For example, the insecure individual who may trust only one person or be able to relate to only one individual may, through this relationship, develop sufficient trust to move out into the community. Also, the problem which the individual has (which may be embarrassing to him because of its severity or because of the areas of concern) may be more easily brought out as the depth of relationship with one person increases and positive transference develops.

Reviewing the advantages and disadvantages of this problem within the context of an emergency telephone service, I feel that the following guidelines are appropriate in working with this type of caller.

1. The one-person caller should not be encouraged. The emphasis should be placed upon calling the agency for assistance rather than calling an individual person. I feel that an analogous situation would be for an individual who is being robbed to call the police station and request to talk to a specific policeman or call a fire department and request that a certain fireman come to put out his fire. If a telephone service is to maintain its integrity as an emergency service, it must be responsive as a unit to individuals in crisis. At the same time, I recognize the importance and value of the conversational-friend relationship that each individual appears to need. This, however, is not the area of responsibility of a crisis phone service. Rather than providing this service to an individual, the service should help him develop it within his circle of friends or community. By focusing the individual on his home environment for conversation and friend relationships, we are decreasing the possibility that a dependent relationship will develop and with it a distortion of the emergency telephone service.

2. If a person calls requesting a particular counselor, everything should be done by the counselor who takes the call to develop a relationship with this individual rather than giving in to his wish to talk to a specific person.

3. During each telephone call, the counselor should make references to the agency and to calling the agency for assistance rather than calling a specific person at the agency. In addition, at the end of the telephone call, a statement should be made to the caller regarding the fact that if he wishes, he can again call the agency, not the person, for assistance and that there are a number of individuals at the service who are able to take his call and to work with him in any crisis problem he may have. In addition, the telephone therapist should not fall into the trap of giving out personal information about himself to the caller, for this will enhance the conversational aspect of the call. To do so gives the caller de facto permission to develop a friend relationship with the counselor.

4. The process of selecting counselors to work at a telephone service should include looking at the insistent needs of the counselors who are applying for this position. An attempt should be made to obtain individuals who are secure themselves and who do not need dependent relationships with other individuals to maintain their integrity, value or importance.

5. During the call the interaction with the client must be continually focused on the problem that he is having and in assisting him in working toward a solution or amelioration of the condition. The telephone therapist must be alert to the test that the caller will give him to determine whether or not he (the caller) can move the telephone relationship into a conversational area. If the telephone therapist is alert, and is secure in himself, he will move toward terminating the call when the individual goes beyond the problem and into a conversation relationship.

6. Each counselor must be constantly on guard so that personal information such as the names, addresses or phone numbers of individual counselors working at the center are not given out to people who call the center. In addition, in no case should the time when any specific counselor is working at the

center be given out to a caller, either by the counselor himself or by other counselors who work at the center.

7. Finally, recognizing that there may be times when a one-person relationship is desirable for a caller, I feel that before a counselor is allowed to develop this type of relationship with a client, the decision as to its value and need should be made at a consultant or clinical director level. It appears to me that this should only be done when the caller requires the consistency in working with a specific person or when the tenuousness of the relationship requires contact with one individual. When it is decided that this approach is to be used, a careful study should first be made of the individual who is calling, his specific needs and the type of person who would be most appropriate for handling this type of caller. Then a clinical plan for obtaining the appropriate therapeutic relationship should be developed with the selected counselor to insure that it will be carried out. The rest of the telephone counselors should then be apprised of the treatment plan. It should be emphasized that this procedure should be the exception and not the rule. Only a few callers require this type of approach.

In summary, it does not appear to me to be appropriate that a crisis phone service should allow its emergency responding ability to degenerate to a mere conversational, supportive relationship. By permitting this type of relationship to develop, the phone service is reducing the effectiveness of its function and in many cases enhancing the pathology of the individual who is calling or feeding the psychological needs of the counselor working on the telephone.

PART IV
THE TELEPHONE COUNSELOR

INTRODUCTION

This section is concerned with the individuals who work as counselors in telephone counseling services. There have been two main disagreements here. The first has been whether telephone counseling services should use professionals or nonprofessionals as counselors. Several centers have restricted their counselors to professionals and endeavor to hire full-time counselors who are paid to be counselors. Other centers have used volunteer nonprofessional counselors. The latter course has become popular partly because there is often a scarcity of professionals in a community who are willing to work at the agency, and partly because most centers are poorly funded and must rely on volunteers to operate the service.

Although pragmatic reasons may have prompted centers to diverge on this issue, there are now empirical and theoretical arguments being advanced to argue for the use of the professional as opposed to the nonprofessional and vice versa. The following two chapters present the arguments for both cases.

A second issue involved with selecting the type of counselor has centered around whether in order to treat a particular kind of problem, the counselor has to have or have had that problem. Occasionally, a suicide prevention center has opened with the thesis that for adequate counseling the staff must be or have been suicidal. Increasingly, ex-drug-addicts are used as counselors for current addicts. Alcoholics Anonymous and Recovery (oriented to the neurotically ill individual) espouse this principle.

If a moderate position is adopted, then there can be no argument here. Clearly, adequately trained and supervised ex-addicts can serve, for example, as useful co-counselors for treating current addicts. However, when an extreme position is adopted, then the arguments are less tenable. Some teen hotlines operate on the assumption that only teenagers can counsel other teenagers. Other teen hotlines operate on the assumption that with adequate selection and training, people of all ages can counsel teenagers. The latter position is in agreement with that of the editors. The arguments for and against this position are not presented here because of the difficulty in obtaining a reasoned chapter arguing for the use of "like to treat like." Since this may reflect our bias, we felt the need to raise the issue at least in this introduction.

The remaining two chapters in this section deal with less controversial issues; the selection and the training of telephone counselors.

Chapter 18

ASCENDING TO "LOWER" LEVELS: THE CASE FOR NONPROFESSIONAL CRISIS WORKERS

RICHARD K. McGEE AND BRUCE JENNINGS

At THE BEGINNING of the 1970s there could be no mistaking the full force of the nonprofessional revolution in the helping services. Extensive reviews of the role for new, lesser trained manpower in nearly all areas of health, educational, social, and humanitarian enterprises have been provided by both scientific researchers and casual observers (Ewalt, 1967; Grosser, Henry, and Kelley, 1969; Guerney, 1969; Reiff and Riessman, 1965; Sobey, 1970). Nowhere has the role of the nonprofessional been more in evidence nor more fully utilized than in the growing field of suicide prevention and crisis intervention services (Heilig, Farberow, Litman and Shneidman, 1968). Anyone who reflects upon the development of suicide and crisis services during the 1960s may arrive at his own personal opinion as to the most important factor which permitted or stimulated this social service phenomena. However, in the opinion of many, the present writers included, it was the repeated success of the nonprofessional volunteer in the Los Angeles Suicide Prevention Center which made possible the development of a new form for delivering helping services to persons suffering an acute personal crisis. It was the eminent Louis Dublin (1969) who made the point with his usual dramatic eloquence at the First Annual Conference of the American Association of Suicidology: "The lay volunteer was probably the most important single discovery in the fifty-year history of suicide prevention. Little progress was made until he came into the picture."

223

So enthusiastic has been the acceptance of the nonprofessional in some quarters of the crisis intervention service movement that there has been a tendency to conclude that the nonprofessional is clearly and unequivocally superior to the professional person from any discipline for this particular role. Such a position should not be espoused without careful study and evaluation of many issues, both theoretical and practical, together with an objective analysis of empirical data. At least two positions may be taken on the continuum of attitudes toward the volunteer. At one extreme is the position just mentioned, that the nonprofessional is basically superior in the delivery of crisis services to the professional. Another position is that the professional is clearly the superior person, but that due to the shortage of professional manpower and the great demand for services, our society will have to accommodate by accepting inferior services where the alternative may be no service at all. Such a position holds that if there are sufficient professional personnel, they should perform the functions, but in their absence, the nonprofessional may be used as an aide to assist the professional care-giver.

The purpose of this chapter is to examine these issues and some recently accumulated data and offer a rational base upon which to draw an informed conclusion in favor of the nonprofessional as the most appropriate crisis intervention worker. The arguments come from various sources: dogma, precedent, practical considerations, and laboratory research.

DOGMA

Students who have attended one of the semi-annual training institutes at the Los Angeles Suicide Prevention Center (Heilig, 1970) have become familiar with an oft-quoted principle known as "Litman's Law." Briefly stated, this law holds that

The more severe and acute the suicidal crisis is, the LESS one needs to be professionally trained to manage it effectively.

This principle is not merely idle talk, articulated for its "shock value," although it does produce an element of surprise in the neophyte upon first encounter. Rather, Litman's Law is the result of serious reflection upon the observations and experiences of the staff at the Los Angeles center, both in their own work with acutely suicidal people and in their supervision of non-professional volunteers performing the same clinical functions. Litman and his colleagues have found that whereas both professional clinicians and the lay volunteers can manage acute crises effectively, the skills, training, theory, and other characteristics which distinguish the professional from the layman are simply unnecessary for the task. What matters most, especially in the more acute cases, are those traits of human concern for people, good judgment, and determination to intervene which cut across disciplines or professional-nonprofessional categories.

Farberow (1966) leans more toward the nonprofessional in his evaluation of the first year's experiences with the Los Angeles volunteers. He says,

> We found that they were often able to offer a relationship to the patient which was on a more direct and a more friendly level than that of the professionals. There seems at times . . . a sense of professional detachment which is developed by professionals. This, we find, often gets in the way. The volunteers did not have this kind of barrier. (p. 12)

Caplan (1961) has described this barrier as the "professional armour" developed during and as a result of professional training. It serves to protect the clinician from the vulnerability which arises when his own personal identification with the problems of the patient interferes with the professional work of being a therapist. Caplan further sees this professional distance as a distinguishing feature of the professional. "An essential difference between an amateur and a professional is that the professional has this distance, and deals objectively rather than subjectively with the problems of his clients" (p. 24).

Farberow is not alone in the belief that the professional persona or armour is a disadvantage in crisis intervention work. Edwards (1970) described the result of using full-time, paid non-professional counselors in the Fulton-DeKalb County (Georgia) Emergency Mental Health Service. Many of these counselors had been on the job for twelve to fifteen months and had logged over 2,000 calls. He reported that they had lost their original anxiety over taking emergency calls from suicidal people, and consequently, in his opinion from monitoring their work, they had lost their effectiveness as crisis counselors. According to Edwards, "They have begun to sound just like a psychiatrist on the telephone." Edwards further declared that the nonprofessional counselors are "the real professionals" in the crisis intervention field. As a psychiatrist charged with the awesome responsibility of establishing and directing a suicide and crisis intervention program to serve the entire metropolitan Atlanta area, Edwards is in a position to make valid judgments in such matters.

Caplan (1964) has described the theory and technique for crisis intervention therapy, and he shows why professional level expertise is unnecessary. He argues that the crisis is a present, real-life drama in which the patient is struggling with stresses in the here-and-now environment. It is not necessary nor appropriate to handle such cases by delving into the deeper layers of the unconscious or by probing the childhood and other earlier experiences for symbolic or latent meanings. Primary process data are irrelevant. Hence, much of the area in which a professional clinician is accustomed to working and the avenues to understanding problems wherein he is most comfortable are not the ones which offer him or the patient the best chance for healthy resolution of the crisis. In a sense, the professional clinician is disarmed and forced to take on a role which does not utilize his years of training and skill. He is forced to take on the role which the nonprofessional is already best equipped to play. The latter, by definition, lacks the skills and knowledge and the habitual tendency to be led into a deep interpretative inquiry of the psychodynamic etiology of the patient's problem.

To completely understand this position, it is only necessary to escape from the cognitive trap which places personal crises, sometimes called "problems of living," in the category of psychopathological disorders. Whereas a neurosis or a schizophrenia may require the application of a given type of treatment program, a personal crisis is another type of human ailment and correspondingly requires a different type of amelioration. Elsewhere, Caplan has warned that the symptoms of a crisis, namely, increased anxiety, signs of depression, agitation, confusion, may mimic the symptoms of mental illness, but they are not the same and should not be confused with them.

To summarize, the opinions and attitudes of some of the outstanding authorities in the field of suicide prevention and crisis interventon have assigned to the nonprofessional an unequaled value in this form of helping service. It must be recognized that this position takes nothing away from the experienced professional clinician. In fact, it recognizes him even more for his special skills which other lesser trained personnel cannot perform; it recognizes that the society needs such skills in quantities which far exceed the supply. The position merely states that there are some problems which people face which can be handled better by nonprofessional personnel because of the nature of the problem, and its consequent form of treatment, and because of the nature of the helper. Acute suicidal cases and personal crises require not the expertise of a diagnostician and therapist but the availability of immediate warmth, personal involvement, firm direction, and gentle but forceful action. Such behaviors are not generally in the clinical repertoire of a professional person when he is acting out his professional role. This is not to say that professionally trained persons cannot be as warm, sensitive, involved as the nonprofessional. It is the professional role which inserts the armour or distance between the helper and the client. The dogma resulting from these attitudes of prominent leaders of suicidology—all of them professional persons—holds the nonprofessional volunteer is free of these barriers and is therefore best equipped to use his lesser training in more effective intervention as a crisis worker.

PRECEDENT

One of the arguments which speaks most heavily for the nonprofessional person is that he has emerged in so many centers around the country as the only person willing to take on the task.

Resnik (1964) argues that the professional practitioners and societies failed to pick up the challenge when it was presented, and therefore the nonprofessional moved in to fill a vacuum which was created by an expanding need and a professional resistance to meeting it. Even the very early programs used nonmental health personnel. The National Save-A-Life League in New York began in 1906 with the support of the clergy. While they were certainly professional persons, these ministers pioneered a new form of finding cases and serving people in suicidal states. To be sure, they had the cooperation of local psychiatric practitioners when needed. While some may argue about how often such support is needed, the fact remains the league began a new form of service. Dublin (1963) reports that some churches in Chicago began operating telephone lines for suicidal people. Not much is known about these programs, and one can assume that due to changes in leadership, the impetus behind the program was lost. However, in 1959, the FRIENDS, Inc., in Miami developed the first program which was clearly based upon the power of the involved nonprofessional in a helping relationship. Resnik (1964, 1968) has described the FRIENDS program in detail.

Almost simultaneously with the development of FRIENDS, Chad Varah began writing of his success with the Samaritans in England. That program has spread throughout the United Kingdom, due primarily to the validity of the nonprofessional extending a befriending relationship to whomever is in need (Varah, 1965).

In the mid-1960s, when the suicide prevention center movement was first getting started, one concentration of activity could be found in Florida and the Southeast. The establishment of WE CARE, Inc., in Orlando, Florida, in 1965 marked the beginning of a type of crisis service designed to become a part of local community mental health services (McGee and McGee, 1968). Soon after WE CARE was started, other programs were initiated on the same model. The Brevard County Suicide Prevention Center was the second example (McGee, 1968) and the Lifeline program in Miami followed. By 1970 there were suicide prevention services in nineteen cities of six states in the Southeast. All but two of these programs use the nonprofessional person as the primary crisis worker.

Two surveys have been taken of the centers around the country (McGee, 1967). Questionnaires were mailed to all known centers operating in November of 1967 and in March of 1969. Returns from both of these surveys revealed that over 80 percent of all suicide and crisis intervention programs utilize the nonprofessional in some direct service capacity with people who call in on the publicized telephone number.

Consequently, the history of the suicide prevention center movement shows that the volunteer is a most significant factor in permitting such programs to be developed. Had the volunteer nonprofessional been found unacceptable, unable to meet the challenge, the programs could not have survived and multiplied as they have. Some communities such as Halifax County, North Carolina, which had no local professional manpower in the mental health field, were nevertheless able to begin and maintain a viable crisis intervention service because of the availability of the nonprofessional (Altrocchi and Batton, 1968; Altrocchi and Gutman, 1968). It is especially noteworthy that the Suicide Prevention Center in Knoxville, Tennessee, began its service utilizing the professional members of the local mental health clinic staff. After little more than a year of operation they began recruiting some nonprofessional personnel to take over. The professionals who began and operated the service came to realize that their services could be better used as consultants, and they went looking for the nonprofessional to assume their role. One can hardly conclude that these professionals deliberately elected to begin providing an inferior service to their community. Rather, the conclusion is obvious that they recognized that the nonprofessional could do the job as well, if not better than they. However, if the nonprofessional can do the job *as well as* the professional, but does it on a volunteer basis rather than for extensive fees or salaries, that does seem to be doing it *better* for most communities. The precedent established by the early centers and continued throughout the massive spread of new centers across the nation clearly implies the advantage of the nonprofessional.

PRACTICAL CONSIDERATIONS

Of course, an immediate association with the practical advantage of the nonprofessional volunteer is that he eliminates the costs of salaried professionals. While this is certainly true to some extent, it is neither completely accurate that the volunteer is cost-free to a program, nor is this economic argument the most important of the practical considerations. In the first place, the volunteer must have some professional guidance in the form of clinical case consultation or administrative management. The programs using the volunteer exclusively have found that they must employ a person just to coordinate the activities of the nonprofessional staff. Volunteers are by no means a free or even inexpensive way to operate a crisis intervention program. The distinct advantage in communities where there are professional personnel already working in clinics and other settings is that the professional is freed to utilize his time for consultation activities, program development activities, and other professional tasks which are becoming recognized as more appropriate for the professional practitioner than one-to-one patient care. This was the original rationale for the use of nonprofessionals in the Los Angeles Suicide Prevention Center (Heilig, Farberow, and Litman, 1968), and it is still a major advantage of the system.

In addition, there are more potential volunteers available in every community than there are professional personnel. Between ten and ninety persons must be available to be scheduled for duty shifts each week in twenty-four-hour crisis intervention services. The actual number needed depends upon the length of shift per day and the number of shifts covered by each person per week. In the Suicide and Crisis Intervention Service in Gainesville, Florida, the schedule requires the filling of sixty-nine time periods each week. It is a difficult task even with nonprofessional workers who volunteer their time for community service; it would be impossible if professional personnel were required.

Some efforts have been made to add crisis intervention duties to the workload of professional personnel who are already on duty in other roles. Such attempts have been made using nurses and aides in hospital emergency rooms, nurses or residents on psychiatric units of inpatient settings, and the professional staff of outpatient mental health clinics. Typically, such efforts have been unsatisfactory, and the practice has been to bring in the nonprofessional volunteer to handle the crisis intervention and suicide prevention functions.

A third practical consideration relates to the fact that professional personnel are rarely adequately trained for the crisis intervention function. Each psychologist who has successfully dealt with a suicidal depressed patient in psychotherapy, or every psychiatrist who has capably managed antidepressant medication to control a personal crisis is not, thereby, automatically an authority in suicidology. There are very few university graduate or medical schools in the nation which have established even one course in crisis intervention or suicidology. The social work profession has been the group most identified with the practice of crisis therapy, but psychology and psychiatry have tended to overlook such training, either in didactic or in experiential form. Naturally, both psychiatric residents and psychology interns have been trained in psychotherapy with depressed and sometimes suicidal patients, but these patients come from a far different population than the typical individual who calls on the suicide or crisis telephone line. Very recent developments in the Center for Studies of Suicide Prevention at N.I.M.H. have been in the direction of establishing a national curriculum in suicidology (Resnik, 1971), but the consequences of awakening academic institutions to the need for, as well as the availability of, such educational material for professional trainees are not yet apparent in even the current students, much less the already graduated practitioners.

Finally, a further practical consideration of using nonprofessionals relates to the healthy skepticism which still prevails concerning them. Such skepticism is felt not only by the professionals who look askance at their competence, but also by the community at large which generally responds with stereotyped concepts about personal misery. The nonprofessional, being a part of the general public, feels and shares this skepticism about his own ability to handle acute personal crises. All of these attitudes contribute to a readiness for thorough screening and continuous evaluation of on-the-job performance. It is true that not all suicide and crisis centers perform as extensive or as elaborate performance evaluations as are desirable, but the fault here lies in the lack of suitable performance criteria and measurement methods (McGee, 1971). Nearly every center performs some type of routine screening, even perfunctorily; some have instituted very elaborate screening programs. On the other hand, it is rare to find such careful screening of professional people in community mental health agencies. Until the most recent times, when academic programs have begun to produce more professioanl people than the available public money permits to be employed on limited budgets, the mental health professional was in complete control of his marketplace. Only the curriculum vita was important, and that was most often a formality used to exclude the most inadequately trained. The vita only reveals experience, with no comment on competence. The general rule was that a clinic in need of a psychiatrist or a hospital in need of a psychologist would take the first one who was willing to work for the low salary they had to offer. Further, who has ever heard of on-the-job quality control of professional competence? Unless a person is so noxious and inept in his personal style that even the secretaries can detect his danger to patients, there is no formal system whereby the professional clinician must account to his superiors for what he does during the fifty-minute patient hour. Of course, there are the state licensing boards and the national specialty boards which certify competence—one time. Who is to say how well some competencies are preserved fifteen or thirty years later? All professionals resent being supervised by or responsible to members of other disciplines, and in the interests of harmony, such procedures are not found in the typical community mental health agency.

This is not the case in the suicide prevention or crisis intervention center which utilizes the nonprofessional workers. These people are tenacious in their demands for supervision and feedback from consultants or staff supervisors. It has been observed in several centers that the lack of satisfactory amounts of evaluation and in-service training will result in a marked diminution of volunteer morale and enthusiasm for the task; they will drop out if they are not given the kind of continuous overseeing from more experienced personnel which permits appropriate levels of anxiety to be maintained. Rarely does a system develop with a built-in quality control phenomena such as is found in the use of nonprofessionals in the helping services. It is a distinct practical advantage over the use of the professional worker who ordinarily eschews supervision and evaluation of his clinical work as soon as he leaves the training role.

The practical considerations which point to the advantage of the nonprofessional over the professional are more than economic. It is true that the volunteer costs less, but it is not possible to dispense with professional manpower altogether. They are necessary for consultation and/or administrative management of the programs which use the nonprofessional. The other advantages of the volunteers are that they are more readily available than professionals in the quantity which is demanded by the typical weekly schedule in suicide and crisis programs. Further, they can easily be provided with the specific training for their role, which is a form of training the typical professional practitioner, especially in psychology and psychiatry, does not have from his own academic preparation. Finally, the nonprofessional brings with him a built-in need and desire for continuous performance evaluation to which professional personnel will neither submit nor subject one another.

EMPIRICAL DATA

With the generally recognized manpower shortage in all areas of mental health care, a number of investigators began experimenting with the use of lay persons in a wide variety of patient relationships. Knickerbocker and McGee (see Chap. 24) and Knickerbocker and Fowler (1971) have reviewed the literature on the measurement of therapist behavior which facilitates effective outcomes in therapy. There is now extensive evidence that lay persons can offer moderately high levels of warmth, empathy, and genuineness in several patient populations, including hospitalized and outpatient neuropsychiatric patients, normals, juvenile delinquents, and children (Carkhuff, 1968). Truax and Carkhuff (1967) have shown that of these three therapist-offered conditions, warmth is the most potent factor as a predictor of successful outcome.

Inasmuch as these dimensions had not been previously observed systematically with volunteers in the role of crisis intervention telephone workers, Knickerbocker and McGee (Chap. 24) compared their performance with that of professional persons working in the same center, under the same work conditions. All subjects, whether professional or nonprofessional, had received the same basic training course before becoming workers in the center. Their ratings were made blindly by groups of raters who had no knowledge about the purposes of the investigation or the professional status of the worker being rated. Ratings of empathy, genuineness, and warmth were made using the Truax method (Truax and Carkhuff, 1967) and the method developed by Lister (1970).

The results revealed clearly that in all three dimensions, the nonprofessionals were as high in their scores as the professionals. There were no significant differences between the two groups in amount of empathy or genuineness as measured by the Lister ratings or in the amount of genuineness as measured by the Truax method. However, on both rating methods, the lay volunteers were significantly superior to the professionals in amount of warmth they offered to callers.

Such data offer an unequivocal verification of the impression which Farberow (1966) reported when he said the volunteers offered "a relationship which was on a more direct and a more friendly level than that of the professionals." It is important to note that it is in the dimension which counts the most towards successful outcome of the helping relationship that the nonprofessional is most clearly superior, under the conditions observed in this study.

SUMMARY AND CONCLUSIONS

There was a time when the volunteer nonprofessional was valued because he was more plentiful than the professional. If he were given some supervision and careful training, it was felt that he would probably do little harm, and he might do some good in helping relationships. It was a time of consciously altering the strategy of mental health service delivery. The original strategy had been to train as many highly competent professional people as possible to staff the mental health services which began developing in more affluent communities in the 1940s to facilitate rehabilitation of GIs and their families following World War II. The goal was to *minimize the number of losses* due to inadequately trained personnel. In recent years, the strategy has required modification because of the great number of people needing many more kinds of help than the former model can provide. The goal has become to *maximize the number of wins.* So the volunteer nonprofessional was seen as a person who could possibly add a few more wins than losses to the accounting of services delivered.

Almost immediately the nonprofessional began to attract the attention of some of the professional community with the fact that he has something unique to offer in a situation which may be especially suited to his own talent. Rather than be a substitute for unavailable professionals, the nonprofessional became recognized as necessary and valuable *in his own right.* In some fields more than others, the nonprofessional is considered even more advantageous than the professional whom he replaces. Suicide prevention and crisis intervention is such an area of activity. The evidence is overwhelming. There are practical advantages, there is a substantial theory or impressionistic opinion resulting in a dogma, and there are empirical research results which demonstrate that the nonprofessional is superior to the professional in these functions. With such evidence in the field of suicidology, the movement to lower levels of training is the only rational response which the profession can make in its ascent to higher levels of service. In this case, ascending to lower levels is a paradox with which we can live comfortably.

REFERENCES

Altrocchi, J. and Batton, L.: Suicide prevention in an underpopulated area. Paper read at American Association of Suicidology, Chicago, March 1968.

Altrocchi, J. and Gutman, V.: Suicide prevention in an underpopulated area. Paper read at Southeastern Psychological Association, Roanoke, April 1968.

Caplan, G.: *An Approach to Community Mental Health.* New York, Grune & Stratton, 1961.

Caplan, G.: *Principes of Preventative Psychiatry.* New York, Basic Books, 1964.

Carkhuff, R. R.: Differential functioning of lay and professional helpers. *J. Couns Psychol., 15:*117-126, 1968.

Dublin, L. I.: *Suicide: A Sociological and Statistical Study.* New York, Ronald Press, 1963.

Dublin, L. I.: Suicide prevention. In E. S. Shneidman (Ed.): *On the Nature of Suicide.* San Francisco, Jossey-Bass, 1969.

Edwards, C. H.: The identification, training and utilization of paraprofessional key personnel in the delivery of crisis intervention services in non-metropolitan areas. Paper read at Mid-South Conference on Crisis Intervention and Suicide Prevention, Athens, Ga., January 1970.

Ewalt, P. L. (Ed.): *Mental Health Volunteers.* Springfield, Thomas, 1967.

Farberow, N. L.: The selection and training of nonprofessional personnel for therapeutic roles in suicide prevention. Paper read at Southeastern Psychological Association, New Orleans, April 1966.

Grosser, C.; Henry, W. E., and Kelly, J. G.: *Nonprofessionals in the Human Services.* San Francisco, Jossey-Bass, 1969.

Guerney, B. G. (Ed.): *Psychotherapeutic Agents: New Roles for Nonprofessionals, Parents, and Teachers.* New York, Holt, Rinehart & Winston, 1969.

Heilig, S. M.: Training in suicide prevention. *Bull. Suicidol.* No. 6, pp. 41-44, Spring 1970.

Heilig, S. M.; Farberow, N. L.; Litman, R. E., and Shneidman, E. S.: The role of nonprofessional volunteers in a suicide prevention center. *Community Ment. Health J., 4:*287-295, 1968.

Knickerbocker, D. A. and Fowler, D. E.: A system for evaluating the performance of crisis workers: Paper presented at American Assoc. of Suicidology, Washington, March 1971.

Lister, J. L.: A scale for the measurement of accurate empathy, facilitative warmth, and facilitative genuineness. (mimeo) University of Florida, 1970.

McGee, R. K.: A community approach to crisis intervention. In R. K. McGee (Ed.): *Planning Emergency Services for Comprehensive Community Mental Health Centers.* (mimeo) Gainesville, University of Florida, 1967.

McGee, R. K.: Community mental health concepts as demonstrated by suicide prevention programs in Florida. *Community Ment. Health J.,* 4:144-152, 1968.

McGee, R. K. (Chm.): Assessing the performance of suicide prevention center programs and personnel. Symposium presented at the meeting of the American Association of Suicidology, Washington, March 1971.

McGee, R. K. and McGee, J. P.: A total community response to the cry for help: We Care, Inc., of Orlando, Florida. In H. L. P. Resnik (Ed.): *Suicidal Behaviors: Diagnosis and Management.* Boston, Little, Brown, 1968.

Reiff, R. and Riessman, F.: The indigenous nonprofessional. *Community Ment. Health J. Monograph,* No. 1, 1965.

Resnik, H. L. P.: A community anti-suicidal organization. *Current Psychiatric Therapies, Volume IV.* New York, Grune & Stratton, 1964.

Resnik, H. L. P.: A community antisuicide organization: The friends of Dade County, Florida. In H. L. P. Resnik (Ed.): *Suicidal Behaviors: Diagnosis and Management.* Boston, Little, Brown, 1968.

Resnik, H. L. P.: Critical issues in suicide prevention. Paper read at American Association of Suicidology, Washington, March 1971.

Sobey, F.: *The Nonprofessioanl Revolution in Mental Health.* New York, Columbia University Press, 1970.

Truax, C. B. and Carkhuff, R. R.: *Toward Effective Counseling and Psychotherapy: Training and Practice.* Chicago, Aldine, 1967.

Varah, C.: *The Samaritans.* New York, Macmillan, 1965.

Chapter 19

THE USE OF THE PROFESSIONAL IN TELEPHONE COUNSELING

ANN S. McCOLSKEY

IN CONSIDERING CRISIS intervention models, one is met with a bewildering variety of examples, serving a variety of purposes and value systems under that broad rubric. If, however, the various models are arrayed along two dimensions, a professional-lay dimension and a volunteer-compensated dimension, some order is introduced into the universe and rational comparisons can more readily be made. These distinctions are not always clearly rendered; for example, "volunteer" is sometimes loosely contrasted with "professional," in discussion of crisis intervention models, as if these were antonyms. It should be clearly kept in mind that they are not and that two orthogonal, unrelated dimensions are involved. Volunteers may be professionals, subprofessionals, preprofessionals, and para-professionals—every variant of trained worker—as well as lay helpers, in crisis intervention programs.

The professional-lay dimension is of course the primary dimension, insofar as the character of a particular crisis intervention program is concerned; the volunteer-compensated dimension is a secondary, utilitarian dimension. There are other secondary descriptive continua that can be introduced, in schematizing crisis intervention programs. There is a continuum of breadth or comprehensiveness of services, for example, ranging from narrowly conceived, brief, superficial intervention in suicidal crises (limited to rescue efforts and/or referrals to other agencies) or stopgap drug therapy at one end of the continuum to continued psychotherapeutic care and comprehensive, social-environmental management at the other end. There is also a continuum of directness-indirectness (of interventive efforts), ranging from direct, face-to-face encounters to indirect phone contacts. If crisis intervention models, extant and theoretical, are arrayed along the primary professional-lay dimension and categorized as broadly professional or nonprofessional in character, the other three dimensions can be utilized to pinpoint secondary differentiating characteristics of programs to facilitate comparative analysis.

NONPROFESSIONAL CRISIS INTERVENTION PROGRAMS

Considering first the broad category of nonprofessional crisis intervention programs, it may be stated that, from a theoretical point-of-view, the concept of a program of this type represents a contradiction in terms—that there is no logical justification for an emergency service manned by unskilled workers. Logically, if professional training in one of the mental health disciplines is considered a requisite for management of psychological problems of any degree of severity, then adjustmental crises or acute problems demand the utmost, not the least, in expertise. Conceptually, the notion of using untrained persons to intercept crisis reactions is as illogical and hazardous as attempting to stem a massive hemorrhage with a Band-aid.®

Suicide Prevention Programs

The argument has been advanced, nevertheless, that in a specific type of adjustmental crisis, a suicidal crisis, untrained persons can be taught specific responses and/or that naive caring is enough (McGee, 1966a). As a result, suicide prevention programs, soliciting suicidal calls and deploying benevolent lay people to intercept them by phone have sprung up with accelerating frequency over the past decade and a half, inspired chiefly by the establishment of the Los Angeles Suicide Prevention Center in 1958. This pioneer center was founded by the N.I.M.H. as a support facility for the ground-breaking research efforts of Farberow and Shneidman in the previously tabooed area of suicidal behavior. Subsequently, the L.A.S.P.C. staff cautiously began to experiment with the use of volunteer nonprofessionals with their suicide prevention program (Shneidman *et al.*, 1970) to relieve the staff of some of their burgeoning clinical responsibilities and facilitate research, and this feature of the program caught the public fancy. A grass-roots suicide prevention movement, in effect, resulted, sweeping the country with near-evangelical fervor and little rational restraint. It unfortunately has not been clearly recognized that the popular variant of the L.A.S.P.C. suicide prevention model bears little resemblance to the original—that the nonprofessional volunteers at the L.A.S.P.C. execute a restricted function (answering phone calls during the day) under the watchful eye and direct supervision of the professional staff, and also that there is a little-touted cadre of preprofessional graduate students who handle all the night calls, so that the total L.A.S.P.C. operation is a complexly organized, highly professional, research-oriented suicide prevention program which has little in common with the popular, free-standing, lay-operated answering service bearing the same generic name.

The contagion of the popular suicide prevention movement, even if transitory, demands careful, critical study of the phenomenon. It may be noted, first, that a recent survey (McGee, 1968) of forty programs across the country (about a 75% sample) reveals that only 31 percent are now operating with a wholly nonprofessional staff and that over two-thirds of the programs have become in part or entirely professional in composition, providing empirical evidence that the basic concept of a non-professional emergency service is not viable. Concomitantly, another more detailed appraisal of a smaller sample of suicide prevention programs (Whittemore, 1970) reveals the same trend toward professionalization and a related change in the direction of broadening of the original suicide prevention base to embrace crisis intervention. Most of these programs have expanded their titles to include crisis intervention or have given up the narrower suicide prevention appellation entirely. At the same time, utilization statistics demonstrate that less than 10 percent of the calls to these ostensible suicide prevention centers involve suicidal attempts, and only one-fourth involve either attempts or threats. (Nearly 40% of the tiny fraction of calls representing actual attempts, furthermore, are placed by third parties who happen to be on or come on the scene, rather than by the person attempting suicide.) Recent data from the L.A.S.P.C. (Shneidman, et al., 1970) demonstrate the same paradox more emphatically: less than two percent of the calls to this prototypical suicide prevention center involve actual attempts and only 10 percent involve either attempts or impulses. This ubiquitous finding puts in clear question the theoretical rationale for suicide prevention as a unique type of clinical operation, identifiably different from crisis intervention, and therefore supports the argument that there is no logical substitute for wide-ranging professional skills in this or any type of emergency mental health program.

Another line of evidence challenging the rationale for suicide prevention is that emerging from research on the apparent antithesis between the suicide attempter and the suicide completer or the unsuccessful and the successful suicide, to put it in paradoxical terms. A number of studies (e.g. Beall, 1969) describe the typical attempter in statistical language as a woman who tends in personality pattern to be a dependent hysteric, protesting against the actual or threatened loss of or rejection by a significant other, and employing nonlethal methods. The typical completer is described statistically as a man who manifests independence in interpersonal relationships and underlying feelings of alienation and who employs lethal methods. It has been remarked that the act of suicide, for the completer, represents an assertive rather than a defeatist action—an active, ideological commitment to death; while, on the other hand, the attempter's suicidal gesture represents an attention-getting "cry for help," as Farberow and Shneidman (1961) have poetically termed it—a desperate but self-aborting effort to escape life stress while clinging to life. It follows (as Seiden [1971] and others recently have recognized) that it is the attempter, not the completer, who is attuned and responds to the naive helping efforts of a suicide prevention service while, ironically, the completer, the putative target of such a service, is unaffected.

The so-called helping efforts of the lay suicide prevention worker, which are necessarily circumscribed and have become somewhat ritualized, and which include attempts to ascertain the lethality of suicidal intent by direct questioning, followed by either rescue efforts or referral to mental health professionals, may be worse than ineffectual with the genuinely suicidal individual; they may be offensive, further alienating the potential completer and firming his suicidal resolve. Szasz (1971) and others (e.g. Macks, 1971) lately have protested against the coercive intervention of zealous suicide prevention workers and have questioned the ethics and clinical propriety of involuntary rescue or referral. The practice of direct interrogation regarding the lethality of a caller's suicidal intentions appears particularly suspect. Such questioning may alienate the genuinely suicidal individual or it may have a dangerous power of suggestion for the hysteric (as may the overly enthusiastic promotion of a suicide prevention service).*

At the same time, there is evidence that lethality ratings by untrained workers have poor predictive power and therefore no utility, for they have been found to vary directly with and to reflect the degree of inexperience and level of anxiety of the worker rather than the gravity of the suicidal crisis. It has been demonstrated, conversely, that lethality can be assessed with a very high degree of precision by an experienced psychologist (Shneidman, 1971), and the unarguable conclusion is that professional competence is a requisite for the practice of any of the functions subsumed under suicide intervention, and that there is no mechanical shortcut to nor substitute for professional competence.

It has also been found (Murphy, *et al.*, 1969) that many or most of the callers to a suicide prevention center have previously had or are currently receiving some type of professional help, which is consistent with the hypothesis that the actual consumers of this type of service are dependent-hysteric suicide attempters raher than completers. This finding suggests that the lay worker's

---

* Callers have been known to profess to be suicidal in order to justify use of suicide prevention services (McGee, 1966a).

practice of automatically referring these already psychiatrically or psychologically sophisticated callers for professional help is redundant, and the concomitant finding (Murphy, *et al.*, 1969) that follow-through on such referrals is limited supports this judgment.

Apart from consideration of the theoretical or clinical implications of lay-operated suicide prevention services, there is, of course, a pragmatic question of economy. The appeal of the volunteer nonprofessional lies at base in the low cost, on paper, of his services. There are high, indirect or intangible costs of utilizing untrained volunteers, however, to substitute for or supplement professionals in the delivery of critical, emergency services. The involved professionals paradoxically spend as much or more time in recruiting, selecting, training, and supervision of nonprofessionals as they would in providing direct services, and there is simply an indirect rather than a direct expenditure of professional time and skill. If the nonprofessionals are uncompensated volunteers, there is also a cost in morale of the workers over a period of time, compounding the problems of recruitment, training, and supervision: there is invariably a very high turnover and attrition rate among voluntary nonprofessionals. The absence of compensation inevitably affects worker morale, particularly when there are compensated and uncompensated staff, and there is also a subtle morale factor involved in the covert role conflict that is typically induced in the fledgling, nonprofessional mental health worker in the course of his brief training and exposure to acute adjustmental problems and crisis situations in the lives of others. As he gains experience, however superficial or peripheral, a sense of professional pride and ambition is prematurely awakened and he comes to think of himself as part of a professional service, and yet he has no licit professional status. At the least, suppressed frustration and envy of legitimate (and adequately compensated) professionals are felt, while ultimately many are driven to abandon their anomalous roles. The position of the unpaid nonprofessional in an emergency mental health service becomes, in time, untenable.

A parenthetical observation from the L.A.S.P.C. experience and two other experimental projects in nondegree training of ancillary mental health personnel is that a minimum of two years of study and training (involving both course work and field training) is apparently required (McGee, 1966b; Rioch, *et al.*, undated). Since in each of these three experimental projects the trainees were college educated (or better) and the training was at a graduate level, a master's degree in psychology or social work could have been earned in the same time or less, and the conclusion again appears to be that there is no short-cut to professional competence in this field.

This complex of theoretical, empirical, and pragmatic arguments against the use of nonprofessionals in crisis intervention programs comprises virtually a mandate to base whatever model is adopted at or near the professional end of the professional-lay descriptive dimension.

PROFESSIONAL CRISIS INTERVENTION PROGRAMS

Suicide Counseling Associations

Turning to consideration of professionally staffed crisis intervention programs, there are, first, voluntary associations of professionals in suicide counseling which have emerged spontaneously in this country and abroad at intervals over the past half-century (see Farberow and Shneidman, 1961). These are at base social welfare programs with a religious flavor, usually sponsored by social agencies or church-related organizations. They frequently include mental health para-professionals (ministers, physicians, nurses, lawyers, and educators) along with social workers, psychologists, and psychiatrists as mental health professionals; there sometimes is a nucleus of paid professionals as a regular staff. Short-term, emergency counseling is offered either indirectly (by phone) or directly (in person), in identified suicidal crises. These programs are narrow in reach by definition and are limited in an operational sense by their voluntary and loosely organized character. The use of volunteer professionals represents, of course, a significant paper economy, but entails a devitalizing sacrifice of efficiency and control. Attrition among the volunteer professionals is high, and the viability of programs of this ilk is a direct function of the degree of dedication and emotional stamina of their leadership. Typically, there is a low survival rate.

Emergency Psychiatric Services

A different crisis intervention model utilizes professionals on a compensated basis, providing for better coordinated services and more sustained participation. One variant of the compensated professional model is the emergency psychiatric services type of program (Furman, undated; Lamb, *et al.*, 1969; Weisz, *et al.*, 1968). These services typically are linked to a hospital inpatient facility and are based in the hospital emergency room and patterned after E. R. services. The staff ordinarily consists of psychiatric residents, who provide brief diagnostic screening for hospital admission or stopgap chemotherapy to E. R. walk-ins or via home visitations. The model is superficial and limited in its conceptualization of crisis intervention in terms of rudimentary, medically oriented surveillance rather than broader, psychotherapeutic management. Programs of this type have been inspired (in the financial as well as ideological sense) chiefly by the Community Mental Health Services Act of 1963, which stipulated that emergency mental health services must be provided in order for any facility to qualify for federal funds as a community mental health center, and they have proliferated in the past decade as a kind of bandwagon phenomenon without a great deal of conceptual programming.

Crisis Counseling Programs

An alternative model involving compensated professionals is what may be termed a crisis counseling model. In contrast to the emergency psychiatric services type of program, this is a conceptually broader, psychotherapeutically oriented rather than medically-diagnostically oriented model, with a concomitant focus on indirect, verbal intervention by phone rather than direct, face-to-face encounters, and with at the same time a focus on more in-depth, psychological response to acute adjustmental problems or crisis situations. There are few unequivocal examples to date of this progressive model, but, as previously intimated, many suicide prevention programs appear to be evolving into a broader, compensated-professional-crisis intervention format and hence to be converging on the crisis counseling model. None of the contemporary crisis counseling programs, however, satisfies a criterion of comprehensiveness of care, although there is *conceptual* breadth, for none can be classified as comprehensive because of the short-term, time-limited character of their psychotherapeutic services. Invariably they depend upon referral to other professionals or mental health services for longer-term or follow-up counseling. In a rare instance, provision for continued psychological care is made in indirect fashion, by housing separate crisis intervention and regular outpatient services under the same programmatic roof, so that crisis cases can be followed at least within the same facility if not by the same professional (*cf.* the program of the Massachusetts Mental Health Center),* but there is still in such a case a clininally inefficient break in the continuity of care and an artificial, conceptual distinction between crisis counseling and regular psychotherapy. Ideally, the crisis counseling model will provide for continuity of care by utilizing the same professional staff for emergency and follow-up psychotherapy and thus will satisfy the threefold criterion of comprehensive, compensated, professional service.

A Comprehensive Crisis Counseling Program

One program in Florida emulates the comprehensive crisis counseling model: the Escambia County Community Mental Health Center in Pensacola. So far as can be determined, it is unique in this respect and therefore bears detailed examination and description for heuristic purposes.

At the core of the Escambia County program is a duality of roles assumed by the professional staff of the outpatient unit of the center, as a logical consequence of the fact that emergency mental health services are conceptualized as an integral aspect of or an extension of regular outpatient services,

---

* See *Emergency Services.* U.S. Government Printing Office. U.S.P.H.S. Publication #1477.

not as a discontinuous system. In this program, every staff member in rotation takes a shift on a twenty-four-hour emergency or crisis intervention schedule which has been tabbed "Crisis Call." The professional on Crisis Call is responsible for managing all calls received during his shift, whether day or night and whatever the nature of the call or contact (whether emergency or routine, by phone or walk-in). No operational distinction is made between after-hours calls and calls during center office hours, as is necessarily made when services are provided by different emergency and regular outpatient staffs. Day or night, the staff member on Crisis Call executes the same, full range of professional functions, assessing the degree of urgency and the psychological needs in each case, responding as immediately and actively (in a psychotherapeutic sense) as is required, and offering further counseling or consultation as needed.

The telephone is the preferred medium for crisis counseling (or crisis consultation) within this framework, bridging physical distance and the ritualistic delays of traditional scheduling-by-appointment; immediately clarifying needs and coordinating helping efforts in the course of third-party referral or consultation; and dispelling some of the stigma and negative mystique of mental health services for the naive caller. Walk-in crisis cases are also seen at the center during the day, but are not solicited actively, for experience demonstrates that the typical walk-in client is *not* in crisis and is more likely to have stopped by the center out of curiosity or on idle impulse, or to have been arbitrarily remanded to the center by another social or health agency, or private professional, in mechanical fashion, for no clear reason. If a crisis is experienced in a walk-in case, it is frequently experienced by a third party (parent, teacher, spouse) who conveys the resisting patient into the august presence of the professional for judgment (as "crazy" or "sick") and treatment (perceived as magical exorcism or as restraint, by confinement or chemical means). Partly for this reason, counseling and psychotherapy in this program are family and relationship centered, rather than individually focused, and consultation with allied "caretaker" agencies and para-professionals is emphasized. The program is comprehensive in this sense as well as in the sense of continuity of care.

At night, the telephone is the exclusive medium for Crisis Call and reliance is placed explicitly and realistically on indirect, verbal intervention rather than direct confrontation. If, however, physical intervention in some form is required (e.g. in the event of a serious suicidal attempt), the Crisis Call staff member can, of course, call on other emergency resources in the community.

Crisis Call has its own phone number to enhance visibility of the service in the community and to identify and expedite urgent calls. All calls are screened through the center switchboard and receptionist during daytime office hours and through a commercial answering service at night and on weekends. The staff member on call, day or night, must remain accessible by phone at all times; at night, however, he takes calls in his home, relayed to him by the answering service.

The mode of reimbursement for night Crisis Call is via compensatory time. This means of reimbursement is not only enormously economical (128 hours a week of professional time on night Crisis Call costs but 21 hours of compensatory time), but also appears to have some psychological advantages over monetary compensation from the staff's point of view. Time off from daily responsibilities is highly valued by professionals, and it also appears to lend a certain dignity to overtime work. From an accounting and administrative point of view, compensation in the form of time is a more flexible commodity than money, and it has the distinct advantage of being an invisible and readily absorbed expense, requiring no direct, budgetary defense or justification. This highly effective system of compensation, of course, is an outgrowth of the unique duality of roles assumed by the outpatient staff in this program.

It may be concluded that the comprehensive crisis counseling model functions in an efficient manner from both clinical and mechanical points of view. The only drawback, if it be such, is a subtle one that arises from the overlapping roles played by the staff: some center clients perceive the night Crisis Call staff as being "on call" for other staff (in the medical, group practice tradition) rather than as providing an ancillary, outreach service, and this results occasionally in abuse of the service and exploitation of the night staff—in the latter's opinion. The problem is, however, resolved on an individual basis by the night Crisis Call staff member, with the caller and/or his regular therapist, when it occurs.

Preliminary utilization statistics on night Crisis Call tend to validate the conceptual underpinnings for this crisis intervention model and confirm the impression of clinical effectiveness. The average frequency of calls per evening is two (which is consistent with projections from other crisis counseling programs, taking into account a local population of about 200,000); this rate appears to reflect a sufficient need for and use of the service without overburdening the night Crisis Call staff. More significantly, virtually all (90%) of the night calls are appropriate, in the sense that they are of a clinical rather than information-giving character and require half to three-quarters of an hour of phone counseling or consultation, on the average. Furthermore, fully half of the calls are classified as "extremely urgent" and three-quarters are classified as either "moderately" or "extremely urgent." Night Crisis Call therefore appears to answer a genuine and unique need, and the impression is that the active and appropriate use of and positive response to the service by the local community is a direct consequence of its professional character and the feature of continuity of care. It is of interest, in this regard, that in over two-thirds of the cases, follow-up counseling is planned, while in 20 percent, a single, intensive, phone counseling or consultation session suffices. Only about 12 percent of the calls entail referral to other emergency resources in the community. It may also be noted, incidentally, that some callers explicitly recognize and make use of the protective shield of anonymity that can be offered by a phone counseling service, and that some also use night Crisis Call on a repeated basis to the exclusion of other, direct modes of psychotherapeutic help —providing testimony for the unique effectiveness of indirect phone counseling.

It may further be noted that fewer than half of the night callers (41%) are new to psychotherapeutic help while the majority have had some prior contact with mental health professionals (at the center or elsewhere). It could be argued from this that this program largely is tapping a population of already-identified consumers of mental health services and that its value therefore is attenuated. This however, is a common finding among crisis intervention programs of all types, as previously has been suggested, and appears more simply to bear out the axiom that most individuals making an unstable adjustment have a history of unstable adjustment.

The conclusion from this comparative analysis of contemporary crisis intervention models and detailed exposition of the comprehensive crisis counseling model is that this model, satisfying as it does the criteria of compensated professionalism and breadth of concepts and services and featuring phone counseling or indirect intervention, approximates an ideal crisis intervention type.

REFERENCES

Beall, L.: The dynamics of suicide. *Bull. Suicidol.*, pp. 2-16, March 1969.

Farberow, N. L. and Shneidman, E. S.: *The Cry for Help*. New York, McGraw-Hill, 1961.

Furman, S. S.: *Community Mental Health Services in Northern Europe*. U.S. Government Printing Office. U.S.P.H.S. Publication #1407.

Lamb, H. R.; Heath, D., and Downing, J. J.: *Handbook of Community Mental Health Practice*. San Francisco, Jossey-Bass, 1969.

Macks, V. W.: Suicide prevention: mental health 'oppression.' *Social Work, 16*:102-104, 1971.

McGee, R. K.: Development and organization of suicide prevention centers. Community Mental Health Services Symposium, Atlanta, 1966a.

McGee, R. K.: Non-professionals as mental health workers in counseling and testing. American Psychological Association, New York, 1966b.

McGee, R. K.: The manpower problem in suicide prevention. In N. L. Farberow (Ed.): *Proceedings of the 4th International Conference for Suicide Prevention*. Los Angeles, Delmar, 1968.

Murphy, G. E.; Wetzel, R.; Swallow, C., and McClure, J. N.: Who calls the suicide prevention center? *Am. J. Psychiatr., 126*:314-324, 1969.

Rioch, M. J.; Elkers, C., and Flint, A. A.: *Pilot Project in Training Mental Health Counselors*. U.S. Government Printing Office. U.S.P.H.S. Publication #1254.

Seiden, R.: Quoted in *Behavior Today*, page 3, March 29, 1971.

Shneidman, E. S.: Perturbation and lethality as precursors of suicide in a gifted group. *Life-Threatening Behavior, 1*:23-45, 1971.
Shneidman, E. S.; Farberow, N. L., and Litman, R. E.: *The Psychology of Suicide.* New York, Science House, 1970.
Szasz, T.: The ethics of suicide. *Intellectual Digest, 2*:53-55, 1971.
Weisz, A. E.; Staight, D. C.; Houts, P. S., and Voten, M. P.: Suicide threats, suicide attempts, and the emergency psychiatrist. In N. L. Farberow (Ed.): *Proceedings of the 4th International Conference for Suicide Prevention.* Los Angeles, Delman, 1968.
Whittemore, K.: *Ten Centers.* Atlanta, Lullwater Press, 1970.

Chapter 20

SELECTING THE TELEPHONE COUNSELOR

GENE W. BROCKOPP

CRISIS INTERVENTION IS hard work. To do a competent job, the most highly trained professional needs to use all of his skill and experience in the fast-moving, arduous process of assisting an individual who has come to him with a critical life problem. To engage in the same process over the telephone is often more difficult as the interviewer must base his decisions on only the verbal and covert verbal cues. Each center has the task of finding people who will be able to perform this task with understanding, skill, objectivity and involvement. From the population of the community, each center must select individuals who can feel and express the basis human qualities which will enable them to relate to and work with a person in crisis. In this chapter we will discuss some of the problems related to the selection of individuals who work on a telephone emergency service.

PROFESSIONAL VS. NONPROFESSIONAL

One of the first decisions that a crisis service needs to make is whether or not the individuals answering the telephone will be selected from a professional population or from the general population of the community. Almost all of the more than 200 centers in the country use volunteers to work on the telephone. A few programs (for example, the Philadelphia and Washington crisis centers) use only professional individuals who are specifically trained in one of the mental health disciplines. The question of which group functions better on the telephone has not been definitely answered. There is no sound empirical evidence to indicate that professional individuals function better than non-professional individuals on an emergency telephone service. The few studies that have been completed are on such highly specific and unique groups that it is questionable whether the data from the studies can be applied to any other group in the country. In the cities where only professional individuals are used on the telephone service, justification for this practice is stated in terms of feelings and experience, rather than in terms of factual data. At the same time there is also no scientific basis or justification for the use of volunteers in the center. This decision is often based on the feeling that these individuals can do an adequate job on the telephone, and that since they are volunteers they reduce the cost of the operation. To further blur the line between these two groups, Dublin states that the nonprofessional is the true "professional" of the suicide prevention movement and that the so-called mental health professional is really the untrained individual in the field. With very little data to indicate which is the true professional or which group is most effective in working with this population, I would like to state my opinion regarding the relative use of professional or nonprofessional as a worker in the emergency telephone service.

At the Buffalo suicide and crisis service, we have trained more than 400 volunteer counselors over the past three years for our twenty-four-hour telephone service. About one-half of these can be classified as professionals; that is, individuals who are presently practicing in one of the mental health professions, such as social workers, psychologists, nurses, or who are advanced students in these fields. The other half were either under-graduate students in a variety of subject areas, people from the community who maintained a regular job in the community, or housewives who worked at the center on a part-time basis. Our experience has been that there is very little difference between the work of the professional and the nonprofessional person when they are using the crisis intervention model in working with a client on the telephone. The professional person has some advantages in that he has a theory to guide him in his therapeutic relationships with people. He also has an understanding of dynamic psychology and therefore some method of placing the behavior of the patient into a meaningful context. His diagnostic skills may assist him in determining the severity of the person's problems and increase his ability to evaluate the client's need for assistance. At the same time, these skills can often be a hindrance. For telephone crisis intervention work forces the professional out of the traditional therapeutic model into a much more problem-solving type of relationship. His training, which is more designed to assist him in working with "sick" people, may result in his being unable to see the patient in terms of his strengths rather than his weaknesses. Also, as mentioned in previous chapters, it is most important that the person working on the telephone be able to relate to the client through his "humanness." Often the academic training and therapeutic techniques that individuals acquire in the process of professional training reduce their ability to relate in a "real" way with the client.

The nonprofessional person also has difficulties. Although he does not need to unlearn certain therapeutic techniques, he must do something equally difficult; he must learn to "listen with his gut" and respond to the feelings that he has about the individual in crisis, for he does not have the technical skill that the professional does, and therefore cannot rely on head-knowledge about the individual. Being untrained in mental health and being told for many years that only professional people can handle individuals in difficulty, the nonprofessional person is often quite anxious and concerned whether or not he is doing a good job. This increased anxiety may cause him more problems and greater difficulty in doing a good job than any other single thing.

Given a nonprofessional individual who is mature in his feelings, has sufficient sensitivity to develop good interpersonal relationships and enough intelligence to act judiciously, we feel that the quality of the crisis counseling is about the same as that of a professional person who is open and has not lost his "humanness." Either of them can develop the technical skills necessary to work on an emergency telephone service and do so with the concern, intelligence and objectivity that are necessary in crisis intervention work.

In the Buffalo Suicide and Crisis Service we do not differentiate between the so-called professional and the nonprofessional person on any of our services. We classify all individuals who work on the telephone as volunteers. Our criteria for selecting them is not in terms of their professional background, but in terms of their characteristics as human beings and their ability to relate to people in a positive, expectant and innovative manner. Regardless of the individual's background or previous experience in the mental health or other related areas, he must go through the same selection process, the same training program and be subject to the same type of supervision, scrutiny and regulations. The experiential evidence we have indicates to us that this basis for selection results in highly qualified, responsive telephone workers.

METHODS OF FINDING VOLUNTEERS

Initially the center had difficulty recruiting sufficient volunteers to maintain the telephone service. To reach the widest number of potentially good volunteers, speeches were given in various classes in psychology, social work, medicine, and nursing at the universities and colleges in Erie County. In addition, each time a speech was made in a community organization or business group, a request for volunteers was made. This resulted in sufficient individuals being recruited for the telephone service. We were, however, quite concerned about attracting individuals to the center who would have opinionated points of view, or people who would not have the basic personality traits which would allow them to work effectively at the center, but who might want to engage in this type of activity for the personal therapeutic value it would have for themselves. As the service continued, our confidence in our ability to select individuals and to train them for the telephone service increased and we began to explore different means of recruitment of volunteers. For example, an ad was placed in the local newspaper under the "Personal" column which read as follows:

Part Time counselors for day work with telephone counseling service. Work 4-8 days per month, ½ day shift o.k. No salary but

$1.00 per hour expense money. We provide training & supervision. We are looking for warm, sensitive people who can relate to others and who are open to learning. Some college desirable. Age no factor except must be over 18. Call Miss Hanon, Suicide Prevention & Crisis Service. Mon. thru Fri. 9 A.M. to 5 P.M. 854-1966.

At the same time, ads were placed under "Help Wanted—Male" and "Help Wanted—Female" which would direct the individual to the larger, more inclusive ad in the "Personal" column. We ran the ad for a three-day period of time and obtained more than 180 responses. Each person was sent an application form to complete and return to the center. Over ninety application forms were completed and returned to the center.

At the present time, as a result of the high quality training programs we have established and the increased visibility of the center in the community, we have more individuals who wish to work for the center than we can train and use. Virtually every day brings additional applications from people who have heard about the service and want to work at the center. As a result the process of finding volunteers has changed into a process of selecting volunteers from the many individuals who apply for training.

CRITERIA FOR SELECTING VOLUNTEERS

We feel that the criteria for the initial selection of volunteers should be extremely broad and should be restricted only by a few conditions. For example, we do not allow anyone under eighteen years of age to work on the telephone service. Although this minimal age was initially an arbitrary one, we feel that it is justified for the following reasons. We find it is difficult to find individuals below eighteen years of age who have sufficient maturity of thought and action to enable them to work on a telephone emergency service. Their experiential background, both with life in general and with crises in particular, is naturally quite limited. Although they respond quite freely and innovatively to individuals in crisis, their background often hinders their seeing the client's problems in the perspective of his chronic life situation and understanding the difficulties which he may have been having for a long period of time. In addition, we find that the majority of individuals under eighteen who are working on emergency telephone service, are those who have had a history of positive experiences, a sense of mastery over their environment, and a future which looks bright. The result is that they sometimes take a flippant view toward the individual who is in chronic serious crisis situations. Another reason for not using the individual under eighteen is the legal question that may arise from having an underage person working in a crisis service, giving advice and direction to an individual who is in a serious situation. It was felt by our insurance underwriter that the service itself could be faulted and possibly sued if it used individuals on the telephone service who are not of legal age.

The second criteria that we use to exclude individuals from the telephone service is the personal characteristics that may hinder his active and/or objective participation as a volunteer. In this criteria we are concerned about a number of areas. For example, questionable emotional stability as evidenced by the previous behavior of the individual or his active involvement in psychotherapy at this time. If a person has made a suicide attempt in the past three years, he is automatically excluded from the volunteer service until the seriousness of the attempt and the means by which he has resolved the difficulty which resulted in his making the suicide attempt can be ascertained by a careful evaluation of his behavior. The same is true of an individual who is presently in therapy. We will not allow any individual to work on the telephone service who is presently in a therapeutic relationship unless (1) the therapist with whom he is working agrees to his employment as a volunteer, and (2) after an intensive evaluation we feel that the individual would be able to undertake the stress of working on the telephone service, not be a deterrent to individuals who are calling the center, or have his involvement result in exacerbation of his emotional problems. Each of these cases is evaluated individually. No one who has made a suicide attempt or is in therapy is automatically excluded. We are equally concerned about individuals who have a heart condition, have been subject to epileptic seizures, have a speech impediment or a physical handicap which may hinder their effective operation on the telephone service. Each special condition is evaluated in terms of both the impact of the continuous emotional stress on the person and the potential effect of the condition on the client who is calling the center.

The other criteria we use for selecting volunteers are (1) the individual, if selected and trained, will work at the center for a period of time; (2) an individual must agree to the process of continued supervision of his work at the center and be able to maintain a schedule whereby he can put in a minimum of one 6-hour shift every two weeks; (3) the person has to agree to sign a pledge of confidentiality and an agreement that his work at the center can be used in the ongoing research program of the center.

THE PROCESS OF SELECTION

As the first step in the selection process, each individual who wishes to work at the center is sent an application form to complete and return to the center. Shortly after the application form is received and reviewed by the supervisor of the volunteer program, a call is made by him or by another clinical staff to the individual, at which time additional information about the person's interest in the center, reasons for wanting to work at the center or questions raised by the application form are discussed with the individual. At the same time the person calling from the center is listening to the characteristics of the applicant's telephone voice, his ability to "come across" over the telephone as a person, and the quality of his voice (such as timbre and tone) are evaluated. We are looking for individuals whose enthusiasm for life and concern for the other can be transmitted through their voice, individuals who can transmit through their nonverbal communication a sense of hope and expectancy, and individuals whose speech impediments, if any, will not detract from the communication to the point that they will call attention to themselves.

On the basis of this short interview, most individuals who apply as volunteers are requested to come to the center for a personal interview with the Supervisor of Volunteer Services. This interview will be the first of two, each conducted by a different individual on the clinical staff. The initial interview focuses on giving the prospective volunteer information on the center, his work as a volunteer, the expectancies of the center for him, the responsibilities that he will have as a volunteer, and an evaluation of his potential as a telephone worker. The second interview focuses much more on a clinical evaluation of the individual's ability to work as a crisis intervener on the telephone. The questions that were raised on the application form are brought to the individual's attention, and he is given the opportunity to expand or enlarge any of the items in question. At the end of the second interview, the applicant is informed that he will be contacted within a few days as to whether or not he will be accepted for one of the training programs. Using the four pieces of information (the application form, the evaluation of the individual's telephone voice and the two clinical interviews), the supervisor, together with the clinical person who has interviewed the applicant, determines whether or not this individual is qualified and suitable for working on the telephone on the basis of the collected data and their "gut" responses to him as a person. Although this selection process may appear to be arbitrary and somewhat unsystematic, we have found that the result of obtaining individuals who are successful at working on the telephone is more efficiently accomplished by this method than by giving the applicants a series of psychological tests and a psychiatric examination. To our knowledge, no set of tests or evaluations have been devised which will adequately predict success in working on telephone emergency service. Our experience indicates that a multiple clinical evaluation is the most efficient selecter of volunteers who will be successful crisis interviewers.

The selection process, however, is not completed when the individual is permitted to enter the training program. We emphasize to the applicant that the process of selection will continue through the training program. We also tell him that he is under no obligation to work at the center after he has completed the training program (although we have used this as one criteria of his selection). At the same time we inform him that we, through the training program are continually evaluating his work and his suitability for working at the center so that through the process of training he must select us and we must select him. The training program itself is designed to help weed out individuals who are able to verbalize or intellectualize but are unable to function in a pragmatic situation. By specific role play situations a person will be asked to confront some of the problems he has had difficulty resolving. Through this process, approximately 10 percent of the individuals who begin the training program decide not to continue in the work at the center as volunteers.

After the person has completed the training program, he is placed on a probationary status for a period of six weeks. During this period of time he must work under the supervision of a senior volunteer. His calls, worksheets and contacts with clients are carefully evaluated and analyzed with him, and suggestions are made by his supervisor regarding improvements he can make in his telephone contacts. The quality of his work is evaluated by both the clinical director and the supervisor of volunteers. After the six-week probationary period, the individual becomes a regular volunteer at the center.

If his work continues at a high level of competence, and the individual shows the ability to be a supervisor of volunteers, he may be selected by his clinical supervisor as a candidate for the position of senior volunteer. To be placed in this position, a person will again need to move through a selection process whereby both his supervisor and at least five volunteers recommend him for this senior position. Once he is selected, he goes through an advanced training program on the supervision of volunteers.

CRITERIA FOR FIRING VOLUNTEERS

Even though it is most disagreeable, each center will need to prevent certain individuals from continuing as telephone crisis interveners. Relieving a volunteer of his duties is extremely difficult, perhaps even more difficult than relieving a person from a paid position. We strongly feel that volunteer workers at a center should be treated in the same way we treat paid workers. Their selection, training, supervision should be of a high quality. If their level of performance deteriorates or for some reason becomes destructive to individuals calling the center, their services, like those of any other person, need to be terminated. To facilitate this process and to decrease the negative elements, we have instituted the following criteria for releasing an individual from the volunteer service at the center: (1) poor quality performance on the telephone after direction and supervision has been given to the volunteer, (2) consistent failure to show up for supervision, or inability to utilize supervisory sessions, (3) attitudes which interfere with or are opposed to the philosophy and purpose of the Suicide Prevention and Crisis Service, (4) irresponsibility, especially as indicated by a failure to be present for the shift accepted by the volunteer, (5) violation of the confidentiality code of the SPCS, and (6) refusal to give sufficient time to perform the required functions of the volunteer.

If the volunteer violates any of the above stated principles, he is called in by the supervisor of the volunteer services, apprised of the apparent violations, given an opportunity to correct a misconception of his work or to express his feelings about his violations of the code and his willingness to improve his work at the center. If the supervisor feels that there is some justification for the individual violating the above policies, the volunteer is placed on inactive status for a short period of time, after which he is allowed to return to full status as a volunteer. If the violations continue, the volunteer is dismissed from the service.

By placing responsibility on each of the volunteers for maintaining excellence and respectability, we are able to provide a high quality service to the community. The volunteers "police" each other to a high degree and are quick to call attention to violations of rules and regulations committed by their fellow volunteers, since they are concerned about the well-being of the person calling in to the center and the need for him to obtain service of the highest quality at the time of his crisis. The result is an elite corps of individuals who measure up to the highest standards of the words "professional volunteer."

Chapter 21

TRAINING THE TELEPHONE COUNSELOR

GENE W. BROCKOPP

T HE APPROPRIATE TRAINING necessary to prepare a person to work effectively on the telephone with individuals who are in a state of crisis or contemplating a suicidal act is still an unknown factor. Little has been written on the subject. None of the more than 200 centers have the resources to undertake the type of study which would be necessary to clearly delineate the characteristics of a program which would result in a competent trained "professional volunteer."

The result is that each center has had to develop its own program of training based on its experience and those of the other centers with which it has had contact during the initial phase of its development. Often these training programs are continued regardless of their efficacy. Rarely are they subjected to careful scrutiny and substantially revised.

At the Erie County SPCS we believe that a training program should be a direct reflection of the way the agency sees itself, its function in the community and its concept of the suicidal or in-crisis person. The program we have developed has changed radically over the past three years as a result of the experimental data and experiential evidence we have gathered. During this period of time, the program has evolved into a fairly structured unit which is conducted within the context of a small task-oriented experiential group. However, the quality as evidenced by the on-the-job expertness of the more than 400 volunteer counselors we have trained is the only "real" data we have of the appropriateness of our program. Unfortunately, we have been unable to do the type of study which would be necessary to back up this training program with experimental evidence.

PHILOSOPHICAL ASSUMPTIONS

The training of any person is based on certain implied or stated assumptions. These will determine the selection of the individual to be trained, the method to be utilized, the attitude-knowledge outcome to be achieved, the social-cultural setting in which the person will work and the function of the center in the community. At the Erie County SPCS the training program is based on the concept that an emergency telephone service should provide more than a listening ear" in the community (although that by itself is a remarkable achievement). We feel that an emergency telephone service is best conceptualized as telephone therapy within the crisis intervention model. That is, we feel the interaction on the telephone should be therapeutic to the caller and have both a direction and a goal. The direction should be to ascertain and utilize the caller's strength and those of his environment to enhance and sustain him through the crisis. The goal is to ameliorate, change, modify and hopefully improve the psycho-social condition of the caller. We call this process life-space counseling. We feel that this type of therapy can be effectively learned by any mature person who has interpersonal sensitivity (the ability to listen with your "gut") and sufficient intelligence to act judiciously. We believe that one of the most damaging things that professionals have done is to imply and state that people should not trust their feelings in trying to help a fellow human being. We neither subscribe to nor follow this concept in our training program. Rather, we attempt to utilize the strengths of the trainees and their life experiences in a small task-oriented discussion group and assist them to begin making inferences about crisis behavior based on their feelings and the knowledge they are given in the training program. We feel that both the training-learning and the working setting should be permeated with the concept that people will tend to make the correct and appropriate response if it is assumed that they will do so. A corollary to this is that an incorrect or inappropriate response made in the context of a helping, concerned relationship will usually have minimum negative effect.

The focus of the training program is to increase the volunteer's interpersonal sensitivity and his ability to use himself as a therapeutic tool in his interaction with a person in crisis. We build on the trainee's natural ability and normal desire to be a helping person and assist him to integrate these into a therapeutic style which is appropriate and comfortable for him. One of the more difficult tasks is to help the volunteer to learn to listen objectively so he will avoid developing a premature conclusion about the nature of the caller's problem. We emphasize the need of the telephone therapist to fully survey those forces in the client's life space which are contributing to his problem and those which can be enlisted to help with the solution before developing with the caller a method for ameliorating his difficulty. Further, throughout the training program, we emphasize the concept that every effort should be made to help the client develop a solution which does not utilize any agency or social organization. Those solutions which can be accomplished with the least involvement of the formal mental health or social agency community tend to be the best ones. At the same time we will give the client all the support he needs to match the intensity and severity of the crisis he is having.

THE TRAINING PROGRAM

After the prospective volunteers have gone through the selection process (see Chap. 20), between fifteen to twenty are grouped into a training unit and two staff members are selected to be their trainers. Although these two staff members will utilize other members of the staff for specific aspects of the training program, they have the primary responsibility for the training of this group of volunteers and for integrating each of the individual segments into a total program.

The program consists of nine, 2½ to 3-hour didactic and experiential sessions typically offered on a twice-a-week basis. Over the past two years the structure of the training program has varied quite widely in the way it is presented to the trainees. We have used all-day sessions, twice-a-week programs, once-a-week programs, and a number of combinations of the above. At the present time, we feel that a program which operates on a twice-a-week basis for approximately three hours each session is most profitable in terms of trainee learning, building concepts regarding telephone therapy, and maintaining interest in the service. If the volunteers are expected to work in our day program, the training is offered during the day; if at night, the program is given in the evening.

The training program is constructed to allow time for practicing of the concepts developed through role playing. This is done both in front of the whole group and in small groups of volunteers. As the group progresses, we add the psycho-dramatic elements of alter ego, doubling and mirroring to the process to show the levels of interaction that are part of each therapeutic interaction.

During the training program, each trainee is expected to spend two, 3-hour periods at the center observing the work of volunteers on the telephone and listening to their interviews with clients. This helps the prospective volunteer see the relevance of the training he is receiving and increases his involvement in the center's functions.

Each of the nine sessions has a major theme and a number of minor ones interwoven into the session. The following is a brief summary of each session.

Session 1

The first session is divided into three units. The first short unit formally introduces the volunteer to the center. The trainees are given a tour of the facilities of the center, a talk on its background, development, and the concepts on which it operates. They are also given an idea what their job will be like, what their responsibilities and privileges are, and the types of calls in which they will be involved and how their work relates to the other functions of the center. Material they will use in the training program, including the manual for volunteers, is presented to them.

The second major part of the session is devoted to the volunteer. Using a variety of group approaches, we explore his expectations, fears and concerns about working at the center and about his using himself as a being working with people in crisis. We help them confront themselves with their own feelings about suicide, death, drugs and crises and the reasons why they want to be involved in this type of program. Through this process, we try to help the new volunteer clarify some of his ideas and expectations and increase his motivation for either working at the center or leaving the program. During the latter part of this unit, the trainees are asked to pair-off and get to know one another. Through this dyadic relationship, the volunteer begins the process of interviewing and through the process discovers a number of common bonds between himself and other individuals in the group. In the discussion period that follows, two themes are usually brought out: (1) a general fear of giving the wrong advice to people in crisis situations, and (2) the expectation of personal growth and development on the part of the new volunteer. The trainer usually reinforces and clarifies both of these issues, making the distinction of responsibility *to* the client, not for the client. The overall result of this discussion is to increase their feeling of competence and community and to facilitate a free exchange among the members of the group.

The last unit of the first session builds on the communication process begun in the interviews by presenting a brief lecture on communication. The lecture emphasizes two points: Communication is a multi-level phenomena and one *cannot* not communicate. Examples of the use of silence, phrasing, tone, and other aspects of verbal and nonverbal communication are discussed and applied to the work on the telephone.

The first session ends with the volunteer signing up for his first three-hour observation period at the center.

Session 2

The second session emphasizes the concept of crisis intervention with a discussion of the theoretical and practical aspects of the process. An understanding of "crisis," its effect on an individual's life and on the person's psychological state, is emphasized along with the process by which intervention may occur and what it is intended to accomplish for the person. The PIE model of proximity, immediacy and expectancy is emphasized. Role playing is developed around various crisis situations. It is usually during these role plays that the volunteers are introduced to the intake form which the agency uses to record calls. Each time a role-play situation is used, the group not directly involved in the dyadic relationship is expected to complete an intake sheet on the caller as if they were taking the call. By continually engaging in this process, we emphasize the need for information gathering and reduce this process to a more mechanical and automatic procedure.

Session 3

The focus of the third session is the telephone as a therapeutic instrument. The basic advantages and disadvantages of the telephone in crisis counseling are developed for the trainees (for example, the lower defensiveness on the part of the caller, the anonymity and immediacy of the telephone communication). Usually a tape of examples from the center or from other published materials is used to explore the telephone therapy process.

The remainder of the session consists of a series of role-play situations in which one trainee assumes the role of caller and the other the role of the telephone counselor. The "callers" are given a variety of calls to play in placing the call (1) to portray different types of callers at a Suicide Prevention Center, (2) to bring out the possible processes for working on the telephone, and (3) to confront individuals in the group with types of calls they may have to deal with, which may relate to some of their personal concerns and questions (for example, calls having sexual content, obscene language, legal problems). The trainees are placed in a back-to-back configuration during the role play, so that the only available communication is through verbal contact. After each role play the group analyzes the communication in terms of how well the people were communicating, the clues about how they felt and the differences between the verbal and nonverbal clues in the communication. Each of the trainees is asked to evaluate how he felt in the "telephone call" and how he felt he was responding to the other individual. During each of the analyses of the calls, the trainees are asked to formulate strategies for dealing with different types of calls or various ways of handling a specific type of caller.

During this session, emphasis is also given to the first few minutes of a call with the focus being on how the telephone therapist begins to develop a "set" for the caller and how the relationship is defined within the first minute of the telephone conversation.

Session 4

During the fourth session, a model for conducting a therapeutic interview over the telephone is presented to the volunteers. The model that we use stresses four points.

1. How much time do I have? The initial question each telephone therapist should ask himself upon picking up the phone is "How much time do I have before I must make a decision regarding the disposition of the caller?" We feel that after an individual can come to grips with the concept of time and realizes that he has time to work with the person who is calling, he can reduce his anxiety and deal effectively with the other areas of the call.

2. Formulation of the caller's problems. We emphasize the need of the telephone therapist to explore quite widely the caller's difficulty, being open to the whole range of possible problems an individual may have before focussing on the specific problems the individuals are bringing to the telephone therapist.

3. Assessing the caller's resources and the forces which have moved him into a crisis situation. We feel that this aspect of the interview should focus both on the positive and the negative aspects of the individual's life, so that the telephone therapist can attend to both his needs and his fears in order to develop a therapeutic plan which will maximally use his personal and interpersonal resources with minimal reliance on the community at large.

4. Developing a treatment plan. This is pulling together the above other three points, focussing the individual in the direction which we feel is most appropriate for him in terms of the problem he has presented and the resources available to him. During this session we discuss techniques for obtaining information about the caller and ways in which calls can be ended.

We again focus heavily on role-playing situations and may

add to the role-play process alter egos to help the volunteers listen more carefully to what is going on in the caller and in the telephone therapist.

Session 5

The fifth session of the training process focusses on suicide and the suicidal process. Information on suicide, its epidemiological and statistical aspects are given to the trainees and questions are answered about the individual who may make a suicide attempt or commit suicide. The trainees' individual concerns about suicide are also explored along with how they may feel about talking to an individual about life or death situations. A discussion of lethality along with various methods of evaluating the lethality of a suicidal situation are given to the trainees.

The last half of the session is devoted to role playing involving suicidal situations with each role playing being designed to teach certain aspects of the suicidal process or to develop ways of working with suicidal individuals.

Session 6

The sixth session focuses on drugs, their use and abuse. A drug information booklet developed by the center staff is read as a basis for the discussion of this session. Chemicals ranging from Coca-Cola® to heroin are discussed and the drug experience is examined as a process involving an interaction between the user's personality attitudes, environment and the type of chemical that he has consumed. Ways of responding to bad trips and helping a caller through bad trips are discussed along with the "flash-back" process and techniques that can be used for turning a bad trip into a good one. Time is also spent talking about psycho-active drugs and in conceptualizing some major ideas of drug therapy.

During the last half of this session, role play around drug problems are developed along with some increasingly complex, emotionally charged situations, in which the therapist is called on to use a number of the techniques which have been developed and explained in the previous training sessions.

Session 7

The focus of this session is an examination of community resources and referral techniques. The use of various resource books and an understanding of the agencies in the region are explored with the trainee. He is also assisted in recognizing situations that require immediate emergency medical attention or other outside intervention. The process of tracing a call, using the police, or making a referral to social or clinical agencies is also explored. Emphasis is given to the making of an appropriate referral to the short-term, intensive psychotherapy unit which is part of the center's services. The use of various reference books, both the formal ones developed by the community and the informal ones devised by the center staff, are explained to the trainee. The process of making a report and the major referral agencies in the region is described in detail. The trainee is assisted in recognizing emergency situations which may require immediate medical or police attention. The process of tracing a call, using the reverse telephone directory, enlisting the help of the police or emergency squad is explored through role-play situations. Emphasis in the session is given to making an appropriate referral to the short-term intensive psychotherapy unit which is part of the center's service to the community.

Role playing during this session focuses on the last few minutes of the telephone call. Method of closing off a call without antagonizing the caller are discussed. The use of the last few minutes of the call for permission giving for subsequent calls are also developed by the trainees.

Session 8

This session explores the special problems of the emergency telephone service. The trainee is given methods of working with problem callers (callers who are chronic callers, cranks, depressive, masturbating, intellectualizing) and is assisted in seeing each of these callers in terms of the real meaning of their call. Other seductive problems they will be facing will also be discussed. These include the one-person caller, the caller who wants personal data on the volunteer and the caller who wants data on their boyfriend, wife, who may have called the center.

Session 9

Review, Summary and Evaluation. During this session the trainee evaluates his training experience through a review of the concepts which have been developed through the training program. At the same time he discusses his readiness to assume telephone counseling duty at the center. These areas are usually explored in a dyadic relationship between the trainees. Administrative procedures of working at the center are then explained. These include the problem of parking, scheduling for work, use of various forms, supervision of work, confidentiality of information, the ongoing research program and the need for maintaining accuracy of records. The expectations of the center for continued input by the volunteer into the program and participation by the volunteer in the scheduled advanced seminar is then expressed.

At this time the trainee is given the option of leaving the program and not working on the telephone. We emphasize that the trainee must freely choose to work at the center and that the center must also freely choose him as a person it will want to represent it to the person in need and to the community.

The newly trained telephone counselor is required to sign up for a minimum of one 6-hour duty every two weeks with a maximum of two, 6-hour units in any one week. He is also required to tape record all the calls which he takes during this period of time. After he has served for two, 6-hour periods he meets with his supervisor to analyze and review his calls. If it is felt by both the supervisor and the volunteer that he is doing an adequate job on the telephone, he is placed on the regular volunteer schedule. His work at the center, however, is continually monitored. For every two, 6-hour units he works at the center, he will meet one hour with his supervisor and go over a sample of his calls, discuss his difficult calls and the intake sheets he has completed. In addition, each telephone therapist is required to attend regular monthly seminars which deal with specific treatment plans for high frequency callers, discuss different types of treatment programs, types of problem callers, review areas of telephone counseling, or extend their knowledge of the field of crisis intervention.*

---

* On the average, volunteers work on the telephones at the center about six months before leaving the volunteer staff or moving to other types of work at the center. After one year, less than 20 percent of those in a given training group are still working as telephone counselors at the center.

PART V

EVALUATING TELEPHONE COUNSELORS AND TELEPHONE SERVICES

INTRODUCTION

THE NEED TO EVALUATE all programs, and in particular mental health programs, goes without question today. Not only is there a demand that we account for how wisely money has been spent, but also our curiosity alone should motivate us to ask whether a particular program has had its desired effects and to further ask by what process it has its effects.

It is too early to wonder about the process by which telephone counseling services have an effect on the community. We are still preoccupied with finding ways of documenting the ways in which they affect the community, if any. The initial chapter in this section provides a broad overview of the kinds of procedures that telephone counseling services can utilize in order to evaluate their service. The remaining three chapters focus upon one issue of evaluation; how do we measure the level of competency of the counselors working at telephone counseling services? Each of the three chapters describes a different method of achieving this aim.

There are other issues of evaluation, but we have chosen to focus upon the performance of telephone counselors since we feel that this is by far the most important area for evaluation and the one for which agencies should be held accountable. The service provided by the agencies is counseling and this is therefore the primary behavior of the agencies which should be inspected. Furthermore, it happens that this is currently an area in which research interest is focused, and so we are able to report facts and methods rather than mere aspirations.

Chapter 22

THE EVALUATION OF TELEPHONE COUNSELING SERVICES

DAVID LESTER

IT IS BECOMING INCREASINGLY important in mental health programs to evaluate the treatment procedures utilized. Partly because funding sources, public and private, are demanding feedback as to how beneficial their money has been to the community, and partly because in the past too many programs have had claims made for their usefulness that were undocumented or, when documented, found to be unsubstantiated, few programs can exist today without advancing some data to justify their continued funding.

On the other hand, faced with the demand that a program be evaluated, administrators are often hard pressed to find meaningful ways to do so. Inspection of the annual reports of telephone counseling services reveals that the most common way of demonstrating the effectiveness of the service is to present data on its activity. If an agency made contact with n clients, then this is seen as evidence of its usefulness to the community and justification of its continued funding. The astute observer who compares several annual reports will quickly note that the number n varies between fifty and 25,000 among different telephone counseling services, and yet each agency is satisfied with its performance.

A documentation of activity, though of interest, will not do as a measure of effectiveness for several reasons. First, the services rarely if ever have any notion of what the need of the

Parts of this chapter are based on Lester, D.: An evaluation of suicide prevention centers. *Int. Beh. Sci.*, in press and Lester, D.: The myth of suicide prevention. Paper presented to the University of Maine, April 1971.

community might be. Although the service may be counseling 100 patients a month, there may be 1,000 or even 10,000 in the community in need of help. Secondly, the service may not be counseling those to whom it is directed. Suicide prevention centers counsel large numbers of patients but the evidence available indicates that they rarely receive calls from the individuals in the community who are about to complete suicide (rather than those who are about to attempt suicide). Thirdly, there is no indication that those patients counseled received adequate, beneficial counseling. The patients calling the service might conceivably be helped more were there no telephone counseling service to call. Finally, telephone counseling services might be doing harm in the community, for example, by impeding the development of independence in its clients.

The presentation of data on the volume of activity of the service by itself is insufficient to answer these points. Better methods of evaluation must be used.

THE OBJECTIVES OF A PROGRAM

It is obvious that in order to evaluate a program, its objectives must be clearly stated. Though obvious, this is rarely the case. Occasionally, the name of the agency implies an objective. A suicide prevention center has the unavoidable implication that, at the least, it will prevent suicide in the community. (That this implication is unavoidable may account for why many suicide prevention centers have reoriented themselves as crisis clinics!) Other services, such as teen hotlines, have no objectives implied in their title.

It would be a useful exercise for a telephone counseling service to try to formulate its idealized objectives, as Suchman (1967) has called them. What changes does the agency hope to effect in its community? The suicide prevention center might reduce the community's suicide rate or its attempted suicide rate; the teen hotline might reduce drug use, illegitimate births, absence from school for emotional reasons, the incidence of delinquency, and so forth; a crisis intervention service might reduce admissions to psychiatric facilities, reduce recividism in former psychiatric patients, speed up the referral process in which a distressed individual in the community is referred to an appropriate helping agency, and so forth.

For an agency to be forthright enough to state its idealized objectives is a courageous act, for most likely these objectives may not be reached. (It would be wise, nonetheless, to be aware of the idealized objectives, even though they are not advertized.) The experience of telephone counseling services indicates that they release a flood of response from the community that indicates a vast amount of emotional distress among the members of the community who hitherto had no resources to turn to. However, there are no data yet that counseling these patients has any general or specific effect on the mental health of the community.

As an illustration of this, suicide prevention centers have had the definite aim of reducing the suicide rate in their community and their experience here is discouraging. Two rigorous studies have examined the effect on the suicide rate of the opening of a suicide prevention center. Weiner (1969) compared two Californian cities with centers with two cities without centers and found no differences in the change in the suicide rate. In fact, only one city had experienced a significant change; Los Angeles with a suicide prevention center had experienced a significant increase in the suicide rate. Bagley (1968) in England compared fifteen towns with centers to fifteen towns without centers and found that the former towns had experienced a decline in the suicide rate as compared to the latter towns. The results of the two studies, therefore, conflict. Any individual suicide prevention center that tries to document publicly its effect on the suicide rate is gambling and no center in the United States has successfully yet claimed to have reduced the suicide rate in its community.

Several explanations have been proposed to account for the failure of suicide prevention centers to reduce the suicide rate of their communities: the inaccurate reporting and recording of suicidal deaths (Douglas, 1967) and the possibility that suicide prevention centers encourage by suggestion the emotionally distressed individuals in the community to commit suicide, in much the same way as the reporting of suicides in the press may suggest suicide as a viable resolution of mental distress to some people (Motto, 1970).

The evaluation of idealized objectives is, therefore, rarely attempted.

LESSER OBJECTIVES

A telephone counseling service can formulate lesser objectives for itself. For example, if a service addresses itself to a particular subgroup of the population, several possibilities are available.

1. The potential clientele can be asked whether they have heard of the service, whether they have used it, and what their image of it is. For example, Motto (1971) found that 80 percent of a sample of depressed and suicidal patients admitted to a psychiatric unit had heard of the local suicide prevention center, but that only 11 percent had called it. Evidence from Los Angeles (Weiner, 1969) shows that only 2 percent of completed suicides had called the suicide prevention center.

2. Who calls the center? If the center is addressed to a particular clientele, do these people call the service? For example, the typical completed suicide is old, white, and male. The typical caller to the Chicago suicide prevention center was young, black, and female (Maris, 1969).

3. The evaluation may be even more tangential to the idealized objectives of the service. Are the calls coming from the appropriate areas of the community? For example, if the suicide rate is high in a particular locale in the community, does the center receive a high proportion of calls from that locale. In Buffalo, Lester (1971) was able to demonstrate that this was occurring. The monitoring of the areas where calls come from to the agency enables the agency, if it desires, to adjust its advertizing and out-reach activities accordingly and so provides useful feedback to the agency.

CATEGORIES OF EVALUATION

Aside from the objectives of a program, Suchman (1967) has noted that programs can be evaluated in terms of different categories of effect. These categories represent different criteria by which a program may be judged. To date, very little research or evaluation of telephone counseling services has been conducted for any of these criteria. However it may be informative to list the criteria mentioned by Suchman.

1. *Effort.* What is the quantity and the quality of the activity that takes place and how does this compare to the counseling resources? This, of course, varies from service to service. The suicide prevention and crisis service of Buffalo serves a community of about one million and receives some 24,000 patient calls a year on its three telephone services (suicide prevention service, teen hotline, and problems-in-living service). The service is staffed by about seventy-five volunteers. The quality of the service is unknown.

2. *Performance.* What is the effect of the effort put out by the service? Do people receive help from the service? Very few studies have attempted to follow-up callers to telephone counseling services and assess the impact of the service. Murphy *et al.* (1969) interviewed a sample of callers to a suicide prevention center who had called on their own behalf and found that only about half had followed through on the advice given to them by the counselor.

3. *Adequacy of performance.* Is the performance of a service sufficient to cope with the community need?

4. *Efficiency.* Could the service provided by the agency be better provided by a different kind of agency or by an agency with a different structure?

5. *Process.* How does the agency produce the results that it does?

EVALUATION OF THE INTERNAL OPERATIONS OF A TELEPHONE COUNSELING SERVICE

So far, the methods of evaluation discussed have been unsuitable for the majority of telephone counseling services. To evaluate idealized objectives is a gamble. To evaluate idealized and lesser objectives is expensive To evaluate in the areas suggested by Suchman is to break new ground for telephone counseling services and most services are not equipped to do this. What can telephone services do in order to evaluate their services if these alternatives are not feasible?

A number of telephone counseling services that do evaluate their performance focus upon low-level objectives concerned primarily with the internal operation of the agency, the administrative functions, and the performance of the counselors. There are many possibilities here and a number of them are described below.

The Internal Operation of the Agency

1. How long does it take to obtain a counselor at a telephone counseling service? Lester (1970a) called a telephone counseling service at different hours during the week and noted how long it took a counselor to answer the telephone and how often he obtained a busy signal. In this way, a center can identify peak periods of activity and monitor the performance of its counselors. McGee *et al.* (see Chap. 2) called different centers in the south-east United States and noted the time that passed until a counselor was obtained. This latter study provided data on the speed with which a center can respond to a call depending upon its system for answering calls: an answering service, use of a local agency such as the fire station, locating the counselors at their homes or in the center, and so forth.

2. The success in referring patients to other resources can be noted by finding out the proportion of referrals who show at these resources. The Suicide Prevention and Crisis Service in Buffalo can refer patients to its own crisis clinic, and Lester (1970b) noted the proportion of referrals who showed. Over several months, this varied from 29 to 56 percent. The success in referring patients can also be noted for each counselor. Following up on this finding, Lester (1970c; Lester and Priebe, 1971) tried to identify from the data on the initial contact sheets completed by the counselors when a patient first calls those characteristics that distinguish shows from no-shows.* Slaikeu

---

* Shows were older, less likely to be single, and more likely to be calling on the suicide prevention line than other lines.

et al. (1971) are pursuing this by carrying out a content analysis of the telephone calls during which shows and no-shows were referred to the crisis clinic.† In this way it is hoped to provide feedback to the counselors as to the factors likely to lead to a patient failing to follow through with the referral made for him.

3. The completeness with which patient records are kept can be assessed. Do counselors obtain the information from patients that the center requires? Kolker and Katz (1971) have found at their suicide prevention center that if a counselor fails to note down the age of the caller, then he is also less likely to collect information necessary to recontact the patient if this is necessary (if the patient hangs up, if the line inadvertently gets disconnected, or for a follow-up contact). Whittemore (1970) compared samples of initial contact sheets at different centers and noted that whereas the sex of the patient was noted in 99.9 percent of the calls he checked, the age was not noted for 16.9 percent of the callers, marital status was unknown for 10.4 percent, and religion was unknown for over 75 percent.

4. Whittemore (1970) in his comparison of ten centers has provided data on the kinds of callers and calls that different centers receive. For example, Whittemore found that the proportion of anonymous calls at the ten centers varied from 18 to 63 percent. The proportion of calls with no suicidal involvement varied from 43 to 79 percent. Telephone counseling services can easily collect their own data and compare the data to those from the ten centers studied by Whittemore.*

5. Many centers ask counselors to rate the improvement of the patients as a result of the telephone contact. This rating can provide some data as to how well the counselor feels that he is performing.

6. Although it is obvious that the cost of the service is not necessarily related to the adequacy and quality of the service, the cost per telephone contact can easily be computed and compared with other centers.

---

† The major finding here is that patients who themselves suggest a referral are more likely to show.

* K. Whittemore, Fulton-DeKalb Emergency Mental Health Center, 99 Butler Street, S.E., Atlanta, Georgia 30303.

7. Motto (1969) has devised a set of standards for suicide prevention centers in terms of the adequacy of the administration, staffing, and evaluating of the program, the training and supervision of counselors, consultation resources, and the ethical standards. Ross and Motto (1970) have applied these standards to a number of centers and attempted to set a minimum requirement that centers should meet. Centers can easily apply these standards to their own operation.

Lester (1970a, 1970b, 1970d) has provided sample data for many of these criteria for the internal functioning of a center from the suicide prevention and crisis service of Buffalo and these data can be used for comparison.*

The Adequacy of the Counselor's Performance

A separate and crucial area for evaluation is the adequacy of the counseling provided by the staff of a telephone counseling service. Most centers require some kind of supervision of counselors and this is, of course, crucially important. However, it is also necessary to devise standardized means of evaluating the effectiveness of counselors. Not all centers can obtain adequate supervisors for counselors and not all supervisors are competent. The availability of standardized evaluation procedures would enable centers to make additional checks on the competence of their staff and, furthermore, enable centers to compare their performance with that of other centers. Three methods of evaluation are being developed at the present time.

1. Fowler and McGee (Chap. 23) have devised a technical effectiveness scale.† This scale focuses upon the technical aspects of the counselor's performance: did he get the name of the patient or sufficient information that he could recontact the patient if necessary, did he obtain sufficient information so as to be able to evaluate the suicidal lethality of the patient?

2. Knickerbocker and McGee (Chap. 24) have explored the use of the Truax and Carkhuff dimensions of counselor

---

* Reprints of these articles by Lester are obtainable from the Suicide Prevention and Crisis Service, 560 Main Street, Buffalo, New York 14202.

† For information write to McGee at the Center for Crisis Intervention Research, 804 S.W. 2nd Avenue, Gainesville, Florida 32601.

effectiveness: genuineness, respect, concreteness, self-disclosure, and empathy. They have demonstrated that these dimensions can be reliably measured, but as yet there is no evidence that these dimensions make for efficient telephone counseling or crisis intervention. These dimensions of therapeutic behavior may be more appropriate for face-to-face traditional therapy than for crisis intervention by telephone. For example, the level of functioning of a sample of counselors at the Suicide Prevention and Crisis Service in Buffalo has been noted on all five dimensions (Lester, 1970d), but the only dimension that appears to be related to whether a patient shows or fails to show for an appointment at the center is the dimension of concreteness. However, these dimensions of counselor behavior can be measured quite easily. Knickerbocker and McGee were able to obtain highly reliable ratings after training judges for only two hours. The dimensions of counselor behavior are described fully by Carkhuff (1969).

3. Williamson *et al.* (Chap. 25) have devised a series of simulated patient calls. In these, an actor calls the counselor (who may or may not be informed that the call is a test call) and presents a rehearsed role. The response of the counselor to this standardized call can then be evaluated.*

The first two methods enable the counselor to be evaluated while actually counseling patients, if the calls can be taped or if the rater can listen in to the call. The third method requires a special call to be placed to the counselor for purposes of evaluation but has the advantage of being a standardized patient simulation.

IN CONCLUSION

The kind and amount of evaluation that a telephone counseling service does will obviously depend upon the budget and available staff time. All centers should have some evaluation of their performance. It is becoming accepted (McGee *et al.*, Chap. 2; Whittemore, 1970) that the most effective counseling

---

* Information about this method is obtainable from Dr. J. Williamson, Department of Medical Care, School of Hygiene, Johns Hopkins University, 615 North Wolfe Street, Baltimore, Maryland 21205.

takes place at centers where counselors are on duty twenty-four hours a day at the center and where they take calls directly, without the mediation of an operator or answering service. At the very least, a center should evaluate the adequacy of counseling of the staff.

The larger issues are of importance too. Do telephone counseling services have an effect on the mental health of the community or, for that matter, of their patients? What did distressed individuals do before there were telephone counseling services to turn to? What kinds of help and programs must we offer the individual in a crisis (suicidal and nonsuicidal) in order to help him? However, to answer these kinds of questions (which are related to the idealized objectives mentioned earlier) requires a large expense of time and money, which is beyond the reach of most telephone counseling services. At the present time, several of the major suicide prevention centers are initiating research projects addressed to these questions and so partial answers to these larger issues may be forthcoming in the next decade.

REFERENCES

Bagley, C.: The evaluation of a suicide prevention scheme by an ecological method. *Soc. Sci. Med.*, 2:1-14, 1968.

Carkhuff, R.: *Helping and Human Relations.* New York, Holt, Rinehart, & Winston, 1969.

Douglas, J.: *The Social Meanings of Suicide.* Princeton, University of Princeton Press, 1967.

Kolker, H and Katz, S.: If you've missed the age you've missed a lot. *Crisis Intervention*, 3:34-37, 1971.

Lester, D.: Steps toward the evaluation of a suicide prevention center: part two. *Crisis Intervention*, 2(suppl to 1):12-18, 1970a.

Lester, D.: Steps toward the evaluation of a suicide prevention center: part one: *Crisis Intervention*, 2(suppl to 2):42-45, 1970b.

Lester, D.: A comparison of patients who show for appointments and those who do not show. *Crisis Intervention*, 2:75-76, 1970c.

Lester, D.: Steps toward the evaluation of a suicide prevention center: part four. *Crisis Intervention*, 2(suppl to 4):20-22, 1970d.

Lester, D.: Geographical location of callers to a suicide prevention center. *Psychol. Rep.*, 28:421-422, 1971.

Lester, D. and Priebe, K.: Patients who show for therapy and those who fail. *Crisis Intervention,* in press.

Maris, R.: The sociology of suicide prevention. *Soc. Prob.,* 17:132-149, 1969.

Motto, J.: Newspaper influence on suicide. *Arch. Gen. Psychiatr.,* 23:143-148, 1970.

Motto, J.: Development of standards for suicide prevention centers. *Bull. Suicidol.,* pp. 33-37, March 1969.

Motto, J.: Evaluation of a suicide prevention center by sampling the population at risk. *Life-Threatening Behav.,* 1:18-22, 1971.

Murphy, G.; Wetzel, R.; Swallow, C., and McClure, J.: Who calls the suicide prevention center? *Am. J. Psychiatr.,* 126:314-324, 1969.

Ross, C. and Motto, J.: Implementation of standards for suicide prevention centers. Unpublished, 1970.

Slaikieu, K.; Lester, D., and Tulkin, S.: Content analysis of telephone calls referring patients to a clinic for therapy. In preparation.

Suchman, E. A.: *Evaluative Research.* New York, Russell Sage Foundation, 1969.

Weiner, I. W.: The effectiveness of a suicide prevention program. *Ment. Hyg.,* 53:357-363, 1969.

Whittemore, K.: *Ten Centers.* Atlanta, Lullwater Press, 1970.

Chapter 23

ASSESSING THE PERFORMANCE OF TELEPHONE CRISIS WORKERS: THE DEVELOPMENT OF A TECHNICAL EFFECTIVENESS SCALE

DALE E. FOWLER AND RICHARD K. McGEE

A SIGNIFICANT DEVELOPMENT of the past decade in the delivery of community services has been the rapid proliferation of suicide prevention or crisis intervention centers. Such programs came into existence in nearly every state, and in all of the major urban centers beginning about 1965, and at the end of the 1960s numbered in excess of 150. There have been a number of factors which have contributed to this movement, but probably none is more potent than the increasing utilization of the lay citizen, the nonprofessional, as a volunteer telephone worker. The role of the volunteer in crisis center development has now been well documented in the literature (Heilig, Farberow, Litman, and Shneidman, 1968; McGee, 1967, 1968).

Heilig *et al.* (1968) described the first experimental approach to the use of volunteers in the Los Angeles Suicide Prevention Center, and they reported the subjective and a priori guidelines used for selecting workers. These included evaluations as to the maturity, responsibility, motivation, sensitivity, willingness to learn, and ability to get along in a group which the applicants

The research reported in this paper was conducted in the Center for Crisis Intervention Research, Department of Clinical Psychology, at the University of Florida. The facilities of this laboratory are provided by Research Grant MH 16861 from the Center for Studies of Suicide Prevention, N.I.M.H. Portions of this project were performed by the senior author as partial fulfillment of the requirements for the M.A. degree, under the direction of the junior author. From *Bulletin of Suicidology*. Reprinted with the permission of the publisher.

revealed during personal interviews. Although many other programs have adopted the use of volunteers, none has offered a systematic method for assessing the applicant's suitability for the work or the worker's performance once on the job.

In an earlier report, McGee (1968) described an elaborate method for rating volunteer performance and attempted to correlate these ratings with data which might be used to predict future success. However, the data for these correlations could be obtained on a sample of only twenty-two volunteers, and the method was considered too complicated to be useful in any practical way by other centers.

The primary difficulty in developing predictors for use in screening new volunteer applicants relates to the lack of performance criteria. Until it can be established what behavioral or personal characteristics are desired, it is impossible to develop predictor measures to select quality personnel. This paper presents both a rationale for a performance criterion and a method for assessing volunteers in relation to it.

CONCEPT OF TECHNICAL EFFECTIVENESS

The argument is sometimes advanced that, like psychotherapists, crisis workers are "born and not made." It is agreed that certain personal qualities which the applicant brings to the task are of such importance that if they are missing, even the best training program cannot make up the deficit. However, every program director also believes that some type of training is necessary before anyone should begin taking calls. This suggests that both specifically learned skills and native personal traits are necessary for crisis workers.

Technical Effectiveness (TE) is therefore defined as the extent to which a person performs those tasks that he has been explicitly trained to perform, and which the center recognizes as the fundamental duties of the worker performing the telephone crisis intervention function. These duties have been outlined in the clinical and research reports from the Los Angeles center (Litman, 1963; Litman, Farberow, Shneidman, Heilig and

Kramer, 1965). In brief, the job of the emergency telephone therapist includes three partially overlapping activities:

1. He must secure the communication. He must involve the caller in the helping process to the extent that the agency can understand the nature of the problem and be of some help. This can mean only that the therapist appears so non-threatening and potentially helpful that the caller elects not to hang up and sever the connection. It can also be expanded to mean that the communication is secured for further contacts to be initiated by the center. In such cases the communication would be secured when the therapist has elicited a name, telephone number, address, or other identifying information to permit a recontact if the communication is broken.

2. The worker must evaluate the caller's condition, particularly the danger that a self-destructive act is imminent. Moreover, in addition to assessing the lethality of the caller, the telephone worker must also determine in nonsuicidal cases whether the problem is an acute crisis, and the nature thereof, or if the case is one of chronic maladjustment and dependency.

3. The telephone therapist must begin to formulate a treatment plan to mobilize the caller. This plan of action may eventuate in a transfer action wherein the caller becomes directly involved with another helping agency which is equipped to manage long-term care or rehabilitation. In many instances, however, the action plan serves only to structure the next few hours and may focus on an immediate visit by members of the center staff to the caller's home, or an interview with the caller in the office, where a more long-range plan of action will be developed.

The measure of technical effectiveness developed in this paper includes these three functions. They are considered necessary (but not sufficient) in the opening of every case handled by a telephone crisis agency. The measurement of those additional qualities and skills which come under the rubric of "clinical competence" form the subject of other investigations currently under way at the Center for Crisis Intervention Research.

Method

The first effort to develop a measure of volunteer performance consisted in writing ninety-four items, each of which referred to a behavior associated with one of the three basic telephone duties. These items were then used by three members of the research team to rate the behavior of volunteers from taped recordings of their performance while taking an initial call from a new client. For these ratings, a pool of eight tapes was selected, each tape having been made by a different telephone worker. The ratings were made on a dichotomous scale indicating the rater's opinion as to whether the behavior did or did not occur during the conversation. The original pool of ninety-four items was then narrowed down to a sample of forty items by eliminating those wherein there was clearly no agreement among the three raters. The revised forty-item form was then used by a group of six new raters listening to the same set of eight tapes. Again the items about which there was easy agreement were identified, and the remaining ones eliminated. Items which were clearly redundant, and therefore highly interrelated, were also eliminated until a twelve-item scale was evolved. These items were then studied carefully for content and were edited and rewritten into language which permitted the most objective response of observable behavior.

The final form of the scale was the result of attempts to use the twelve items in rating a new set of tapes. Four rating sessions were held at which a group of twelve graduate psychology students independently rated from five to ten tapes. After each tape, ratings were compared and a discussion was held about items whereon there was still disagreement; at the end of each session, items were reworded to clarify meanings based on the data generated in the discussions. The final form of the TE scale is the nine-item form reproduced in Table 23-I.

It should be noted that item number 7 of the scale asks if the worker determined whether or not the call was a suicide case. Nearly every suicide prevention program around the country has reported that from 15 to 20 percent of their calls involve a current suicide threat or attempt; the remaining 80

TABLE 23-I

THE FOWLER TECHNICAL EFFECTIVENESS (TE) SCALE

Item	*Scoring Criterion*
1. Can the caller be immediately recontacted?	In order to answer this question affirmatively the call must contain enough information to enable the center to return the call and contact the caller, or to immediately go to the caller.
2. Did the volunteer ask for (or obtain) specific information regarding significant others?	A specific question dealing with the possibility of roommates, parents, neighbors, friends, or relatives must occur in order to answer this question yes. A general inquiry such as "Do you have someone you can talk to?" will not be enough to qualify as a yes answer.
3. Were specific problems identified?	A problem identified to which the center can respond, even if it is not the focal problem, will qualify for a yes answer.
4. Did the volunteer communicate that he is willing to help?	This question may be answered on the basis of both affect and/or content.
5. Did the volunteer develop a structured plan of action or help the caller develop one?	A structured plan of action must lead to some action or event that will involve the caller in an observable behavior.
6. Did the caller agree to the action plan?	A definite commitment must be obtained from the caller in order for this question to be answered yes.
7. Was it determined whether or not this was a suicide case?	Specific inquiry from worker mentioning "suicide" or "kill self"; or spontaneous statement from caller may be scored.
8. (a) Did the volunteer ask about a suicide plan? . . . or (b) If caller voluntarily disclosed the information, did volunteer inquire for further details?	Answer either (a) or (b), but *not* both.
9. Was it determined if caller has made prior suicide attempts?	Specific inquiry must be made by the worker or a spontaneous statement from caller may be scored.

to 85 percent are concerning some personal crisis wherein suicide is not a currently contemplated alternative solution for the caller. Therefore, in approximately 80 percent of the first calls rated by the TE scale, the worker should determine that this is *not* a suicide call. Although he will get a positive score from item 7 for having made that determination, he will not get any score for items 8 and 9, for they reflect interviewing behaviors which are relevant only to suicide calls. The TE scale must be viewed as a two-form instrument—a nine-item scale for suicide cases and a seven-item scale for nonsuicide cases.

In order to use this assessment method fairly across calls, both for the same volunteer and across volunteers, it is necessary to express the score on the scale as a ratio rather than as a raw number. For example, to score a call, the rater assigns a plus or a minus to each item, depending upon whether the behavior did or did not occur. A perfect score would be nine pluses on a suicide call, but only seven pluses on a nonsuicide call. However, a person who receives five pluses would score .5556 (5/9) if the call was a suicide case, but five pluses is a score of .7142 (5/7) when the case is not a suicide call. (The conversion of number of pluses to total TE score for a call can be seen in the frequency distribution presented in Table 23-IV.) If the telephone therapist should fail to determine if the call is a suicide case, a minus is scored for item 7, and items 8 and 9 *must be scored* either plus or minus; the nine-item scale is always used unless the call is clearly established as a nonsuicide case.

Once the scale was completed, several concerns dictated additional analyses to be performed on it. First, could it be demonstrated to be highly reliable across several raters who were not previously involved in its development when applied to new, unselected telephone conversations? Secondly, is it possible that the scale can be used reliably by only one person, instead of a group of raters? Further, can the scale be used to assess telephone worker performance across a group of volunteers; does it yield scores which are consistent within a single person, but still vary between workers? Data were collected to answer these questions.

Results

In order to determine the reliability of the scale across several raters, the Kendall Coefficient of Concordance was computed on three separate sets of data. Table 23-II shows the results of these analyses which clearly demonstrate the inter-rater reliability to be exceptionally good for this type of instrument.

TABLE 23-II

KENDALL COEFFICIENT OF CONCORDANCE VALUES COMPUTED TO
ANALYZE THE INTER-RATER RELIABILITY OF THE TE SCALE

Analysis	No. of Raters	No. of Tapes Rated	Value of W	P
1	3	11	.992	<.001
2	3	14	.904	<.001
3	10	10	.923	<.001

It is doubtful that most suicide prevention or crisis intervention centers around the country can afford the manpower to
create a team of judges who can rate tapes for assessing the
performance of volunteers. What is needed is an instrument that
can be periodically used by one person, usually the volunteer
coordinator, to check on the performance of the telephone staff.
Therefore, one of the judges in the reliability study was selected
and his performance was compared with each of the others in
order to show the feasibility of using only one person as a rater.
Table 23-III shows the Spearman rank correlation coefficients
developed in three separate analyses, using different sets of tapes.

TABLE 23-III

SPEARMAN RANK-ORDER CORRELATIONS COMPARING THE TE
RATINGS OF ONE JUDGE WITH THOSE OF THREE OTHERS

Other Judges	Number of Tapes	Rating of Judge A Compared to Value of rho	P
Judge B	11	.984	<.001
Judge C	11	.960	<.001
Judge E	22	.997	<.001

It is important to know how the scores on this scale are
distributed, and how a series of scores might be used to chart
the performance of individual volunteers. In order to determine
the characteristics of this distribution, the scale was used to
rate the first call taken by each of seventy-six telephone workers.
The frequency of scores obtained are shown in Table 23-IV. It
will be noted that the obtained scores are distributed evenly
along the range of possible scores. It is also evident that the
scale is able to identify groups of subjects who fall into both
ends of the distribution, which may be especially valuable for

TABLE 23-IV

FREQUENCY DISTRIBUTION OF TE SCORES COMPUTED FOR 76
TELEPHONE VOLUNTEERS AT THE SUICIDE AND CRISIS
INTERVENTION SERVICE, GAINESVILLE, FLORIDA

TE Score	Number of Pluses: Suicide Call	Number of Pluses: Non-Suicide Call	Frequency
1.0000	9	7	7
.8889	8	—	6
.8571	—	6	3
.7778	7	—	7
.7142	—	5	2
.6667	6	—	6
.5714	—	4	1
.5556	5	—	6
.4444	4	—	7
.4286	—	3	1
.3333	3	—	10
.2857	—	2	0
.2222	2	—	6
.1428	—	1	0
.1111	1	—	10
.0000	0	0	4

further screening of new personnel early in their role as telephone therapists.

To demonstrate that the TE score can be used to chart the
course of an individual volunteer, three sets of ratings were
selected for presentation in Figure 23-I. Each graph in the figure
represents the cumulative or moving average of the TE scores
obtained sequentially on the first ten new case calls taken by a
telephone crisis therapist.

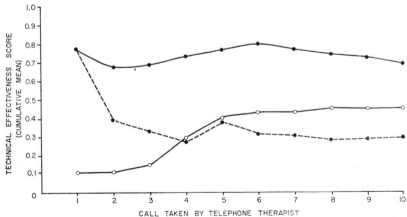

Figure 23-1.   Performance of three telephone therapists on ten consecutive
initial calls.

It is evident that one of the volunteers appeared to learn well in the training program and was able to apply the learning to the actual work setting. This worker began with, and was able to maintain, high performance on the scale. The chart suggests that other workers may begin their work at lower levels, but with increasing experience or with helpful feedback from their coordinator can demonstrate regular improvement. It may be noticed that in all three of these performance curves, the worker reached a plateau after approximately five or six calls. This suggests the possibility that the TE score measures a natural base level of performance after initial training and that it would serve as an index of change resulting from additional training or other efforts to modify worker performance. It might also be used to reflect important decrements in performance which have been noted after workers have been on telephone duty over many months or after having taken a large number of crisis calls.

Discussion

The Fowler TE Scale is a new research instrument with well-established inter-rater reliability. It has been shown to be a feasible method for making systematic observations of volunteer telephone performance, even when only one person is available to make the ratings. The scale is currently being correlated with demographic variables, personality test scores, and other measures of performance in the crisis center. Future papers will discuss the results of these studies.

In the meantime, the TE scale is also a potentially valuable instrument for the practical assessment of personnel in existing crisis intervention agencies. Motto (1969) has indicated the need for setting and maintaining standards for the operation of suicide prevention programs. He cites the Bay Area Association for Suicide Prevention (BAASP) standards for member agencies. This model includes a section on staffing standards and sets the minimum criteria for acceptability. Among them is the requirement that "all staff members who have responsibility for responding to callers must have a minimum of 40 hours of instruction time, or equivalent, including at least . . . handling incoming calls independently with consultation as needed and with regular supervisory review . . ." (p. 36). Motto also urges that pertinent material to document all elements of this staffing standard requirement be available in written form for reference by members of the agency. The TE scale is an easily administered means of making this necessary supervisory review and preserving the information for later reference.

Many crisis centers do not currently tape all incoming calls, but this should not be a major problem with the use of the scale. Nearly all centers do tape occasionally, if only to provide themselves with fresh training material. In such cases it would be possible to require that each telephone crisis worker submit one tape of his work at whatever interval is appropriate in that center. In centers where formal policy or limited technical facilities prevent taping at all, it is possible to complete the TE rating by observing the call being taken or monitoring the call on a speaker phone or extension telephone. Finally, when all else fails, the worker could be asked to role play a case with a partner—as is frequently done in training sessions—and the performance rated on the TE scale. There are a number of possibilities, and every center that has a concern about maintaining a high level of quality control can find a way to employ this method for evaluating its telephone personnel.

SUMMARY

This paper has presented the rationale for a method of assessing the performance of telephone crisis intervention workers. The Fowler Technical Effectiveness Scale is designed to measure the extent to which workers perform the basic functions of securing the communication, assessing the patient's condition, and forming a plan of action. The scale has repeatedly demonstrated exceedingly high inter-rater reliability and can be used by one rater with a high degree of confidence in the results. It yields scores which are stable when repeated on individual workers, and it discriminates a sample of workers throughout the range of possible scores. Its practical use as a measure of training effectiveness, as well as for supervisory evaluation, is highly recommended, and the heuristic value of the instrument as a research tool appears to be unlimited.

REFERENCES

Heilig, S. M.; Farberow, N. L.; Litman, R. E., and Shneidman, E. S.: The role of nonprofessional volunteers in a suicide prevention center. *Community Ment. Health J.,* 4:287-295, 1968.

Litman, R. E.: Emergency response to potential suicide. *J Mich. State Med. Soc.,* 62:68-72, 1963.

Litman, R. E.; Farberow, N. L.; Shneidman, E. S.; Heilig, S. M., and Kramer, J. A.: Suicide-prevention telephone service. *JAMA, 192:*107-111, 1965.

McGee, R. K.: A community approach to crisis intervention. In McGee, R. K. (Ed.): *Planning Emergency Services for Comprehensive Community Mental Health Centers.* Gainesville, University of Florida, Department of Clinical Psychology, 1967.

McGee, R. K.: An approach to the selection of volunteers for suicide prevention centers. Paper presented at the meeting of the American Association of Suicidology, Chicago, March 1968.

Motto, J. A.: Development of standards for suicide prevention centers. *Bull Suicidol.,* pp. 33-37, March 1969.

Chapter 24

CLINICAL EFFECTIVENESS OF NONPROFESSIONAL AND PROFESSIONAL TELEPHONE WORKERS IN A CRISIS INTERVENTION CENTER

DAVID A. KNICKERBOCKER AND RICHARD K. McGEE

SINCE THE MID-1960s, suicide prevention and crisis intervention centers have appeared in steadily increasing numbers throughout the United States. The basic procedural component of every program is the twenty-four-hour telephone service which forms the very core of the crisis intervention effort (McGee, 1969). Using whatever interpersonal skills he possesses, the telephone crisis worker accepts responsibility for constructively helping the caller. Although there are several handicaps inherent in the media—for example, both parties are deprived of visual cues and most nonverbal communication signals—the method has proven its incomparable value to emergency crisis intervention.

Many of these centers still incorporate the words "suicide prevention" in their names. However, the majority of calls received by a center revolve around crisis situations for which suicide is not being considered as an alternative solution by the caller. Nearly every such center receives approximately five general crisis calls to every one call concerning a serious

The research reported in this paper was conducted in the Center for Crisis Intervention Research, Department of Clinical Psychology, at the University of Florida. The facilities of this laboratory are provided by Research Grant MH 16861 from the Center for Studies of Suicide Prevention, N.I.M.H. Portions of this project were performed by the senior author as partial fulfillment of the requirements for the degree of Doctor of Philosophy, under the direction of the junior author. All statistical computations were performed through the facilities and assistance of the University of Florida Computer Center.

298

threat or attempt. Experience has shown that these other crisis calls include such problems as drug abuse, marital difficulties, vocational problems, loneliness, alcoholism, ambulatory schizophrenia, and school and adolescent problems. In addition to assessing lethality, establishing communications, and forming a treatment plan as outlined by Litman, Farberow, Shneidman, Heilig and Kramer (1965), the crisis worker is called upon to provide a great deal of psychological support while establishing a therapeutic climate for the caller.

One of the most potent factors of successful delivery of these services has been the increasing use of lay volunteers as telephone crisis workers. Dublin (1969) has hailed the lay volunteer as the most important single discovery in the fifty-year history of suicide prevention, saying, "Little progress was made until he came into the picture." The success of Los Angeles volunteers has been reported several times (Farberow, 1966; Heilig, Farberow, Litman, and Shneidman, 1968). As early as 1961, the report by the Joint Committee of Mental Illness and Health pointed out the acute manpower shortage and suggested alternatives to the problem of the lack of traditional professional personnel. One early program which trained lay personnel to function as therapists provided clear evidence that nonprofessional workers could perform effectively in facilitating the solution to people's problems (Rioch *et al.*, 1963).

Since these beginnings, many lay-worker training programs have been introduced into health delivery systems. However, only a few have systematically assessed the therapeutic effectiveness of volunteers in terms of process variables related in previous research to established indices of constructive client outcomes. Those that have investigated dimensions such as a counselor's communication of empathy, warmth, regard or respect, and genuineness have yielded the following conclusions:

    1. There is extensive evidence to indicate that lay persons can be trained to function at minimally facilitative levels of conditions related to constructive client change over relatively short periods of time . . .

    2. There is little evidence to indicate that professional trainee products are being trained to function effectively on any dimensions

related to constructive client change over long periods of training . . .

3. Comparative statistics indicate the greater effectiveness of lay and lower level guidance training programs in eliciting constructive trainee change on those conditions related to constructive client change . . . on both identical and converted indexes, lay trainees function at levels essentially as high or higher (never lower), and engage clients in counseling process movement at levels as high or higher, than professional trainees. (Carkhuff, R. R., 1968.)

Research on psychotherapists has shown that they are relatively stable in their level of these conditions across several clients (Truax *et al.*, 1966; Truax and Wargo, 1966). Many other studies point rather conclusively to the therapist as the pulling force in the therapeutic dyad: he may either constructively help the client or destructively contribute to the client's problems (Truax and Carkhuff, 1964, 1967). Of the three therapeutic variables, offering warmth as a condition is the most potent factor as a predictor of successful outcome with verbal patients, followed by genuineness and then empathy in degree of potency (Truax and Carkhuff, 1967).

Other writers have indirectly pointed out the necessity of providing these therapeutic conditions for clients. For Caplan (1961), "the individual in crisis may use an intervention as a source of forward movement or growth" or "regress to the use of maladaptive devices to cope with the crisis." Other authors stress putting the person at ease, providing a lessening of insecurity, confusion, guilt, fear, suspicion, and showing a willingness to become personally involved as major emphases in the telephone contact. These authors also encourage telephone therapists to show interest in the client, discern his feelings, respond appropriately, and remain sensitive to emotional reactions (Litman *et al.*, 1965). The client must be met with acceptance, patience, and warmth (Kaplan and Litman, 1961). All of the efforts of the telephone crisis worker are directed toward offering constructive rather than destructive client change. The major difficulty at present is the lack of any reliable measure to determine how well the telephone worker performs these functions.

There is now extensive evidence that lay persons can offer moderately high levels of warmth, empathy, and genuineness in several patient populations including hospitalized and outpatient neuropsychiatric patients, normals, juvenile delinquents, and children (Carkhuff, 1968). No assessment has yet been made of lay and professional trainees in crisis intervention and suicide prevention centers. If the above findings also hold for the emergency telephone setting, then the measurement of these therapist-facilitating conditions would provide one badly needed index of crisis worker performance. Therefore, this experiment is an attempt to identify those workers who offer high levels of constructive or facilitative conditions in emergency crisis situations. Thus, it is intended to present both the rationale for a clinical performance criterion and a method for assessing crisis workers in relation to the criterion.

It was hypothesized that on each of the rated scales (accurate empathy, warmth, genuineness, and their summed total conditions score), the nonprofessional volunteer would offer as high or higher therapeutic conditions as professional trainees or professional practitioners.

Previous research also suggested the hypothesis that both groups would function at below the midpoints of each rating scale or at only moderate levels of therapeutic functioning (Carkhuff, 1968; Truax and Carkhuff, 1967; Carkhuff and Berenson, 1967).

METHOD

Subjects. Two distinct volunteer populations were studied at the Center for Crisis Intervention Research. All subjects were clinical associates or staff members at the Suicide and Crisis Intervention Service (SCIS) in Gainesville, Florida. The two groups were comprised of (1) nonprofessional volunteers and (2) professional trainees and professionals. The lay volunteers included sixty-five crisis workers who had never been trained in any helping profession before coming to work at the center. These subjects, from the community of Gainesville, Florida, ranged in occupation from housewives to undergraduate students from diverse disciplines. The second group of volunteers consisted of professional trainees (advanced graduate students in clinical psychology and counselor education with at least some clinical experience at the University of Florida), and professional social workers, and ministers who used pastoral counseling in their profession. This second group were all involved in achieving or maintaining a professional role in a helping profession. Age and sex distribution were observed to be equivalent for the two groups. The nonprofessional group consisted of 42 percent male crisis workers with an overall group mean age of 27.40 years. Similarly, the professional group was made up of 53 percent male crisis workers with an overall mean age of 28.25 years. All subjects were caucasian.

Procedure. A rating method similar to that used by Truax and Carkhuff (1967) was used to assess the performance of the workers. In addition, analagous but more differentiated scales for rating empathy, warmth, and genuineness developed by Lister (1970) were also employed in the hope of developing an effective training device. These sets of scales proved to be highly correlated with one another and thus proved to be measuring the same phenomena. All of the ratings were directed toward the communication of the crisis worker and not the caller.

Raters. Twenty-seven undergraduate students in an introductory psychology course at the University of Florida volunteered to serve as raters. At the outset of the experiment, they were divided into one of three groups, each of which received instructions in rating one of the variables. The raters were given bonus course credit for their participation. All raters were formally trained in their groups for two hours. This training included learning the procedure, defining the scale to be rated, checking their reliabilities in a group discussion situation, and listening to and rating ten previously rated standardized three-minute tape segments. An effort was made to answer all questions the raters might have. They were then asked to memorize the two methods of rating and to make a commitment to rate as honestly as possible. (It was felt that many of the raters overlearned these rating scales using this procedure.) They were then given the following to take home: (1) a practice sheet of written conversations to rate, (2) a copy of Truax's rating stages, and (3) a copy of Lister's component rating method.

Stimuli. The ninety-two segments of taped telephone conversation, each of three minute's duration, were used in the experiment. Each segment was taken from the first through fourth minute of an initial case call to the SCIS. Tape segments were randomly picked from the library of taped calls stored at the Center for Crisis Intervention Research according to the following criteria: (1) the call had to have been at least six minutes in duration, (2) it had to have been received during the first year of the center's operation (which controlled somewhat for experience factors), and (3) the call had to be judged by the experimenters as involving a crisis of sufficient intensity such that therapeutic conditions would be offered appropriately. (Calls about jobs, information seeking, and about other people's crises were excluded.) A break of one minute's duration was left between tape segments to give the rater ample time to make the required rating. The samples were then randomly placed on four reels of Scotch Magnetic Tape and played to the raters on a Wollensak T-3000 tape recorder.

Ratings. The raters rated the tape segments in two 3-hour sessions two weeks apart. Four raters could not attend the second session and were allowed to rate the tapes in an extra session with the experimenter present. Each rater was given a score sheet, materials defining his scale, and an index card with scoring procedures written on it. For each tape segment, the raters first rated according to Truax's stage method. They then rated the same segment on Lister's component method for measuring the same variable. On all scales, the lowest rating was assigned a value of one.

*Measurement scales and rater reliabilities.** The Accurate Empathy Scale attempts to rate the worker's ability to recognize, sense, and to understand the feelings that another person has associated with his behavioral and verbal expressions and to accurately communicate this understanding to him. It was rated

---

* Copies of the rating scales employed in this study and instructions for their use may be obtained without charge by writing to the Center for Crisis Intervention Research, Department of Clinical Psychology, University of Florida, Gainesville, Florida, 32601. A Summary of reliability data from previous research with the scales may be found in Truax and Carkhuff (1967).

as a nine-point scale using the Truax (1967) method and was rated as an additive thirty-eight-point, nine-component scale using the Lister (1970) method. The reliability of all raters combined per segment was .83 for the Truax method and .82 for the Lister method as estimated by Ebel's (1951) formula for intraclass correlations.

The Warmth (caring, respect, or positive regard) Scale consists of expressing to a caller or client an honest concern that what he does is of real importance to the worker. It was rated as a five-point scale (Truax) or as an additive twenty-eight-point, five-component scale (Lister). The reliability of all raters combined per segment was .80 for Truax's method and .83 for Lister's method of rating.

The Genuineness (therapist self-congruence) Scale attempts to measure how the worker expresses what he truly feels in a nondestructive manner without insincere professional role playing. It was also rated on a five-point scale (Truax) and on a fifteen-point, two-component scale (Lister). The reliability of all raters combined per segment was .78 for Truax's method and .82 for Lister's method of rating.

RESULTS

The study hypothesized that lay volunteers offer as high or higher therapeutic conditions (empathy, warmth, and genuineness) over the telephone as professional trainees and professionals in a suicide and crisis intervention center. To test these various hypotheses, eight separate analyses of variance with repeated measures were computed. The results of these analyses are shown in Table 24-I.

The differences in the predicted direction for offered levels of warmth were significant ($p < .05$) using both analysis of variance and the t tests with one tail between means ($p < .01$). It can be noted that between the two groups, the volunteers tended to be as high or higher than the professionals on all of the rated scales using either rating method. These comparisons, together with t tests of mean differences are shown in Table 24-II.

TABLE 24-I

ONE WAY ANALYSES OF VARIANCE FOR TRUAX AND LISTER
THERAPEUTIC CONDITIONS FOR PROFESSIONALS
AND VOLUNTEERS (df=1/90)

Dependent Variables	*F Ratios for Main Effects*
Truax Empathy	2.24*
Truax Warmth	4.37†
Truax Genuineness	0.21
Truax Total Conditions	2.39*
Lister Empathy	1.14
Lister Warmth	2.30*
Lister Genuineness	0.00
Lister Total Conditions	1.05

* p<.10
† p<.05

TABLE 24-II

COMPARISON OF PROFESSIONAL TRAINEES AND VOLUNTEERS
ON TRUAX AND LISTER FACILITATION SCALES a

Scale	*Professional Trainees*		*Volunteers*		*Value of*
	Mean	*S.D.*	*Mean*	*S.D.*	*t*[b]
Truax Empathy	2.42	0.47	2.61	0.58	1.63*
Truax Warmth	2.88	0.41	3.15	0.60	2.42‡
Truax Genuineness	3.08	0.44	3.14	0.62	0.53
Truax Total Conditions	2.79	0.33	2.96	0.53	1.85†
Lister Empathy	16.88	3.40	17.82	4.04	1.14
Lister Warmth	21.23	3.54	22.93	5.33	1.78†
Lister Genuineness	23.96	3.66	23.97	4.69	0.01
Lister Total Conditions	20.68	2.64	21.57	4.17	1.22

* <.10
† <.05
‡ <.01

a The Truax Empathy Scale has been changed into a 5-point scale in this table, and Lister's Warmth and Genuineness Rating Scales have been transformed into 38-point scales by multiplying their scores by constants. Professional Trainees Group n=27, Volunteers Group n=65.

b These tests of t use the individual group variance (between) as the best estimator with df=90.

These results offer additional evidence for the first hypothesis. Table 24-II also offers other evidence suggesting the efficacy of the lay volunteer. The F ratios for Truax empathy, Truax total conditions, and Lister warmth rating are all significant at the .10 level. The *t* tests using the group variance as the best estimator were all significant at the .05 level for these scales. No significant differences were found between the groups or either rating method for genuineness, although the mean was slightly higher on both methods for the volunteer group. It is clear that for these groups of telephone crisis workers, the non-professional volunteers demonstrated as high or higher levels of therapeutic conditions to the caller than members of the professional group.

Hypothesis 2 predicted that both groups of crisis workers should be functioning at below the midpoint of rated therapeutic conditions. According to many authors, this is the minimal level of functioning at which clinical effectiveness can occur (Carkhuff, 1968; Truax and Carkhuff, 1967; Carkhuff and Berenson, 1967). As groups, the lay volunteers provided mean total conditions on Truax's scale at 2.96. The professional group, while lower, also offered fairly high levels of conditions with a mean of 2.79 on Truax's total conditions score. While this prediction of below maximum therapeutic functioning was confirmed, these means were very close to the midpoint level of 3.0 and were exceptionally high ratings in light of other studies (Truax and Carkhuff, 1967). The nonprofessional group averaged over 3.0 on Truax's warmth (3.16) scale and Truax's genuineness (3.14) scale. The professional group scored over 3.0 on Truax's genuineness (3.08) scale. It appears that both lay people and professionals who volunteered as crisis workers brought with them fairly high levels of therapeutic conditions. In general, these people, as groups, both demonstrate the ability to offer the callers relatively high levels of accurate empathy, warmth, and genuineness to facilitate them in their crises.

DISCUSSION

One methodological problem in the study was a relative lack of subjects available for the professional group. This created problems in matching the two groups for levels of experience on the telephone. Unfortunately, the professional group doesn't seem to be volunteering to use the telephone as much as the other workers. They seem to select themselves out of this kind of work in the center and involve themselves with other activities. Another problem is the anecdotal evidence of a "jaded effect" for the professional group. Several of them have commented on becoming so adapted to caller crises from listening to all the tapes during their research activities that they "just don't get too excited or interested in the call." Perhaps this is a phenomena that occurs in many helping professions. However, many studies also point to the opposite interpretation; that it is an imagined event. In reality, many therapists have been found to be consistently effective throughout their careers (Truax and Carkhuff, 1967).

The methodological tools used to measure facilitative therapeutic conditions in the study, the Truax Stage Rating scales and the Lister Component Rating scales, were most rewarding. Lister's rating method was developed for use as a counselor education in-service therapeutic training device. Because of their differentiation, their reliabilty, and the interest they created in their raters, it is felt that these scales can be used as a successful *selection, assessment,* and *training* tool to create more effective crisis workers.

Interestingly, the group differences in offered levels of warmth suggest further research hypotheses. Previous studies (Truax and Carkhuff, 1967) point to the potency of warmth as the most successful outcome predictor for verbal patients. Further research would predict that nonprofessionals as a group obtain significantly more successful outcomes than professionals. Research at the SCIS is exploring this possibility.

Probably the most significant outcome of this study is the demonstration with objective data—for the first time in the literature—on the clinical skills of the lay volunteer on the telephone. Apparently, despite extensive training, sometimes in excess of four years, professional trainees have yet to prove their efficacy on any of the various research rating scales (Bergin and Solomon, 1963; Truax and Carkhuff, 1967). In light of the shortage of professional personnel and the rapid proliferation of suicide prevention and crisis intervention centers, the addition of lay volunteers from the community is welcomed. Too often, these workers have to justify their existence in centers because of their naivete about more sophisticated psychological techniques and jargon. However, even though the professional group tended to offer lower therapeutic conditions to their callers, both groups were relatively high in their averaged ratings of conditions. As telephone crisis workers, most of them seem to be clinically effective in offering a constructive and positive relationship to the caller in crisis.

SUMMARY

Research in suicide prevention and crisis intervention programs has yet to develop a method for assessing the clinical effectiveness of crisis workers on the telephone. In this study sixty-five lay volunteers and twenty-seven professional trainees or professional practitioners in a suicide and crisis intervention center were rated on Truax (1967) and Lister's (1970) accurate empathy, warmth, and genuineness scales. Rater reliabilities were between .78 and .83 with two hours training. Nonprofessional volunteers offered significantly higher levels of warmth ($p<.01$), empathy ($p<.10$), and total conditions ($p<.05$) than professionals over the phone. Both groups were operating at total therapeutic levels slightly less than the midpoint of both rating methods. Results were discussed in terms of the growing need for nonprofessional manpower in the helping professions and as a rationale for using the rating methods in selection, training, and assessment of crisis workers.

REFERENCES

Bergin, A. E. and Solomon, S.: Personality and performance correlates of empathic understanding in psychotherapy. *Am. Psychol., 18*:393, 1963.

Caplan, G.: *Prevention of Mental Disorders in Children*. New York, Basic Books, 1961.

Carkhuff, R. R.: Differential functioning of lay and professional helpers. *J. Counseling Psychol., 15*(2):117-126, 1968.

Carkhuff, R. R. and Berenson, B. G.: *Beyond Counseling and Psychotherapy*. New York, Holt, Rinehart & Winston, 1967.

Dublin, L. I.: Suicide prevention. In Shneidman, E. S. (Ed.): *On the Nature of Suicide*. San Francisco, Jossey-Bass, 1969.

Ebel, R. L.: Estimation of the reliability of raters. *Psychometrika, 16*:407-424, 1951.

Farberow, N. L.: Suicide prevention around the clock. *Am. J. Ortho-psychiatry, 36*(3):551-558, 1966.

Heilig, S. M.; Farberow, N. L.; Litman, R. E., and Shneidman, E. S.: The role of nonprofessional volunteers in a suicide prevention center. *Community Ment. Health J., 4*:287-295, 1968.

Kaplan, M. N. and Litman, R. E.: Telephone appraisal of 100 suicidal emergencies. *Am. J. Psychother.*, pp. 591-599, 1961.

Lister, J. L.: A scale for the measurement of accurate empathy, facilitative warmth and facilitative genuineness. (mimeo) University of Florida, 1970.

Litman, R. E.; Farberow, N. L.; Shneidman, E. S.; Heilig, S. M., and Kramer, J. A.: Suicide-prevention telephone service. *JAMA, 192*:107-111, 1965.

McGee, R. K.: Some reflections on the character of suicide prevention centers. Paper presented at the Annual Meeting of the Montgomery, Alabama Mental Health Assoc., University of Florida, Gainesville, May 28, 1969.

Rioch, M. J.; Elkes, C.; Flint, A. A., *et al.*: National institute of mental health pilot study in training mental health counselors. *Am. J. Ortho-psychiatry, 33*(4):678-689, 1963.

Truax, C. B. and Carkhuff, R. R.: Significant developments in psycho-therapy research. In Abt, L. E. and Reiss, B. F. (Eds.): *Progress in Clinical Psychology.* New York, Grune & Stratton, 1964, pp. 124-155.

Truax, C. B. and Wargo, D. G.: Psychotherapeutic encounters that change behavior: For better or for worse. *Am J Psychother., 22*:499-520, 1966.

Truax, C. B.; Wargo, D. G.; Frank, J. D., *et al.*: Therapist's contribution to accurate empathy, non-possessive warmth and genuineness in psycho-therapy. *J. Clin. Psychol., 22*:331-334, 1966.

Truax, C. B. and Carkhuff, R. R.: *Toward Effective Counseling and Psychotherapy: Training and Practice.* Chicago, Aldine, 1967.

Chapter 25

USE OF SIMULATED PATIENTS IN EVALUATING PATIENT MANAGEMENT SKILLS OF TELEPHONE COUNSELORS— A PROPOSAL

John W. Williamson, Evelyn Goldberg, and Mary Packard

THIS CHAPTER WILL describe the development of a method for assessing the performance of telephone counselors in managing emergent problems telephoned by simulated patients. The background leading to the use of simulations, the selection of patients to be simulated, the advantages, disadvantages and the implications of simulations for evaluating telephone counselors will be discussed.

Originally, the use of simulated patients to contact practicing physicians by phone was developed by the senior author of this chapter as a continuing education method for identifying learning objectives of physicians. As the method was developed, an equally important application seemed to be the evaluation of the competence of counselors who manage telephone emergency calls. This use seemed especially relevant since telephone services have been proliferating throughout the country to provide easy availability of trained personnel to advise persons in crisis. (Flood and Seager, 1968).

In general, literature related to assessing the competence of counselors suggests that the ability to help someone is dependent on the counselor's perceptions of himself, his patient, and the task, as well as his thoughts and reactions toward people (Combs and Sopher, 1959; Combs, 1961). In a study performed to test the validity of some of the hypotheses growing out of this concept, Combs and Sopher showed ". . . apparently it is possible to distinguish good counselors from poor ones on the basis of their perceptual organization (Combs and Sopher, 1963). Application of this concept has facilitated the selection of volunteers to man the telephones of the suicide prevention, psychiatric emergency, teenage hotlines, and poison control centers. The meteroric increase in numbers of these centers over the past few years emphasizes the growing need for evaluating the performance of counselors. Use of simulated patients for assessment would seem important and appropriate at this time.

Simulation is the replication of patient behavior, including any pathological signs and symptoms. Its major value in assessment is that it is possible to keep patient variables relatively constant in order to analyze the response of the physicians or counselors providing care. A variety of simulation methods have been developed during the past years. Some of the earliest methods used an "erasure test" technique wherein a patient problem was described and a series of data request items offered (McGuire and Babbott, 1967). Selection of an item was accomplished by erasing an opaque overlay to reveal, in printed form, data that would have been obtained from a real patient. Subsequent management decisions were then made to obtain additional data or to prescribe therapy by this erasure method. The most recent development of this method has been the computerization of these patient management problems by Miller and Harlass (undated). Patient simulators, in the form of manikins which respond to the treatment given to them, have been developed by Lind (1961) and Denson and Abrahamson (1969) for the purpose of teaching the skills needed in anesthesiology. Sim I (Denson and Abrahamson) is a computer controlled manikin which not only responds as programmed, but from which a printout is available summarizing every student action and every patient response. Other simulations take the form of role playing. Froelich (1969) makes use of this method in teaching medical interviewing, while Levine and McGuire (1970) utilize it as a part of the Certifying Examinations of the American Board of Orhopedic Surgery. Froelich also used, as a part of this course, a series of programmed interviews on videotape or motion picture film, which the student views and to which he responds. Others have both videotaped the student's own performance while interviewing as a learning experience or have filmed actual interviews with which the students were later tested (Adler *et al.*, 1970; Stoller and Geertsma, 1958).

Most closely related to the work under discussion is the training of persons to act the part of either a patient with a specific condition or a member of his family. For example, Helfer and Hess (1970) trained the wives of medical students to simulate the mother of a seriously ill child. These simulators were utilized to assess the interviewing ability of a group of medical students. Another group trained a professional life model with acting ability to simulate certain neurological conditions for use in teaching and assessment (Barrows and Abrahamson, 1964).

The use of simulations has several advantages. In the assessment situation, simulators provide a convenient and relatively objective methodology. Everyone is exposed to essentially the same patient stimuli and thus everyone can be assessed by the same criteria. In addition, living simulators can give feedback about the physician's performance. This type of assessment can tap abilities and emotional responses that often go unmeasured in the usual testing situations. When used as a teaching method, additional advantages include the fact that the simulator can be asked to repeat a procedure, the student cannot interfere in the health of an actual patient, and areas in which better teaching is needed are more easily ascertained (Stoller and Geertsma, 1958; Barrows, 1968; Helfer, 1970).

On the other hand, simulation has several disadvantages. It is very limited in scope. Trained actors can simulate neurological problems and emotional problems, but not heart murmurs, large livers, skin lesions, arthritic nodules, for example. It is a costly and complex procedure to recruit and train an actor or develop a patient management problem for an erasure test or computer application. Erasure tests have the serious problem of "cueing" or suggesting management interventions that the physician might not have considered in actual practice. Finally, when faced with a simulated patient in a test situation, there is a definite anxiety factor on the part of the person being tested that could bias the results of the evaluation.

The use of a simulator in assessing the telephone counselor has the benefit of almost all of these advantages and relatively few of the disadvantages. The counselor's anxiety associated with being assessed is controlled since he never knows which patient call is a simulation. Also, there is no cueing factor as in erasure tests since with a real patient the counselor must generate his own questions and advice.

What can be assessed by the use of a simulated patient seeking help over a telephone for a crisis situation? Being constrained to audio communication, verbal as well as certain nonverbal information can be recorded and analyzed. Thus, it is possible to determine the adequacy of patient data the counselor elicits as well as analyze the content, timing, and relevance of the recommendations. The counselor's sensitivity to the patient's feelings and the appropriateness of his affective communication can also be studied.

Such methods as tape recordings provide a complete record of the counselor-patient encounter which solves the problem of obtaining assessment measurements. The most difficult problem is the establishment of assessment criteria for identifying the strengths and weaknesses in the measured performance. The following sections will deal with several dimensions of this problem.

In general, there does not seem to be agreement on a "best" interview method that counselors should use, although many authors are in agreement that certain characteristics are common to all effective interviews. The person with the crisis is asking for help or enacting a state of helplessness because he feels, rightly or wrongly, that he cannot handle the situation (Schwartz, 1969). The counselor must be able to elicit sufficient information to both understand the problem and the patient's capacity to deal with it. Thus, the alleviation of the caller's anxiety and his recognition and movement toward positive alternatives depends in great part on the cognitive and affective abilities of the interviewer.

Cognitive ability is reflected in the verbal content of the

conversation with the patient. It includes the counselor's data gathering skill, his ability to analyze the data and formulate the problem, as well as his ability to identify the most effective measures to help the patient deal with the problem.

Affective ability relates to the emotional part of communication. Though it is difficult to completely separate affect from cognition, for the purposes of this work, affective ability will refer to the counselor's skill in perceiving feelings and creating empathy. Through the use of both his cognitive and affective abilities, an interviewer can assure to some extent the compliance of the caller.

To assess the judgment of telephone counselors handling emergency patients' problems, an evaluation procedure has been devised to both identify the important emergent health problems involving contacts by telephone as well as the means for evaluating a telephone counselor's performance in managing such problems. Important health problems refer to those problems where counselor performance could have a marked detrimental or beneficial effect on the patient's health. Threatened suicide, childhood poisoning, acute chest or abdominal pain represent broad classes of such problems. A priority list of such health conditions would likely have to be developed locally to be most relevant to the specific patient population and health problems handled at the telephone counseling center being evaluated.

Given such a patient problem of high priority, an instrument can then be developed for use by a patient simulator to assess the competence of a telephone counselor in managing such problems. This instrument will consist of five parts:

1. an instruction booklet,
2. a case summary,
3. a patient script,
4. response tabulation sheet,
5. scoring and summary sheet.

In actual use, the patient simulator would have studied the instruction booklet and case summary. When practice sessions indicate sufficient consistency and mastery of the "patient to be simulated," he calls the counseling center to be evaluated and presents the chief complaint. In subsequent dialogue, conducted by the counselor, the simulator responds to all questions and advice as directed in the "patient script." After the call is complete, the counselor's performance is scored and recorded on the scoring and summary sheet together with any recommendations for either counselor's education or improvement of the patient simulation. The following section will describe and illustrate the above five components of this instrument.

The instruction booklet would provide a brief summary of the operational procedures in conducting an assessment of the telephone counselor's performance (Fig. 25-1). The patient simulator would have been trained previously, so the instructions with each instrument would be brief and serve more as a check list reminder.

The case summary is a condensed description of the patient

INSTRUCTION BOOKLET

Instructions to Examiner

1. Read the entire model thoroughly.
2. When you feel you are familiar with the role to be played, place the phone call using the following guidelines:
   a. A detailed case summary and script are provided as guidelines to the conversation and your responses.
   b. The presenting complaint is at the top of the script. This is what you will say when the physician or counseling center answers the phone and offers to help you.
   c. Answer questions using the appropriate responses. When you give a clue in your response, the clue is underlined in the script and the content of the interviewer's next question should be about or contain the underlined information. If it is, go to the sheet with the information about which the question was asked.
   d. If the interviewer does not detect the clue and continues questioning, you have three choices from which to respond:
      1. Answer according to the information in the case summary.
      2. For the question asked, choose the appropriate sheet with the necessary information.
      3. Hang up, if you feel the caller would.
   e. If the interviewer later asks for information given in the original clue, use the information provided on the sheet designed for that clue.
   f. Throughout the test call, check all information asked by the interviewer.

Figure 25-1.

and health problem making up the content of the patient simulation script to be described in Figure 25-2. This document should

CASE SUMMARY

Rhonda Roberts

Rhonda Roberts is a thirty-one-year-old woman who having lived with her mother all her life has recently moved into an apartment to live "a life of her own."

Although the results of extensive testing were negative, Rhonda fears she has cancer and uses this as a rationalization for her limited social life and few (if any) friends. Her fear of impending illness has prompted her to think of moving home.

Four months ago, Rhonda impulsively made a serious suicidal attempt to "pay back" a boyfriend. At her mother's urging, Rhonda refused any psychiatric help while in the hospital since she is *not* "crazy." She was and still is taking pills for nerves but is not aware of the proper or safe dosage and takes whatever she needs. She has little understanding of her emotional problems and refuses to discuss them.

Figure 25-2.

facilitate a more reliable and accurate simulation by presenting all of the medical and psychiatric facts about the case being simulated. In addition, it also includes the patient's typical modes of reaction, degree of compliance, and other characteristics to help the simulator understand the patient's personality.

The patient script is the document detailing the patient's initial remarks or complaints together with subsequent verbal and affective responses the simulator is to provide in reaction to the telephone counselor's specific inquiries and/or instructions (Fig. 25-3). This document is designed to include responses to nearly all relevant questions and instructions that may be mentioned by the counselor being assessed. All items to be included would fall in the following four categories:

Category A. Those items (questions or instructions) that are considered essential for the patient to achieving a successful final health outcome in terms of his longevity or personal functioning.

Category B. Those items not essential for achieving a successful health outcome but which would be important to the patient by facilitating decreased length and/or expense of medical care and/or increased comfort.

Category D. Those items not likely to be harmful to the

PATIENT SCRIPT
(Rhonda Roberts—Acute Depression)

Outline of Sections

I. Elaboration of Conflict

II. History and Reaction to Illness

III. Medication History

IV. Relationship with Mother and Other Family

V. Psychiatric History

VI. Precipitating Event and Relationship with Men

VII. Suicide Attempt

VIII. Alternatives

IX. Modes of Intervention

Illustrative Section

V. Psychiatric History

Item Category	Question	Patient Response
B	Questions exploring suggested previous experience with psychiatrists	Oh, it's nothing . . . it's not important . . .
B	Ever see a psychiatrist	Well, just once. It was all a big mistake.
A	Reason for seeing psychiatrist	It was all a mistake.
A	Elaboration	It was just that I was in the hospital and they wanted me to see one.
B	Reason for hospitalization	Oh, I'd just done something silly.
B	Specific nature of incident	I just took too many pills—by mistake of course.
B	Outcome	They put me in the hospital for a few days til I got better.
C	Reason for not seeing a psychiatrist	Because I didn't need to, that's why.
B	Possibility of seeing a psychiatrist now	NO. I'm not crazy. I don't need one. I told you that.
		If above topic is continued, hang up.

Figure 25-3.

patient in terms of final outcome but which would increase length and/or cost of medical care and/or cause added discomfort.

Category E. Those items likely to cause or risk harm to the final patient outcomes, in terms of the patient's longevity and/or functional capability.

Note that Category C (items neither harmful or helpful) are omitted from the script, as they would be infinite in number and of little value to the simulator. If the counselor asks for such an item of information, the simulator would record the question on the response tabulation sheet and provide a neutral reply, e.g. "I don't know."

The items are developed under direction of a group of experienced specialists in the relevant health area. For example, a suicide script would be developed by a panel of suicidologists and/or psychiatrists. Only those items whose content and rating (Categories A-E) for which at least four out of five members of the consultant panel agree are included in the final script. Although the group strives to include as many relevant items as possible in each of the four categories, operational use will undoubtedly identify additional items that can be added later. In this way, the instrument can be continually upgraded and improved with use.

After all the items are listed and categorized, an appropriate patient response is developed. This response will indicate the information the simulator will provide if the counselor requests. Cognitive, and where important, affective content are specified in the script. For example, if the counselor made direct inquiry regarding sexual activity, the script would instruct the patient simulator as follows, Affect—Controlled anger; Verbal—"I don't want to talk about it!" In this way, nearly every response of the simulator is programmed to provide the same stimuli to each telephone counselor evaluated.

The response tabulation sheet has been developed to permit recording of the specific questions and instructions given by the counselor (Fig. 25-4). The items rated A, B, D and E are recorded by number, whereas C items are recorded verbatim for later analysis. There is space to list the simulator's subjective feeling response to the counselor. Finally, there is space to record any comments or observations that might be useful in assessing either the counselor's performance or the instrument itself.

The scoring and summary sheet indicates the number of items requested in each of the information categories A thru E as compared to the total possible for each category (Fig. 25-5).

TELEPHONE COUNSELOR EVALUATION

Response Tabulation Sheet

Page __1__ of __3__

Elk River
Suicide Prev. Center *801-246-3831* *21 June 1971* *2:10 p.m.*
Counselor's Name   Phone #   Date of Call   Time

Suicide #2 - Rhonda Roberts   *Mary Kard*
Simulated Patient   Patient Simulator

DIALOGUE RECORD

Time	Item #	"Patient" Affect Response	Time	Item #	"Patient" Affect Response	Time	Item #	"Patient Affect Response
2:15	36			21				
	14			36				
	23	annoyance						
	71							
2:30	21	imitation						
	72							
	64	empathy						
	53							
	47							
2:45	27							

"C" ITEM AND COMMENT RECORD

Time	"C" Item	Record Item Verbatim
2:37		What did you have for lunch today?
2:45		The counselor seems nervous and unsure.
2:46		You should listen to the radio more.
2:52		Couldn't find response #26 fast enough — had long pause.

Figure 25-4.

Note that C items are also tabulated to provide an index of irrelevant data requested (or advice given) by the counselor. Diagnostic scores (information gathering) will be tabulated separately from those related to therapeutic management. Affect scores will be reported in terms of general subjective impressions of the patient simulator until more standard methods can be developed. Use of the "semantic differential" and "adjective

Elk River SCORING AND SUMMARY SHEET *Rhonda*
Suicide Prev. Center _21 June 1971_ _Mary Kard_ _Roberts_
Name of Telephone   Date   Patient   Simulated
Counselor   Evaluated   Simulator   Patient

COGNITIVE SCORES

Item Category		Dx Score	Total Poss.	Rx Score	Total Poss.
A	Essential	3	6	2	3
B	Desirable (not essential)	6	10	3	5
C		12		4	
D	Undesirable (not harmful)	1	4	2	5
E	Harmful	0	1	0	3

AFFECTIVE SCORES

	Yes	?	No
Did the counselor establish rapport with you, i.e. did you like him?			✓
Did the counselor stimulate a feeling of confidence in his judgment and ability?			✓
Did he (she) hold your attention more than 75% of the time?	✓		
Did you feel you understood at least 3 out of 4 of his questions and advice?	✓		
Would you likely have complied with this counselor?		✓	
Would you have done the opposite of his recommendation?			✓

RECOMMENDATIONS/COMMENTS

Figure 25-5.

check lists" are currently being studied for this purpose. The final space on the score sheet will be for comments and recommendations of the evaluator regarding the counselor's overall performance.

In this present stage of development, many aspects of this evaluation instrument need to be studied, especially reliability and validity. Reliability will be affected by the ability and training of the simulator, who must have an adequate knowledge of the personality he is portraying and must respond in a standard way to subsequent evaluations. This is a difficult task and yet one of utmost importance as indicated by several investigators (Stoller and Geertsma, 1958; Helfer and Hess, 1970). Once patient simulators are trained, it would seem essential to monitor the reliability of their performance. Perhaps a group of experts could "observe" and evaluate sequential interviews by means of tape recordings. From such procedures, information regarding reliability could be obtained. If more than one simulator is used, intersimulator as well as intrasimulator reliability must be measured.

Ascertaining the validity of this instrument presents a more difficult problem to overcome than does reliability. In addition, there are two problems of validity involved in this work, i.e. does the instrument really portray a person in crisis? Secondly, does the instrument actually measure that which it purports to measure, i.e. patient management skills of the counselor? The use of judges to decide "construct" or "face" validity from the content of the scripts is an attempt to handle the first problem. As the work goes forward, hopefully concurrent validity might be measured from peer rating or eventually actual patient follow-up to determine outcomes in similar "real" patients. However, such studies are merely speculative at the present time.

When finalized, scripts and simulators can be utilized as evaluation instruments for persons other than telephone interviewers and for purposes other than evaluation. For example, they will be useful in testing and training students and in assessing and educating both practicing physicians and other professionals. In addition, they can serve the purposes of training tools for a variety of types of allied health personnel.

The educational application of this instrument could be readily exploited at present if educators can accept the degree of face validity of this method. In any event, much work needs to be done to further develop and test the use of simulated patients to assess telephone counselors. From our experience thus far, the results look very promising and seem to justify continuing and expanding effort in this direction.

REFERENCES

Adler, L. M.; Ware, J. E., and Enelow, A. J.: Changes in medical interviewing style after instruction with two closed circuit television techniques. *J Med Educ*, 45:21-28, 1970.

Barrows, H. S.: Simulated patients in medical teaching. *Canad Med Ass J*, 98:674-676, 1968.

Barrows, H. S., and Abrahamson, S.: The programmed patient. *J Med Educ,* 93:802-805, 1964.

Combs, A. W.: A perceptual view of the nature of 'helpers' in personality theory and counseling practice. In *First Annual Conference on Personality Theory and Counseling Practice.* Gainesville, University of Florida, 1961, pp. 53-58.

Combs, A. W., and Sopher, D. W.: The self, its derivative terms and research. In Juenzli, A. (Ed.): *The Phenomenological Problem.* New York, Harper, 1959, pp. 31-48.

Combs, A. W., and Sopher, D. W.: The perceptual organization of effective counselors. *J Counsel Psychol, 10*:222-226, 1963.

Denson, J. S., and Abrahamson, S.: A computer-controlled patient simulator. *JAMA, 208*:504-508, 1969.

Flood, R. A., and Seager, C. P.: A retrospective examination of psychiatric case records of patients who subsequently committed suicide. *Brit J Psychiat, 114*:443-450, 1968.

Froelich, R. E.: A course in medical interviewing. *J Med Educ, 44*:1165-1169, 1969.

Helfer, R. E.: An objective comparison of the pediatric interviewing skills of freshmen and senior medical students. *Pediatrics, 45*:623-627, 1970.

Helfer, C., and Hess, J.: An experimental model for making objective measurements of interviewing skills. *J Clin Psychol, 26*:327-331, 1970.

Levine, H. G., and McGuire, C. H.: The use of role-playing to evaluate affective skills in medicine. *J Med Educ, 45*:700-705, 1970.

Lind, B.: Teaching mouth-to-mouth resuscitation in primary schools. *Acta Anaesth Scand (Suppl), 5*:63-81, 1961.

McGuire, C., and Babbott, D.: Simulation technique in the measurement of problem-solving skills. *J Educ Meas, 4*:1-10, 1967.

Miller, G., and Harless, W. G.: Computer simulation of patient management. Unpublished, University of Illinois Medical Center.

Schwartz, D. A.: Therapeutic intervention in crisis. *Int Psychiat Clin, 6*:297-315, 1969.

Stoller, R. J., and Geertsma, R. H.: Construction of a final examination to assess clinical judgment in psychiatry. *J Med Educ, 33*:837-840, 1958.

Date Due